D1625075

Rudy, !

Blessings.

Prov 1:5

WHAT PEOPLE ARE SAYING

This erudite, eloquent, and immensely thought-provoking work gets to the heart of the deepest passions and aspirations of the human heart: What does it take to be considered great?

This is indispensable reading for anyone who wants to live life above the norm. This is a profound authoritative work, which spans the wisdom of the ages, and yet breaks new ground in its approach and will possibly become a classic in this and the next generation.

This exceptional work by Dave Martin is one of the most profound, practical, principle-centered approaches to this subject I have read in a long time. The author's approach to this timely issue brings a fresh breath of air that captivates the heart, engages the mind and inspires the spirit of the reader.

The author's ability to leap over complicated theological and meta-physical jargon and reduce complex theories to simple practical principles that the least among us can understand is amazing.

This work will challenge the intellectual while embracing the lay-men as it dismantles the mysterious of the soul search of mankind and delivers the profound in simplicity.

Dave's approach awakens in the reader the untapped inhibiters that retard our personal development and his antidotes empower us to rise above these self-defeating, self-limiting factors to a life of ex-ploits in spiritual and mental advancement.

The author also integrates into each chapter time-tested precepts, giving each principle a practical application to life making the entire process people-friendly.

Every sentence of this book is pregnant with wisdom and I enjoyed the mind-expanding experience of this exciting book. I admon-ish you to plunge into this ocean of knowledge and watch your life change for the better.

- Dr. Myles Munroe
BFM International, ITWLA, Nassau, Bahamas

The 12 Traits of the Greats outlines principles of life, personal development, success, leadership and so much more. I've had a lot of great coaches in my day that made me great in baseball. This book will make you great in life!

- **Darryl Strawberry**
Baseball Great
3-Time World Series Champion
MLB Rookie of the Year

This book proves why Dr. Dave is America's #1 success coach. If you want to get on the highway of success this is a must read.

- **Scot Anderson**
Successful Entrepreneur
Author of *Millionaire Habits in 21 Days* & *Think Like a Billionaire*

Once again, Christian Inspirational Guru Dave Martin brings wisdom, wit and wonder to life with his powerful teachings. If you want to be the BEST you can possibly be, Dave Martin's book, *The 12 Traits of the Greats* will set you on a fast track to super stardom. Making Dave's foundational principles a part of your daily habits – and taking action steps that lead to success – will catapult you to greatness beyond your imagination!

– **Marc Mero**
Inspirational Speaker
Former WWE Wrestling Champion
Author of *How to be the Happiest Person on the Planet*

In this significant and very readable book, Dr. Dave Martin will teach you how to go places you have never been before - and coach you in the traits that will keep you ahead in these turbulent times and create exciting new opportunities and possibilities.

– Obed Martinez
Lead Pastor, Destiny Church.TV
Founder of Passionate Pastors

Most Christians know they were created for something greater. Few know how to actually attain it. In *The 12 Traits of the Greats*, Dr. Dave Martin has shown us the way. With his incredible insight, Dr. Dave shows us that greatness isn't just something to be admired in others. It's something to be attained for ourselves.

Steven Furtick
Lead Pastor, Elevation Church
Author, *Sun Stand Still*

Dave Martin truly brings IT because he believes IT. He's one of the few speakers I've heard who walks the talk. In Dave's new book *The 12 Traits of the Greats* again he BRINGS IT! In every chapter he is spot on...you will learn to live your life at the next level.

- Diamond Dallas Page
3-time World Champion Wrestler & Fitness Guru

Dave Martin has captured the essence of twelve of the most important keys to success in life. These will work for anyone in any circumstance. They will work for you. If you want a new opportunity in life, if you need a change, if you are looking for a way to get to your next level of success, this book will help you. *The 12* is clear, concise and focused on the issues that really matter. You'll love it.

- Dr. Casey Treat
Pastor of Christian Faith Center, Seattle, WA

Two words describe the contents of this book—"Distilled Wisdom". Dr. Dave Martin has distilled a lifetime of his personal experiences of running with the greats and allows us to view our lives through that grid. You'll measure yourself, make necessary adjustments and become an illustration of a great in Dr. Dave Martin's next book! If growth is what you want then *12 Traits of the Greats* is your prescription—read and grow.

- Dr. Samuel R. Chand
Leadership Architect
Author of *Cracking Your Church's Culture Code*

Dr. Dave Martin is an amazing walking testament of the extravagant favor of God. I've seen God increase him in quantum ways over the last decade that I've been blessed to call him friend. It is solely because of the principles he lives by that are outlined in this book- that have helped so many and will certainly equip you as well.

- Israel Houghton
Grammy Award Winner

Why read Dave Martin's *12 Traits of the Greats*? Because you want to do the very most and the very best with the time and the life you have. Because we all need direction and inspiration to achieve that. And because in these pages - in plain but powerful language - is the way to get there. Read it and see change. Read it and be changed.

- Simon T. Bailey
Brillionaire
Author of *Release Your Brilliance*

Dave Martin has written a handbook on life...concise but deep, practical yet powerful. No matter what juncture you're in, this book reminds us all that it's never too late to be great!

- Lynette Lewis
Speaker and Business Consultant
Author of *Climbing the Ladder in Stilettos*

Dr. Dave Martin has experienced effective leadership from a plethora of people, places and perspectives. It is this experience that Dr. Martin draws upon in his new book *The 12 Traits of the Greats*. Dr. Martin gives us an insider's look at what it takes to be a GREAT leader. Each chapter gives you a hands-on, practical approach to becoming a better leader. *12 Traits of the Greats* is the one resource every leader needs to read this ministry season.

- Pastor Troy Gramling
Lead Pastor of Potential Church

Dave Martin's teaching has transformed not only me but my family and business life as well. I appreciate his wisdom and incredible sense of humor. He captures your attention and allows you to create a new crease in your brain in regards to leadership.

- Gillian Ortega
Mary Kay Inc.

Dave Martin takes us on an in-depth journey into really understanding the traits of the greats. There's nothing quite like an engaging, powerful, inspirational, and spirit-filled book. For anyone looking for a great guide to living their best life, this is the coach. Definitely a must-have!!

- Liza Mucheru-Wisner
NBC's *The Apprentice*, Season 10

The Twelve Undeniable Qualities of
Uncommon Achievers, and How You Can
Master Them In Your Life... RIGHT NOW!

THE 12 TRAITS OF THE GREATS

DR. DAVE MARTIN

HARRISON HOUSE PUBLISHING

Unless otherwise indicated, all Scripture quotations are taken from the *King James Version* of the Bible.

Scripture quotations marked NKJV are taken from the *New King James Version*. Copyright © 1982 by Thomas Nelson, Inc. Used by permission. All rights reserved.

Scripture quotations marked NIV are taken from the *Holy Bible, New International Version* ®. Copyright © 1973, 1978, 1984 Biblica. Used by permission of Zondervan. All rights reserved.

Scripture quotations marked The Message are taken from *The Message*. Copyright © 1993, 1994, 1995, 1996, 2000, 2001, 2002. Used by permission of NavPress Publishing Group.

14   13   12   11   10   9   8   7   6   5   4   3   2   1

The 12 Traits of the Greats: The Twelve Undeniable Qualities of Uncommon Achievers, and How You Can Master Them In Your Life... RIGHT NOW!

ISBN: 978-1-60683-313-1

Copyright © 2011 by Dave Martin

Published by Harrison House Publishers
P.O. Box 35035
Tulsa, Oklahoma 74135

Printed in the United States of America. All rights reserved under International Copyright Law. Contents and/or cover may not be reproduced in whole or in part in any form without the written consent of the Publisher.

CONTENTS

FOREWORD

The dictionary defines a "great" as a person who has achieved importance, distinction or success. Whether it's a professional athlete, musician, historical figure or some other notable person, most people can think of someone who would be considered great. So when it comes to living out greatness, the most important question isn't, "Who is great?" The real question is, "Can I become great?"

If you hit the streets and asked ten different people what it takes to become great, you'd most likely get ten different responses. You'd hear things like determination, work or knowledge. You might hear words like education, intuition or even luck. But the trouble with any of those one word answers is that none of them fully encapsulate the reality of what it takes to become "great".

If you drill it all down, greatness (read here: accomplishment, success) takes a willingness to continually learn and then to put that new knowledge into practice—day in and day out. Greatness doesn't just happen because we hope or believe or think it will. It isn't achieved by relying on luck or circumstance. True greatness takes effort to become a reality in our lives.

Dr. Dave Martin understands this truth more than most people I have ever met in my life. For years, he has pursued knowledge, refusing to settle on what he has already learned. He passionately and purposefully seeks to improve his life by seeking to learn. But he doesn't stop there.

He pushes to find new ways to utilize that knowledge and then impart it to others around him. Literally millions of people around the world have benefited from Dave's teaching and direction, not because he knows so much, but because he trains and equips others how to use that knowledge. Simply said, he has put feet to his knowledge.

And once again, Dave is putting his knowledge into practice. Through the pages of this book, he unpacks the 12 most important traits of greatness that he has discovered over the years, and he shows us what it takes for us to become great in our own right.

We've all heard the phrase "knowledge is power," but that's only half of the equation. In the following pages, Dave reveals the other side of that equation—the reality of applying that knowledge.

But before you read further, you need to understand that this isn't a self-help book. You won't find a formula here that you can simply plug into your life. This is not a transcript from some talk show that reveals five steps to a worry-free life.

This book is a bold challenge and call to action, as only Dave can issue. In the opening pages of this book, he confronts us with the reality that in order to discover success, we must be willing to go through the process of change and growth. I call this the spin cycle of success: change, conflict, growth.

In order to experience growth, and ultimately success, in any area of life, we must be willing to change some things. But here's the rub. The implementation of change will undoubtedly bring about conflict. The question then becomes, what do you do in the face of that conflict?

In this book, Dr. Martin presents a blueprint (based on God's Word) with which you can overcome conflict and on which you can build greatness into your life. From the strong foundation of personal responsibility to pillars such as focus and integrity and all the way to the beautiful finish out of living a generous life, this book helps you understand what the greats have understood for years: that greatness is something that anyone can achieve.

So if you are ready for greatness, keep reading. And discover that greatness is waiting for you…if you are willing to go get it!

- **Ed Young**
Pastor of Fellowship Church (FellowshipChurch.com)
Author, *Outrageous, Contagious Joy* (EdYoung.com)

INTRODUCTION

DESIGNED FOR GREATNESS

It was one of the darkest hours in world history. The Nazis, under the brutal leadership of Adolph Hitler, had occupied the vast majority of the European continent. France had been conquered, as had Belgium, Poland, Czechoslovakia, and virtually every other militarized nation on the continent. Refugees had fled to the British Isles, where they stood in weak opposition to Germany's complete domination of Europe.

As German bombs began to rain down upon the British people and as the Battle of Britain began, one lone figure stood between Hitler and his singular control of the continent. That man, Winston Churchill, was not a particularly impressive gentleman. Before becoming British prime minister, his leadership credentials had been less than stellar. He had been a war correspondent and a politician, once departing government altogether after the disastrous failure of one of his key programs. But Churchill had something that few people in the world can claim. He had greatness.

Churchill refused to surrender or compromise in the face of nearly insurmountable odds. He refused to be intimated by what appeared to be an undefeatable foe. He was somehow able to inspire the British people to stand alone in order to do the impossible and to endure the unthinkable, and he was able to maintain a national spirit of hope throughout the darkest hours of the twentieth century. With great finesse and political astuteness, Churchill managed to unite the remaining free nations of the world and enlist their essential help in a battle he could not have won without them. And he managed to maintain the support and confidence of the British electorate during times when their economy, their infrastructure, and their way of life teetered on the brink of extinction.

Greatness is a quality that endures.

Greatness is a quality that endures. It is a quality that demands respect, admiration, and allegiance. Greatness is a quality that appears on the human scene far too infrequently, yet which changes the human landscape when it finally does appear. Every discipline has its great achievers. When we think of great leaders, we think of Washington, Lincoln, Churchill, and Roosevelt. When we think of great warriors, we think of Napoleon, Patton, Lee, and Alexander the Great. Great thinkers include Socrates and Thomas Paine. Great scientists include Einstein, Edison, and George Washington Carver. Every adult in our country can list for you the greatest writers, actors, athletes, and musicians who have filled the landscape of popular American culture. And every child can tell you the name of that one great teacher who most impacted his life.

What causes these people to stand out on the horizon of history or to rise above their contemporaries in our hearts and minds? Because they were great! They possessed "something"—we can't really put our finger on it—that set them apart and caused their work to endure and their legacy to enlarge with the passing of the years. They were bigger than life; perhaps they still are. They were remarkable in their magnitude, degree, and effectiveness.

I contend that greatness and fame are two different things and that they aren't prerequisites for one another. In the same way that famous people aren't always great, so great people aren't always famous. In fact, I would argue that the majority of the world's great people are people who are not in the media spotlight. They live unknown to you and me in Albuquerque and Portland, in Syracuse and Port Orange. They are teachers and salesmen. They are parents and church ushers. They aren't pursued by the paparazzi or hounded for autographs, but they have accomplished the purposes for which they were designed and they have achieved the dreams that God placed within their hearts. And while doing these amazing things, they have changed their children, their friends, their communities, and the lives of many others they have impacted along life's way.

Greatness is not an easy attribute to define or to capture, because it is multifaceted. While some people are great at art or baseball, others are great at public speaking or cooking. But I'm not referring here to *performance* as much as I am *character*. I'm not exploring what a person *does* as much as I am exploring what a person *is* and how that person comes to affect the people around him. God is great. The Bible tells us so. But His greatness consists not so much of the mighty things He *does* (creation, miracles, salvation) as it consists of *who He is*, the nature of His personality and character. God is described in the Bible as pure, as holy, as righteous, and as just. But

He also is described as loving, as merciful, as longsuffering, and as patient. His works impress us, but His character causes us to worship Him and to desire to be like Him. His acts, therefore, merely reflect His character.

So it is with great people. People of greatness—whether athletes or performers, soldiers or philanthropists—inspire us and motivate us to pursue greatness in our own lives. In spite of the fact that these people come from every walk of life and from every corner of the world, and in spite of the fact that they gain notoriety in every discipline known to man, they nevertheless exhibit certain foundational qualities that are common to all of them. All great people, for example, are focused. All great people are adaptable. All great people are imaginative, wise, and passionate. In this book, therefore, I want to explore the twelve most common traits that make great people great. I want to explore the principles of greatness that set great people apart. I want to look at real-life examples of greatness. I want to tell the stories of great people and how they achieved greatness in their own lives. But most of all, I want to drive home the point that every person is designed to be great. Every child born into the world is born with a seed of greatness that can be awakened and nurtured through proper thinking and persistent effort.

Remember that nobody started life as a great person.

In the pages that follow, you will find reason to laugh and to cry. You will find reason to be angry and remorseful. You will read historical accounts, as well as the musings of those who have impacted our lives over the centuries of recorded history. But more than anything,

I hope the twelve modules of this book will inspire you and challenge you to seek the greatness that is latent within your own life. As you read, remember that nobody started life as a great person. Sure, some of us had greater advantages than others and some of us had environments that were more conducive to achievement. But every one of us started life as a little baby with wrinkled skin, closed eyes, and a great pair of lungs. Then, due to the decisions we made along the way, some of us grew up to be less than impressive while others among us grew up to change the world. And while some started the climb to greatness at a very early age, others didn't even start the journey until they were old.

It's never too late to be great. It's never too late to turn things around in your life. Read and learn. Read and think. Read and put into practice the habits and thought processes of some of the world's most amazing people so that you, too, can become everything you were created to be. Greatness awaits you.

CHAPTER 1

RESPONSIBILITY

TAKING OWNERSHIP OF YOURSELF

One of the most valuable foundational qualities we can admire in the "greats" is their immense willingness to take responsibility for their own lives and their own destinies. All men and women of incredible achievement have understood what you also need to understand: that there is only one person responsible for the outcome of your life and the quality of your life, and that person is YOU. Do you want to be successful? Do you want to do great things with your life? If so, you are going to have to take responsibility for every facet of your life: your achievements, your productivity, your results, your relationships, your health, your income, your debt, your feelings. Everything!

Assuming responsibility for oneself isn't easy in this modern world. We have been conditioned all our lives to blame every external circumstance and every other person around us for the parts of our lives we don't like. In modern America, we start by blaming our genetics, our environment, and the poor job done by our parents. But the blame doesn't stop there. After we grow up and leave home, we continue to blame all our failures and flaws on our spouses, our bosses, our friends, lack of money, lack of opportunity, lack of education, the influences of the media, the lousy economy, and even our

---

You must take responsibility for the outcome of your own life.

---

children. We have been conditioned from birth to look everywhere for the root cause of our difficulties except in the most logical and most realistic place: ourselves.

Although some might not admit it, it's a historical fact that the United States was founded upon Judeo-Christian ethics and laws based on biblical principles. And if there's one thing the Bible teaches, it's personal responsibility and accountability. Yes, the Bible also teaches us to love one another and to care for one another, but these directives are based upon the understanding and presumption that a man will first be inclined to help himself, and the Bible says so in both explicit and implicit ways. Therefore, the Bible and those historical legal codes that were based on the Bible emphatically teach us that each man is responsible for what he does with his own life. He is responsible for his own choices and the outcome of those choices. He alone is responsible for the decisions affecting the quality of his life, his current relationships, lifestyles, and behaviors. If each person was not responsible for his own choices in life, how could there be a final judgment? How could there be rewards in heaven?

So if God is going to hold us accountable one day for the lives we have lived on earth, how can we pretend that we can get away with blaming poor circumstances or other people for the outcome of our lives? That excuse won't work on Judgment Day, and so it won't work now. You must take responsibility for the outcome of your own life. I must take responsibility for the outcome of mine. All of us must hold ourselves accountable right now and judge ourselves and our own decisions and behaviors against the standard of our own potential.

The cold, hard truth is that you are living, at this very moment, the results of your past choices and your past decisions. And just as the present is a reflection of your past choices and decisions, so the future will be a reflection of the choices you make starting today. Nothing else can help you. Nothing else can hinder you. Your life is in your own hands, and your hands alone have the power to shape your destiny.

In accepting total responsibility for yourself, you must give attention to every aspect of life that is important to you. You must give attention to your health, because health won't maintain itself on simple genetics. You must give attention to your relationships, because your relationships won't survive or grow without sacrifice and purposeful effort. You must give attention to your dreams, because

---

In accepting total responsibility for yourself, you must give attention to every aspect of life that is important to you.

---

most dreams die from lack of nurture. You must give attention to your financial status, because nobody else will. You must give attention to everything that matters and you must take responsibility for everything that matters, making yourself accountable right now to God and to the high standards you are setting for yourself.

One of the most important aspects of taking responsibility for all the various components of your life will be your own willingness to confront the obstacles, the circumstances, the people, and the personal challenges that lie between you and the goals you have set in each of these areas. There is no victor's crown without a struggle. There is no prize without a fight. There is no overcomer without something to overcome. The challenges of life are the things that make most people quit and the things that become most people's excuses. But the "greats" don't make excuses. They accept the responsibility of confronting the challenges in their lives.

Most people want to see change in their lives, change for the better. They want to grow. They want to learn. They want to take the stagnant parts of their lives and revive them. They want to win the battles they have been losing most of their lives. In fact, people are so hungry for change that they elected our current president simply because he promised it. "Change you can believe in" was his campaign slogan. You probably are reading this book because there are certain aspects of your life that you want changed, aspects that bring you dissatisfaction or that disappoint you in some way.

But you cannot change what you're not responsible for. As long as the fault for your problems lies with someone else, you can't do anything to change those problems. The person with the power to change something is the person with the authority and responsibility to change it. So if you want change, you have some work to do, just like I have some work to do. Before you can even begin doing that work, you need to accept responsibility for the thing you want to change. You need to admit to yourself that you, and you alone, are able to turn this ship around because you, and you alone, steered this ship into its present waters.

Believe me, there are a lot of millionaires out there who had far worse lives than you or me. Some of them had painful childhoods and terrible parents. Some of them were stymied by physical, mental, or emotional handicaps. Some of them were not gifted with high IQ's or with the benefit of quality educations. Yet they overcame their obstacles, because they realized that the outcome of their lives was in their own hands. In the United States, every person has an equal opportunity to make his life better than it is, but nobody can make his life better if he isn't willing to take responsibility for his life. I start this book with this sentiment, because no other changes can possibly occur in you or your circumstances until you are willing to own up to your own responsibility to yourself. You must become a participant in your own rescue by taking ownership of your own destiny.

You created the present, and you can create the future.

When you accept the premise that there is nothing you can do about your plight in life, you become chained to the life you have. You become a prisoner to your circumstances. But your deliverance from all your limitations begins when you admit that you are responsible for where you are and that you are the only person who can do what it takes to get out of where you are. Your life can begin to turn around when you realize your choices and decisions put you in your current situation, and therefore, your choices and decisions can turn things around as well.

If you have been through bankruptcy, for instance, your choices and decisions put you there. If you have been through a divorce, your choices and decisions put you there. If you have been through a business failure, your choices and decisions put you there. Of course, there were some outside influences that added to the demise of that aspect of your life and, of course, other people played a role in the failure. But you are primarily the person that you are and you are primarily standing in the place where you are standing because you made the decisions that formed you and your present circumstances. Take responsibility, because the rest of this book will be utterly useless to you if you are convinced that there's nothing you can do about your life and the direction you are heading. You created the present, and you can create the future.

Perhaps you're thinking, *But Dave, you don't understand. You don't know what I've been through. You don't understand what people have done to me.* Don't tell it to me. Tell it to Helen Keller, a blind and deaf-mute who became one of America's greatest writers and political activists. Tell it to George Washington Carver, a slave who became one of our nation's greatest scientists, educators, and inventors. Tell it to all the men who returned home after World War II to build factories, businesses, schools, and churches. Tell it to the founding fathers and early immigrants, who got off boats with nothing more than the clothes on their backs, yet carved a nation out of the rugged wilderness. You also can tell it to Abraham, Moses, Gideon, Jeremiah, and other great men of God who were called from humble origins to do great things in spite of seemingly insurmountable obstacles and resistance. Tell it to any of these people. Go ahead! Whine and complain and detail all your heartaches and disappointments, and see what they say.

If you are like most people, you have all these "reasons" why you cannot be great or why you cannot do great things with your life, and you have hidden behind these "reasons" far too long. In this book, my goal is to help you create ways of breaking free from your limitations to achieve all your God-given potential. But the battle begins in your own mind with the things you are telling yourself right now. So from the outset, I want you to confront this issue and decide whether you want to proceed with the next eleven chapters. The rest of the book won't be quite as harsh or direct as this chapter has been thus far, but it is important that you face your biggest demon first. The biggest demon for most people is their own unwillingness to realistically confront their future. They believe that their future lives will be controlled by the government, by big business, by economic factors, by secretive groups of powerful people, or by sheer "luck." But they don't believe that their futures will be controlled by their own choices and behaviors. I want you to see that it will be. Your future is controlled by you and you alone, regardless of the shifting winds of change that are blowing all around you and regardless of what Washington or City Hall or any other entity is doing.

There is a popular automobile commercial that talks about the two different kinds of people on the road: drivers and passengers. In the commercial, the drivers are having fun and living their lives with passion, but the passengers are just going along for the ride and aren't having very much fun at all. As you know, commercials can be incredibly silly and shallow, and this one is too, to some extent. But there's a point to this commercial that can be transferred into the real world, because, on the road of life, there also are two kinds of people: drivers and passengers. While the passengers just go along for the ride, accepting whatever happens as their "fate" in life, drivers take responsibility for the direction of their own lives. They grab hold of the steering wheel and guide their lives in the direction they want to travel by maintaining control, making decisions, calling the shots, and determining the pathways their lives will take. Whenever they make a wrong turn, they accept responsibility and get back on track. They refuse to relinquish the outcome of their journey to some unseen person or some unknown force. They want the wheel.

Tim is a great real-life example of somebody who learned this principle in time to avoid disaster and turn his life around.[1] In fact, I'd say that Tim turned his life around 180 degrees, because he finally woke up to the fact that he had to take complete personal responsibility for everything that had occurred in his life in the past and everything that would occur in the future.

Tim grew up in a middle-class home with five brothers and a sister. When Tim was eleven, his father was killed in a terrible automobile accident. Tim quickly found the deck stacked against him in life. Like so many young boys, he struggled through high school and college, but then, as an adult, he finally had the personal freedom to act upon the fear, anger, guilt, and other pent-up emotions that had brewed within him as a result of his father's death. So Tim started living in the "fast lane" and supporting his lifestyle by selling drugs. Eventually, Tim was arrested, convicted, and imprisoned for the behaviors he had chosen for himself.

In prison, Tim had a "pivot point" moment. He woke up and came to his senses, realizing that he was pretty messed up and that he had nobody to blame but himself. Yes, life had dealt him a terrible blow, but life had dealt worse hands to other people who had managed to live happy, productive lives. So Tim made a conscious decision to change. He knew he alone was the one responsible for his imprisonment, and he knew he was the only person who could turn his life around. He began to work on himself.

For one thing, Tim realized that he had a lot of suppressed anger. He was angry about his father's death, and he was angry that he had been forced to grow up without a dad. He was angry that the early years of his life had been disrupted and that he had not been able to enjoy the things that other boys his age were privileged to enjoy. He felt sorry for himself and then angry with his father who had

28

died. He was mad at the whole world, which had been so unfair to him and which seemed unable or unwilling to do anything about his pain. Tim dealt with his anger by turning it inward. He had destroyed his life. He had really messed things up.

When Tim finally put all this together in the solitude of his prison cell, he made a decision to accept full responsibility for his past failures and, more importantly, for his future potential. He took definitive steps to change things in his life. He read books. He organized prison talent shows, where he served as the master of ceremonies. And he started telling jokes, because he had a natural talent for humor. Then, upon his release from prison, Tim was fortunate enough to land a great job at a leading talent agency.

Over time, Tim really excelled at his trade. He got noticed, not only for his work, but also for his talent as an actor and comedian. His performance company even approached Disney with Tim's capabilities, and Disney offered Tim a role in a major television program. Tim turned down the offer, however, holding out for something that fit him better. Disney made two more offers that Tim rejected. Tim wanted to take responsibility for the direction of his own life. He had his own idea for a television program, and his idea just didn't match up with Disney's. So Tim turned down their repeated offers and worked instead to make his own personal dream a reality.

Eventually, Tim was able to star in his own television show, a show he conceived that fit his humor and talent perfectly. The show was about a man who was the host of his own handyman program on television, and this new show became a major hit with the American audience. By now, you have probably guessed that I am talking about Tim Allen, creator and star of the number one television show, *Home Improvement*.

Just thirteen years after his release from jail, Tim Allen was starring in the top television program in America (*Home Improvement*), had the leading role in a major motion picture (*The Santa Clause*), and had the number one book on the New York Times Bestseller List (his autobiography, *Don't Stand Too Close to a Naked Man*). I'd call that a turnaround. How about you? And it all began when Tim Allen made the simple decision to accept responsibility for his own life.

Do you think Tim Allen would have become a successful actor, writer, and comedian if he hadn't accepted responsibility for his own life? Of course not! He would have kept traveling the same worn-out path of repeated self-destructive behaviors that landed him in

---

You are completely and solely responsible for everything you are and everything you become.

---

jail in the first place. He would have continued to be angry and to feel sorry for himself. In prison, Allen was no benefit to himself, his wife, his family, his friends, or society. He would have continued to be a source of pain and trouble for all these people and more, but you can see how dramatically he increased the value of his life to the people around him and to himself by simply owning up to his past decisions and accepting responsibility for his future ones. In a moment of revelation, he went from being a drug pusher to being a future box office millionaire. Not bad for an ex-con!

You are completely and solely responsible for everything you are and everything you become. You are completely and solely responsible for everything you achieve or fail to achieve. You are where you are and you are what you are because of yourself, your own thoughts, and your own behaviors. No one else is responsible or can be responsible for the outcome of your life. I know this may be a harsh dose of reality for some people reading this book, but it's true. A doctor starts the healing process by showing you the hard, cold facts derived from your blood tests and x-rays. Then, facing the objective realities of that truth, he tells you what he can do to help you get back on your feet. In this straightforward chapter, I'm trying to do the same thing. I'm trying to kick off this book by enabling you to see yourself and your situation for what they really are. Once you do, I can help you do something about it.

You need to realize that you are doing the work that you chose to do. You are earning the income that you chose to earn. You married the person that you chose to marry. You are living where you chose to live. You have always been free to choose, and you are still free to choose. But in the real world, you have to eventually live with the consequences of all the choices you have made or failed to make. You see, the issue here is responsibility, and this issue is one of the most important issues in life. It is rapidly becoming one of the most important issues in society, too, because most of the political bickering that is so prominent in our country right now finds its roots in the two opposing views that people hold on this subject.

What are the two schools of thought on the issue of personal responsibility? On the one hand, there are those who believe that no one is really responsible for anything. We are all victims of the external factors and uncontrollable internal powers that dictate our plight. Society, genetics, and the government control individual destiny, therefore society and government are responsible for taking care of people and for making many of the decisions that will determine the outcome of their lives. On the other hand, there are those who believe that, in a society, individual responsibility is the most essential element of personal freedom. This group believes that with individual liberty comes individual responsibility and accountability. Therefore, a person is responsible for the consequences of his own choices and behaviors.

Obviously, I fall into this second group and I believe that the Bible supports this philosophy of relationship between society and the individual. For a person to be genuinely happy and fulfilled, that person must be legitimately free. But freedom carries with it a necessary measure of personal responsibility. If you are going to make your own choices and plot your own course, then you have to live with the consequences, both good and bad, of the choices you make. I am not mandated to either share in the rewards of your good choices or carry the burdens of your poor choices. If you are free to go your own way in life, then you must eat the fruits derived from the seeds you have sown.

Greater progress in your life is possible only to the degree that you accept more responsibility in your life. No one else can or will take up your share of the load. Nevertheless, personal responsibility is a funny thing, because the more responsibility you accept, the more often people will be willing to help you. But the less responsibility you take for yourself, the less people will want to lend a helping hand.

Robert Schuller, founding pastor of the Crystal Cathedral, wrote a great book entitled *If It's Going to Be, It's Up to Me*. In that book, we are reminded that nobody is coming to your rescue. If you want things to get better in your life, you have to get better. If you want things to change, you have to change. If you want things to improve or grow or increase, you have to improve or grow or increase. That's the simple divine law of responsibility.

The most wonderful reward you will receive for accepting responsibility in your life is the tremendous sense of freedom and satisfaction that it gives you. When you step up to the plate and accept responsibility for your own decisions and for the circumstances you have created in the past and can create in the future, you will feel more positive about yourself and happier with life. You will feel good about yourself and excited about the future. You will feel like you are finally guiding your own ship and controlling your own destiny. You will feel like you are truly having an impact on your own destiny and that you are no longer a victim of more powerful people or unseen forces. So take responsibility for yourself, and take responsibility for your dreams and ambitions too.

You also should take responsibility for your work. In fact, in every industry, the "greats" act as if they own the place. Even though they may have an employer and draw a W-2 every year from their firm's accounting department, they still think of themselves as self-employed. No matter who signs their paychecks, they work as if they are working for themselves. And regardless of the position they may fill in the company, they are usually among the most respected people there. Why? Because they take responsibility for everything they touch. They never blame anybody but themselves when things go wrong. They never make excuses. They assume responsibility without hesitation.

This kind of person is the backbone of any business, whether he is an owner or a lower-level employee. In his areas of accountability, he looks for new challenges and assignments. He eagerly seeks out fresh responsibilities, and when something needs to be done, he is the one who takes the initiative to do it. He volunteers for new assignments, because he wants to have his hands all over everything that happens in that place. He does his work quickly and he does it well. Yes, he typically wants "credit" for what he does right and for the problems he solves, and he certainly wants to prosper financially and professionally as a result of his efforts, but he also wants the responsibility that goes with these amenities, and he wants the accountability that goes with this level of trust.

No matter where you might be right now in your life—working for yourself or working for someone else—you need to assume 100 percent responsibility for all that falls under your domain. If you don't, you will never really achieve major success in your life. If you don't, nothing else will ever really work out for you. So if you want to create the life of your dreams, you have to take responsibility for your life, its direction, and its outcomes. You have to give up your excuses, your victim mentality, your reasons why you can't do what you want to do, and all the stories you tell yourself and others in order to rationalize your current plight.

Someone recently told me, "Dr. Dave, I heard there's going to be a recession and that it's going to be pretty deep and pretty long."

"Well," I responded, "I choose not to participate."

Believe it or not, even the economy and its impact on your life is, to a great extent, a matter of choice. In fact, everything you experience in your life is a matter of choice, whether it is internal or external. You can't always control what other people do and what happens in the world around you, but you can always choose to control how you are going to respond to it. The outcome of your life is the sum total of all the responses you make to the various situations that arise in your life.

Moses and Pharaoh are great examples. In the book of Exodus (the second book of the Bible), God chose Moses to be His spokesman and His representative to Pharaoh, king of Egypt. Then God sent Moses to tell Pharaoh to release the Jewish people from their slavery, thus allowing them to travel with Moses to Canaan (the Promised Land). When Pharaoh resisted the demands of Moses, God sent a series of ten terrible plagues upon the nation of Egypt in an effort to convince Pharaoh that He meant business and that Pharaoh should comply with His demand. The same ten plagues that built the faith of Moses, caused Pharaoh to resist with ever-increasing stubbornness. Both men witnessed the same ten plagues—the plague of gnats, the devastating destruction of horrific hailstorms, the visitation of the angel of death—yet while Moses' heart softened as a result of that experience, Pharaoh's heart grew more and more rebellious. As someone aptly summarized, "Apparently, the same sun that melts butter, hardens clay."

These two men encountered the same God and witnessed the same miracles. But the outcome of their lives and their eternal destinies was radically different because of the different ways they chose to respond to what was happening around them. One took responsibility; the other lived in denial. One chose to learn and grow; the other chose to dig in and resist. One initially resisted but chose to comply; the other initially resisted and increased his level of resistance. So God elevated Moses and destroyed Pharaoh on the basis that each man was responsible for his own choices!

Regardless of those things in your life that you cannot control (your family history, your genetic makeup, the economy), you will always have control over three important things. You will always have control over the thoughts you think, the images you visualize, and the actions you take. The choices you make regarding these three ongoing areas of your life will determine the very outcome of your life and the quality of your existence. If you don't like the outcome thus far and the quality is not up to your expectations, you are going to have to change one or more of these three components of self-determination. You are going to have to modify what you think, the way you think, your daily habits, your reading material, your conversation, your dreams and fantasies, or something else, because these eventually determine who you are and where you end up.

Wayne Dyer, a well-known author and lecturer, said, "All blame is a waste of time. No matter how much fault you find with another, and regardless of how much you blame him, it will not change you. The only thing blame does is to keep the focus off you when you are looking for external reasons to explain your unhappiness or frustration. You may succeed in making another feel guilty about something by blaming him, but you won't succeed in changing whatever it is about you that is making you unhappy."[2]

You will never become successful as long as you continue to blame someone else or something else for your plight in life. You're the one who ate the junk food. You're the one who didn't say "no" when you should have. You're the one who took that job. You're the one who kept that job after you realized it was the wrong place to be. You're the one who ignored your better intuition. You're the one who

---

You will never become successful as long as you continue to blame someone else or something else for your plight in life.

---

decided to go it alone. You're the one! You're the one who created the thoughts that led to your actions. You're the one who formed the feelings that led to your thoughts. That's why you're where you are. And if you want to change where you are, you are going to have to stop complaining about your life and you're going to have to stop blaming people and circumstances for your life. You're going to have to take a long, hard look at yourself.

The tendency to blame other people and external factors for one's problems reminds me of the elderly man who was lying in a hospital bed, clinging to life and approaching his final moments. During one of those rare occasions when he was conscious and alert, he noticed his wife of fifty-seven years sitting in the chair beside his bed, and he mustered enough strength to whisper to her.

"Honey," he said, "can you come closer?"

His wife got up from her seat and leaned over his face, placing her ear close to his mouth so she could hear what might be his final words.

"You know," he said, "you were there with me when the house burned down."

"I know, Sweetheart," she said. "I know."

"And you were there with me when I lost it all and we had to start over."

"I remember, Darling," she replied.

Finally, he motioned to her to come a little closer. As she leaned even closer into his body so she could discern his words, he said, "You know, Baby Doll, you're bad luck."

Lou Holtz, the former head football coach at six different acclaimed universities, including Notre Dame, said, "The man who complains about the way the ball bounces is likely the one who dropped it."[3] The circumstances you complain about are typically those circumstances you created for yourself through your own thoughts, feelings, and actions, and they typically are circumstances you can change with new thoughts, feelings, and actions. If you really wanted to, you could find a better job. If you really wanted to, you could eat healthier food and less of it. If you really wanted, you could go back to school. You could live in a better house. You could be a better mother or father or friend. The problem is, you just don't want to. At least, you haven't wanted to until now.

And why is that? Why haven't you done those things that can change the quality and direction of your life? Because change equals risk! If you quit your job, you run the risk of being unemployed. If you try that new venture, you run the risk of being judged by others. If you launch that new business, you run the risk of failing and proving to others that your dreams were just a pipe dream after all. If you make changes in your appearance, you run the risk of losing your friends or evoking their disapproval.

Making life changes is both difficult and uncomfortable. So, if you are like most people, you just settle for the easier path in life and stay put. Then you complain about your life. The "greats," however, are people who refused to accept the status quo. They are people whose ambitions were so strong and whose passions were so consuming, they just had to take the risk. They were men and women who realized their lives were 100 percent the product of their own choices, their own friendships, their own work ethic, and their own ingenuity and determination. Nobody else put them where they were when their moment of enlightenment came, and nobody else could get them to the Promised Land. So they accepted responsibility for themselves and started the lonely journey to excellence and greatness.

You can do the same with your life if you will begin where they began. You can realize all the great potential that your Creator has placed within you if you will take responsibility for yourself and then do what's necessary to turn things around. Let's get busy. Let's analyze all the areas where you are potentially falling short and let's reveal the proven things you can do to improve those areas of your life. But I beg you to begin by taking responsibility for yourself. Otherwise, everything from here on is a waste of time.

Chapter 2

Mindset

Dealing with Your Belief System

Experience teaches us that if two people look at the same thing, each of them will see something different. A man and woman can be shopping, for example, and while the wife may see a beautiful new pair of shoes that would be ideal for her upcoming cruise, the husband only sees the price tag. She can see how perfectly those shoes might go with her new dress for the formal night of the cruise and how perfectly her long strand of pearls would accentuate the neckline of that dress. Her husband can only see how close the charge would put him to the credit limit on his Visa card.

The fact that people view the same experiences differently was driven home to me several years ago when a friend of mine told me a story of how he had witnessed a robbery at a convenience store. Immediately after the robbery, the police interviewed my friend to get his eyewitness account of the crime and the prosecutors took detailed information from him regarding the things he had seen.

But in the courtroom, during the trial, the defense attorney played a videotape from the surveillance camera that had been recording the activity that took place in the parking lot that evening. Everything my friend had sworn to was invalidated by the videotape. The details of his eyewitness account just didn't match up with the cold, hard realities of the objective evidence. His eyes and the eye of the camera recorded two different things.

All of us view life through a prism of our own experiences.

ATURDIDO

My friend was <u>bewildered</u> because he was not lying or twisting the facts, and he did not have a vested interest in the outcome of the trial. My friend had reported under oath what he thought he had actually seen. He reported what he remembered from that experience. But through that experience, my friend learned in a forceful way the truth that I want to convey in this chapter: Our view of life is shaped just as much by our perception of things as it is by the objective realities around us.

All of us view life through a prism of our own experiences. All of us view life through a particular paradigm. For better or worse, our view of things is shaped by the mindset we bring to each opportunity life presents to us. Our view of people is shaped by what we have been taught about people and what our past experiences have been with people. Our view of God is shaped by what we have been taught about God and what our past spiritual experiences have been. Our view of politics, art, business, religion, and every other facet of life is shaped by what we have seen, heard, and encountered throughout our lives. To a great extent, therefore, perception becomes reality.

What we come to think about people and things determines the way we see those people and things. The way we "see" life determines our interaction with the thousands of experiences and opportunities that life sets before us. In other words, our thinking shapes our life.

Nowhere is this principle more important than in the way we view ourselves. The way we view ourselves will shape everything about us and set us on a course that is almost irrevocable. In fact, no human being can change the direction of his life until he first changes the way he thinks about himself. Stinking thinking is, without a doubt, the primary hindrance to greatness. But the man who can recognize the way his mind shapes him and who can bring his own mind under discipline to proper thinking is the man who can do almost anything.

At some point in your life, you have probably heard the famous quote by Henry Ford. Ford said, "If you think you can do a thing or think you can't do a thing, you're right."[4] Ford, one of the greatest entrepreneurs and innovators in American history, realized that one's mental attitude totally shapes one's life. The person who thinks positively about himself will, over the course of his lifetime, do greater things and achieve more of his goals than the person who thinks negatively.

All of us have heard our friends and family members bemoan the things in life they view as impossible. In fact, this kind of thinking and this kind of speech are so much a part of everyday life that we hardly pay attention to them. "I wish I could own a house like that," they say, insinuating their own internal doubts that they ever will. Or perhaps they say, "I wish I had a job like that," insinuating their personal faith that they never will. The tragedy with statements like these is that they are true. They are true not because the attainment of such things is impossible for the ones who uttered these lines. Rather, they are true because the belief systems of the ones who spoke these things will make their statements true. These people truly believe they won't ever own a nice home, so they won't. They truly believe they won't ever have the kind of job they long for, so they won't. The only real difference between the person who lives in that beautiful house and the person who admires the house from afar is not opportunity or talent; it's their opposing belief systems, particularly as those belief systems relate to their own abilities and possibilities. While the man living in that house saw the house as an attainable goal, the one driving by in envy saw that house as something far beyond his reach.

Throughout history, the people who have attained success are the people who have been undergirded by a strong, unshakable belief in themselves. They believed in their own talents and abilities. They believed in what they felt "called" to do. And almost always, these great men and women believed in themselves, despite the fact that others around them opposed them or failed to support them.

In the Bible, Joseph had a dream that his father, mother, and brothers would one day bow down to him. Not realizing the full implications of his dream or the enormous amount of time that would lapse before its fulfillment, Joseph was not wise enough to keep his dream to himself. Instead, he immediately shared his dream with his eleven brothers. In fact, he had this dream more than once, and he shared it more than once with his family. This only served to incite jealousy in his brothers, who already saw him as a spoiled brat. Eventually, Joseph's father chastised him for sharing his dream and his brothers hated him more for it. In fact, they hated Joseph so much that they sold him into slavery, and Joseph was carried away to Egypt, where he would spend many years of his life as a prisoner and a slave.

But Joseph never lost faith in himself, his dream, or the unique ability God had given to him to interpret the dreams of others. Eventually, after many years and through enduring persistence, Joseph's dream came true, and his brothers did come to Egypt to bow before him. Through the divine intervention of God, Joseph had become second-in-command in Egypt, and his brothers came to him for assistance during a devastating drought.

People with a positive mindset are able to accomplish amazing things. They are able to make tremendous sacrifices. They are able to endure hardships and resist temptations and distractions. They are able to overcome foes and navigate obstacles. In short, they are able to succeed in life where others fail simply because they see life as an ongoing series of opportunities. They also see themselves as uniquely qualified to seize those opportunities and extract from them every drop of splendor that life can afford. They aren't content with mediocrity. They aren't content with "just good enough." And whether others believe in them or not, they have a tenacious and resilient faith in themselves.

When it came to art, Vincent Van Gogh was such a man. Van Gogh sold only one painting during his short lifetime. Talk about a starving artist! Although Van Gogh made little money from the direct sale of his art and struggled with mental illness and personal rejection throughout his lifetime, he believed in himself as an artist and in the unique quality of his talent. Obviously, it took the rest of the world a lot longer to recognize his talent, but they eventually did. Today, some of Van Gogh's paintings are valued at millions of dollars.[5]

During his life, Van Gogh was rejected as a serious artist, and his lack of acceptance in his field speaks volumes about the way others viewed him while he was alive. Nevertheless, Van Gogh did not embrace this conclusion; he did not see himself the way others saw him. He saw himself as a gifted artist. He held to the hope that the world would eventually embrace his art and appreciate his creative contributions. And while he waited for the rest of the world to catch up to him in his understanding, he believed in the talents God had given to him and he believed in himself.

The same could be said of almost every man and woman of greatness. All of them overcame great opposition and great ridicule. All of them believed in themselves when others around them could not see their potential or their proclivity for greatness. Walt Disney's art teachers told him that he lacked talent, that his silly drawings of animated flowers and wizards would never command the respect or attention of the public. Elvis Presley was told repeatedly that, although he had some talent, he didn't have enough talent or the right kind of talent to succeed in the music industry. The same was said of the Beatles. How would you like to be one of the many producers who turned them down for a recording contract? Whether we are talking about politicians like Abraham Lincoln or sports icons like Babe Ruth, musicians like Benny Goodman, or entrepreneurs like Bill Gates, the truth remains that all these people possessed an almost other-worldly ability to believe in themselves when nobody else would and to press through toward dreams that nobody else could see.

To be great and to achieve your own success in life, you must begin the journey with an unshakable confidence in your own abilities. Whether others believe in you or not, you must believe in yourself. Whether the temporary conditions and circumstances that surround you are favorable or not, you must believe in yourself. In fact, if you follow in the footsteps of the great men and women named above, you probably won't find your circumstances to be perfectly favorable and you probably won't find much encouragement and support from your friends and family members. Nevertheless, your destiny will not be determined by circumstances or the opinions of others; your destiny will be determined solely by your own analysis of yourself and what you believe you can squeeze out of life. This is why people of achievement often overcome great obstacles in order to reach the plateau of success and often confront criticism head-on in their climb to the top. Nobody is able to steal their dreams or fill them with self-doubt or an inferiority complex, because they see themselves as worthy of the prize.

To be great and to achieve your own success in life, you must begin the journey with an unshakable confidence in your own abilities.

Eleanor Roosevelt once said, "No one can make you feel inferior without your consent." That is true. Too many people have succumbed to mediocrity, even though they possessed the potential for greatness, simply because they chose to buy into someone else's view of them. Sometimes it is the people closest to us—a parent, a teacher, a mentor, a friend—who speak the most negative things into our lives and plant the most limited expectations in our hearts. It was that way with Joseph; it was that way with many of the greats; it is that way with most of us. But great people have chosen to ignore the negative appraisals of others and instead to buy into God's view of them.

In fact, right now is a good time for you to realize that there are only three ways to view yourself. It is up to you which of these belief systems you will adopt and pursue. It is up to you which mindset you will choose.

The first way to view yourself is through the eyes of other people. In other words, by adopting this mindset, you choose to see yourself as other people see you, and you choose to define yourself as other people define you. This can be good or it can be bad, depending upon the environment that shaped you and the way your parents spoke to you during your formative years. For most people, however, the appraisal of others has been brutal, to say the least, because nobody can understand what potential lies dormant in another person's heart or what dreams run through another person's heart or what potential lies within another person's character. Consequently, it's simple human nature (at its worst) for others to project upon you the limitations of life that they see in themselves and the failures in life that they have experienced.

The second way to view yourself is through your own eyes. Again, this can be positive or negative, depending upon your view of yourself. In reality, however, most of us, while we were young, had limited interaction with the world, and few of the people who shaped our thinking hold high expectations of life. Consequently, most of us grew up with ever-decreasing expectations of life and of ourselves.

The third way to view yourself is through the eyes of God. To see yourself the way God sees you is the only accurate way to grasp your true identity and potential. According to the Bible, God sees you "in Christ." In other words, He sees you the same way He sees His Son, Jesus. And in God's eyes, you are already a complete and perfect person because Jesus is complete and perfect.

Have you ever noticed photographs of famous people in magazines, and have you noticed how those photos are often touched up and altered? If the magazine wants to cast a certain celebrity or political figure in a bad light, the editors of that publication have a way of finding the worst possible picture of the person, a picture that was taken at the worst possible moment on the worst possible hair day under the worst possible conditions. The subject always has a scowl on his face, he is always dressed terribly, and he looks overweight and angry. On the other hand, if the magazine wants to promote a certain public figure, that magazine will take the best possible picture of the person and then spruce it up by air brushing the imperfections from the subject's face, minimizing the weight of the subject, and improving the "glow" of the person's skin. Photographers these days can use computer technology to fix almost any problem with a photograph, removing almost any imperfection found in a subject.

Well, that's the way God is with you and me. He sees us "touched up," and He has a picture of us that is free from faults and failures. In fact, God sees us "in Christ" as perfect people. In God's eyes, all our warts and moles have been miraculously removed, our hair is perfect, our smile is bright, and we all look thin and buffed. In reality, every man comes into the world with sin in his life, and most of us make things worse for ourselves as we multiply our failures through foolish decisions and poor choices. But God forgives these things. Through Christ, He makes us perfect in His eyes, and that is why He can see us as balanced and complete. He can see us with all the blossoming potential that He sowed into us when He first created us.

Are you aware just how unique you are in God's eyes? There's nobody else like you in the entire world, and there never will be anybody like you. You have a fingerprint that has never been duplicated and never will be duplicated. You have a retinal scan that is so unique, it can be used to identify you with the same accuracy as a fingerprint or a social security number. When God said, "...*Even the very hairs of your head are all numbered...*" (Luke 12:7), He knew something way back then that science is just now discovering. He knew the DNA coding in a single strand of your hair contains numbers that can be used to set you apart from every other human who has ever lived or who will ever live on this planet. There is nobody like you.

God understands your uniqueness, and He knows your potential. Unfortunately, too many of us have listened to our own voices or the voices of others. We have allowed others to identify us and to draw boundaries around our lives, and we have allowed our own misshapen thinking about ourselves to set artificial limitations upon us. But instead of listening to others and to ourselves, we need to listen to what God has to say about us. After all, God can see everything. He can see yesterday and tomorrow at the same time. He can see what's around the bend in your life and mine. He can see what's over the crest of the hill. So if you and I are already a picture of perfect success in the eyes of God—airbrushed without wrinkles, blemishes, or any imperfections of failure—shouldn't we start thinking of ourselves in that way?

To be great and to be successful in achieving your dreams (which are God-given, by the way), you have to believe in yourself. The thing you really need to take hold of is the fact that your belief or lack of belief in yourself is a choice. You have the power to choose what you will believe about your own potential and what you will think about your own life.

The best definition of belief is found, once again, in the pages of the Bible. Who could possibly know more about faith than God? After all, His only request of us is that we believe in Him. So God himself has given us the best definition of real belief and genuine faith. In Hebrews 11:1, God said, "*Now faith is the substance of things hoped for, the evidence of things not seen.*" So faith, first of all, is the internal "evidence" of something that cannot be seen or proven at the moment. In other words, through faith, you don't have to see something in order to know it exists. In addition, faith is the "substance" of something that is hoped for. In time, therefore, true faith will yield the thing that is desired. True faith in the heart will eventually yield results in the physical world.

Faith in yourself, therefore, is the ability to see (before it grows to maturity) your own potential and a vision of where you have the capacity to go (before you actually get there). It is the ability to see clearly in your own heart and mind a picture of what you want to achieve (before you actually achieve it) and what legacy you want to create (before you actually create it). Faith is the ability to see a picture clearly in your own mind of who you are and what you were created to be and to do before you actually become those things, regardless of what others may think of you or say about you. And, if your faith is genuine, you know that the thing you envision is not contrived. Rather, it is a reality in your heart and it will eventually become a reality in the physical world. It is just a matter of time before everyone else can see what you see already.

Eventually, if one's self-confidence is genuine, faith and fact must merge. In other words, anything significant that has ever been achieved in the real world began as a tiny seed of faith within the heart of the one who gave it birth. Faith in oneself and one's ability to do a certain thing was always the point of conception for any great idea or achievement. But just because someone dreamed it, that didn't make it happen. Dreams only come true if faith in yourself is genuine, deep-seated, and based on an honest appraisal of your own abilities and passions. If your faith is based on a pipe dream, it probably won't come true. Faith and fact will never merge.

Let's face it—lots of people have pipe dreams. They see themselves as rock stars when they can't even play a guitar, they see themselves as Hollywood's next great Oscar winner when they have no observable talent for acting, or they see themselves as the next "American

Idol" when they can't even sing in front of an audience. But I'm not talking about pipe dreams here; I'm talking about real dreams, and the difference is easy to discern. While a pipe dream is based on an unrealistic appraisal of one's own passions, abilities, and experiences, a genuine dream of the heart is based upon a compelling inner drive that just won't go away. It's there all the time; it gets clearer rather than dimmer as the years go by, and it motivates the one who holds it to do something to make the dream a reality. These are the kinds of dreams that have given birth to every great invention, achievement, and accomplishment in the history of mankind, and these are the kinds of dreams that are the substance of magnificent accomplishment.

If you have a real dream—not a pipe dream—burning deep inside your heart, that is the seed that can give rise to your destiny. But if you ever intend to give life to that dream and if you ever intend to see it grow to maturity, you have to believe in yourself. Otherwise, your dream will die in the womb. It will never give birth. No dream of your heart can ever grow up unless you believe it is possible for you to turn that dream into a reality and that you are the person who can make it happen. If your dream is real, God would never have given you that dream without also giving you the resources, the talents, the gifts, and the skills that are necessary to succeed at your dream. He would never have given you that driving, gnawing motivation without also giving you the personality and the inner resources you would need to give it life. So believe in yourself, as God believes in you.

Belief in yourself is a choice, an attitude you develop over time, not an accident or an anomaly of nature. Belief in yourself is a deep-seated awareness that, at least in one area, God has made you to be very unique. It is an understanding that you have what it takes—all the resources, all the talents, all the abilities—to accomplish that which compels you. It is a self-confidence that overcomes all opposition and the doubts of naysayers and pessimists who might infiltrate your life. It is a strong positive attitude and belief in who you are "in Christ."

On the surface, this kind of self-confidence might sound like haughtiness or pride. Christians especially have been disciplined to avoid pride, and anything that smells like pride can quickly become offensive to those who want to have good moral character. But I propose that such self-confidence is not prideful. In fact, I would propose that self-confidence is godly. I have already explained to you that a strong belief in oneself should stem from the way God sees

---

Belief in yourself is a deep-seated awareness that, at least in one area, God has made you to be very unique.

---

us. In heaven, God already sees us as perfect. He already sees us as successful. So to embrace a genuine, God-given dream and to pursue it with passion and abandon is not based upon one's own sinful estimation of self. Rather, I propose that it is based on God's high esteem of those He loves.

But let me also help you here by better defining for you just what pride is in the eyes of God. Or better yet, let me explain what pride is not. Pride is not self-loathing or low self-esteem. When the apostle Paul wrote about pride, he said simply, "...*Do not think of yourself more highly than you ought, but rather think of yourself with sober judgment, in accordance with the measure of faith God has given you.*" (Romans 12:3 NIV). If you will notice, Paul never told us that we needed to think of ourselves lowly. He never told us that we needed to hate ourselves. Even though tradition may teach us that humility is synonymous with low self-esteem, the Bible doesn't support that kind of conclusion. Paul never told the believers in Ephesus they should think negatively about themselves. In fact, he told them they needed to think highly of themselves and to see themselves the way God saw them, "in accordance with the measure of faith God has given." But Paul set a maximum limit to their high self-esteem. He warned them they should not think of themselves more highly than they ought. In other words, Paul envisioned a kind of ceiling to self-assessment. He envisioned a ceiling of reality. He wanted God's people to think highly of themselves, just like Paul thought highly of himself (just read the book of 2 Corinthians). But Paul also knew that pride came from a false over-assessment of oneself, so Paul warned the people not to draw conclusions about themselves that ascended above reality.

The key here is to see yourself accurately, and the most accurate picture you can ever get of yourself is the picture that God has already painted of you in heaven. You don't need to focus on the picture you have painted in your own mind, and you certainly don't need to focus on the picture of your life that others have painted for you. Those people, even the closest ones to you, cannot possibly know the height and depth and breadth and strength of the dreams that beat inside your heart. They cannot possibly know the reality of that "seed" God has placed within you. Only you can understand these things about yourself, and only you have the resources and skills to bring those things to fruition. To know this about yourself and to grasp this without apology is to have an accurate appraisal and picture of yourself.

There was a little boy who wanted to play a trick on his grandfather. Like so many other boys his age, this little boy was naturally mischievous. He had recently discovered the strong taste and powerful aroma of Limburger cheese, so while his grandfather was taking an afternoon nap in the bedroom, this little boy sneaked into the bedroom and placed a tiny bit of Limburger cheese in his grandfather's moustache.

When the grandfather awoke, he said to himself, "This bedroom stinks." So he got up and went into the living room. "The living room stinks too," he said. Then he went into the kitchen. "Even the kitchen stinks," he continued. "In fact, the whole house stinks." Finally, the grandfather went outside to get away from the bothersome odor and to get some fresh air, only to discover that he could not escape the harsh odor that was bothering him. "My goodness," he told his grandson, "the whole world stinks."

The point of this story is that, to some people, the whole world does stink. Their attitude controls them. So no matter where they go or what they do, they cannot escape the "stinking world" that drives them crazy. Why? Because they may move from room to room to room, but they always take their attitude and perspective with them. Like a piece of Limburger cheese under the nose, their negative attitudes toward life and themselves cause them to experience everything in life in a negative way.

Habakkuk, one of the prophets of the Old Testament, said, "*Though the fig tree does not bud and there are no grapes on the vines, though the olive crop fails and the fields produce no food, though there are no sheep in the pen and no cattle in the stalls, yet I will rejoice in the Lord, I will be joyful in God my Savior*"(Habakkuk 3:17-18 NIV). In other words, it is a choice to rejoice, just as it is a choice to think positively about life. I will rejoice. I will embrace the vision that is buried deep inside my heart. I will believe that God has given me what it takes to bring that vision to harvest. My attitude is not dependent upon the temporary circumstances that surround me, because those circumstances will rise and fall. Sometimes, there will be grapes on the vine, and sometimes there won't. Sometimes my crops will be abundant and sometimes they will fail. But I will have a positive mental attitude, because I choose to have one.

The only thing holding you back is your own stinking thinking and your own unwillingness to see yourself the way God sees you.

Just as it is a choice to be negative—yes, whiners and complainers and negative people choose to think the way they think—so it is a choice to be positive and to be confident in oneself and one's own abilities to succeed. Why would God give you a heart that dreams and why would God give you a mind that has the capacity to formulate plans for bringing your dreams into reality and why would God place you in a world where dreams come true for others if God didn't intend for your dreams to come true, as well? God believes in you. The only thing holding you back is your own stinking thinking and your own unwillingness to see yourself the way God sees you.

It's a choice to rejoice. It's a choice to think positively—not unrealistically— about life! A positive mental attitude won't make everything perfect. It won't make everything easy. You still have to put muscle behind your dreams to make them come true. But a positive attitude about life and a quiet confidence in yourself are the "non-negotiables" in the pursuit of excellence. Without them, the journey from good to great will never occur.

Ty Cobb was one of the greatest professional baseball players in history. Playing when the sport was in its infancy, Cobb set records that still stand today. He was an amazing man and an amazing athlete. One of Cobb's most enduring achievements was his lifetime batting average. Over the course of his career, Cobb had an amazing lifetime batting average of .367.

When Ty Cobb was forty-nine years old, he was inducted into the Major League Baseball Hall of Fame. In fact, he was part of the very first slate of inductees who became part of that noted institution. Then Cobb continued a fruitful and rewarding life until he died in 1961 at the age of seventy-four.

During the latter years of Cobb's life, a reporter interviewed him about his stellar career and his amazing lifetime batting average of .367. In the course of that interview, the reporter asked Cobb, "What kind of batting average do you think you would have if you were still playing baseball today?"

Cobb told the reporter that he thought he might be able to hit around .290 or so. The reporter began to probe deeper, trying to understand why one of the greatest hitters of all time thought his batting average might drop 77 points in the modern baseball era. Sure, .290 is still a very respectable batting average for a major league player, but what was it that would cause Ty Cobb's overall average to drop at all?

"Is it the fact that they play a lot of night games in modern stadiums?" the reporter asked. "Is it the fact that they play a lot more games and travel more frequently and for longer distances? Is it the fact that these newer stadiums are larger and that most of them have artificial turf? What is it that would cause such a great hitter to think his batting average would drop at all?"

"Oh, no, it's not any of those things," Cobb responded. "I'm nearly seventy years old," he said.[7]

Approaching the age of seventy, Ty Cobb still believed that he could get a hit against a stout, young professional pitcher nearly three times out of ten. That's a positive mental attitude. That's belief in oneself and in the gifts and abilities bestowed by God.

Have confidence in yourself. Have faith in the God who sees you the way you were created to be, not in the way you currently see yourself and certainly not in the way that others see you. You have greatness in you, because God doesn't make junk. Now it's up to you to grab hold of that fact and build your life upon that fact from this point forward.

CHAPTER 3

PASSION

THE ENGINE THAT DRIVES YOUR LIFE

Have you ever attended a party or a church event or have you ever started work at a new workplace or classes at a new school? Have you ever gone somewhere where you were compelled to meet new people? Of course you have! There was a moment when you first met every significant person in your life. But if you would think back for just a minute and reflect on the typical conversation you had with each of those significant people at the moment you first met them, you would undoubtedly have to admit that your initial conversation consisted of three basic questions: What is your name? Where are you from? What do you do?

Most people are comfortable with their names, and most people are okay with their hometowns. But people are all over the board when it comes to their occupations. Some of them are proud of what they do. In fact, if it weren't so tacky, these people would probably wear their uniforms or nametags 24 hours a day so people would know they are a city planner, a congressman, or a professor of economics.

But many other people don't like that question. And I contend they don't like the question about occupation because they don't like the answer they have to give. All too many American workers spend the majority of their waking hours being average, mediocre, or even destructive in their work environment. Instead of doing something to change the world, they live from paycheck to paycheck and from weekend to weekend so they can simply afford to survive, and then every five days, they escape the drudgery that is their workweek. People like this are so consumed with making a living that they are missing life itself. They have no passion for what they do, and passion is the intangible quality that really makes life worth living.

In fact, passion is the fuel that propels men and women toward any significant measure of achievement, excellence, or fulfillment in their chosen fields of labor. Besides, passionate people are the source of real change in the world. The leaders and innovators in every industry share one thing in common: They simply love what they do. They have learned that by doing what they love doing, they are both personally and financially rewarded while simultaneously impacting others in a positive way. So finding passion in life is the single most important predictor of future success and significance. Consequently, the search for passion must be every man's highest priority.

Every man will be remembered for his passion or forgotten for his lack of it. Consequently, I cannot stress enough how important it is to discover the engine that drives your life. But how can you tell what your true passion is? Believe it or not, that's not such a simple thing for the average person. The typical individual has either failed to discover that adrenaline-producing love of his life or he has given up the search in favor of mere survival and occasional hits of pleasure. Nevertheless, there is something out there that can totally take hold of every man and every woman, and there is something out there that can totally consume your heart and mind, giving you a meaningful pursuit to pour your life into while providing you with more joy, satisfaction, happiness, and prosperity than you could ever imagine. But to begin your search, you need to know whether you are being driven by your true passion now or whether you have simply "settled" for what you currently have.

Your true passion should be easy to recognize, because your true passion will grip you emotionally. It will overwhelm you, because you care so much about it. Believe it or not, money will pale in significance when compared to your passion, once you discover it. You

---

*Every man will be remembered for his passion
or forgotten for his lack of it.*

---

will even surrender your life's savings in order to be able to devote yourself to the true purpose God has given you for your life. In the end, the pursuit of money is not the purpose for living; money is simply a means of achieving one's purpose in life. This is why we consistently hear stories about highly paid executives walking away from seemingly perfect careers in order to pursue their personal passions. This also is why men and women alike will spend exorbitant amounts of cash in order to chase those dreams that give them an adrenaline rush. These people have finally come to learn that money itself is incapable of meeting any human need. Our money must be spent so we can purchase that thing which makes us happy.

Unfortunately, too many people fail to grasp this reality and end up living their lives upside down. They accumulate money so they will have money to spend on that which brings them happiness. But instead of working all their lives at jobs they hate so they accumulate the funds to pay for tiny doses of personal pleasure, I propose that these people ought to devote their time to pursuing that which drives their emotional engines. Then money will follow, because people who do what they love doing, do it better than anyone. They end up getting rich while doing what they love to do.

Great achievers know that a life driven solely by the pursuit of money is a life that can provide only limited happiness. Typically, the missing ingredient in the rich man's search for significance is the engagement of deep-seated emotions and the fulfillment of deep-seated needs. But a man's emotions can be satisfied only by the unique reason-for-being which God has assigned to him, and a man's needs can only be met by pouring himself into that purpose for which he was created. Consequently, each person must discover the unique calling that God placed within him before he was born.

Great achievers know that a life driven solely by the pursuit of money is a life that can provide only limited happiness.

Since your passion won't be my passion, I am only a fool if I spend my life trying to duplicate your destiny, because my passion and destiny are as unique to me as my personality and fingerprint. I will never be completely fulfilled or satisfied with life until I stop trying to imitate you and instead find my own destiny. That type of engagement with God's ideal plan for my life will stir my emotions and light a fire of passion deep within my soul.

Recent psychological research has demonstrated an undeniable link between emotions and performance. Good emotions stemming from satisfaction are required for superior performance in virtually every occupation. Whether in the arts, business, or ministry, great performers are driven by positive emotions. Personal feelings of fulfillment, happiness, and significance are the fuel that propels talented individuals to achieve more than their counterparts and reach their maximum potential.

Many people have jobs, but that doesn't mean they have found their purpose or their life's work. Too often, we use the terms "job" and "work" interchangeably, but work and a job are not the same thing. Jobs come and go, but work is something that is part of a person's life for as long as he or she lives. Your life's work will meet all the needs God created work to meet, and your life's work will fully engage you and call upon your full scope of resources and abilities. The difference between a job and work is like the difference between a mercenary and a soldier, between a hireling and a shepherd, between a wannabe singer and a musician. One is there for the paycheck while the other is there even if it costs him everything.

We can better understand the difference between a job and fulfilling work by looking at the original creation in the opening verses of the Bible. In the book of Genesis, long before sin entered the picture, God took the man He had made in His own image and placed that man in a beautiful garden He had sculpted out of the earth specifically for him. But before God would place the man in that garden, there were seven specific things that God designed for the man's pleasure. These seven things—beauty, food, wealth, work, boundaries, sleep, and relationships—were formed to make man's life satisfying and wonderful, and man was made in such a way that he needed these seven things in order to be content and complete.

It is important to note that work was one of these original pleasures. Work was not a curse. Work existed before sin entered the world. It was a blessing and a delight. God *"took the man and put him in the Garden of Eden to work it and take care of it"* (Genesis 2:15 NIV). And God told Adam to *"be fruitful and increase in number; fill the earth and subdue it"* (Genesis 1:28 NIV).

Because sin is now a part of the human experience, the wonderful things God originally created for man's delight have now lost their luster. Although they were designed to meet man's needs, they actually have become part of man's problem. Work is among those blessings of God that have become counterproductive under the curse of sin. Without meaning, purpose, and passion, work is not emotionally satisfying and is more like a prison than an outlet for one's limitless creativity.

Do you care about what you are doing? Is your heart into it? If not, you should know that you will never find your passion with your head or with your wallet; you will find your passion only with your heart. Too often, people finish their labors at the end of each day, physically exhausted and emotionally numb. They endure the week and look forward to the weekend so they can really start living and experiencing the great emotions God formed in them.

Due to the disconnect between one's livelihood and the passion that makes life worthwhile, recent studies have revealed that disengaged employees are now costing their employers millions of dollars every year. In fact, the lack of emotional involvement in the workplace has led researchers to coin a brand new term: absent while present. People actually show up for work, but they aren't really there while they're there. They show up late, take extra long lunch breaks, leave early, and spend most of their workdays surfing the web or chatting at the water cooler. Science has now recognized this phenomenon, customers can sense it when it is present, and the workers themselves realize it is true. Have you ever seen that bumper sticker that says, "A bad day fishing is better than a good day working"? Enough said!

If you are truly afraid of failing at something, then the presence of that fear might be a key indicator that you have accurately identified the thing you really need to be doing with your life.

The symptoms of this tragic syndrome of purposeless living are all around us: blaming others for our own lack of success and happiness, constant feelings that something is missing from one's life, ongoing regrets over lost opportunities of the past, living in the past or the future rather than the present, and doubting one's ability to change one's own life. If the work that awaits you each day doesn't both scare and excite you, then you have probably fallen victim to this pervasive mindset of disengagement, a mindset that has turned our current world into a culture of mediocrity. And if you have fallen victim to this way of thinking, it's probably because you are doing the wrong thing with your life. A little passion can cure all your ills.

Talking about passion, here's a little hint: If you are truly afraid of failing at something, then the presence of that fear might be a key indicator that you have accurately identified the thing you really need to be doing with your life. As human beings, we really hate to fail at something we care about. If I were to fail at the thing I truly love the most, then what would be left for me to dream about or pursue? So to avoid failure, I tend to hide my passion for certain things behind well-crafted defensive remarks like, "It's just a hobby" or "It's just something I do for fun."

As with romantic relationships ("Oh, we're just friends"), we humans tend to protect ourselves from failure in meaningful pursuits by carefully scripting self-talk for ourselves and catch phrases for others that are cleverly designed to keep us from accepting responsibility for our true passions and taking a risk by going after them. But by lying to ourselves like this, we often limit ourselves from recognizing and accepting those passions that can truly ignite our hearts. Why do we do this? Because it is too dangerous to be serious about something we love! I could get hurt. I could have my heart broken. But just as the single adult is eventually forced to choose between living alone for the rest of his life or taking a chance on love, so the person of great potential is eventually forced to choose between the same old path of predictability and safety where everybody else walks or the lonely path of passionate pursuit.

In his book, *The Passion Plan*, (Hoboken, NJ: Jossey-Bass, 2001) Richard Chang describes the four basic characteristics of passion. According to Chang, passion is:

- **Natural**. It is a part of you. You do not need to create passion; you just need to recognize it and place it in an environment where it can thrive.

- **Dynamic**. Passion has the ability to grow and to encompass new areas and spread in new directions.

- **Empowering**. Passion creates vision and energy for living, giving purpose and direction to life.

- **Unconditional**. Passion is unwavering. No matter what, it cannot be extinguished or denied.

It's equally important to know what passion is not. Passion is not:

- **Addiction**. True passion will not blind you to the other needs in your life (i.e. faith in God, healthy personal relationships, recreational time, etc.).

- **Talent**. Having the ability to do something doesn't mean that passion is present.

- **Forced**. You cannot force yourself into being passionate about something.

- **Fleeting**. Passion does not come and go with every new fad or with the seasons of your life.

In my travels and work, I have taught many thousands of people about this subject, and I have had the opportunity to talk one-on-one with hundreds of them. What I have learned is that most people understand the things I have been sharing with you about passion, and they believe what I have laid out for you in this chapter. But the problem lies in the fact that the vast majority of them have a difficult time defining a vision for their lives. After thinking about this problem for many years, I have finally come to the conclusion that most of these people are failing in their search for purpose simply because they are approaching the task backwards. They are trying to define a vision that can stir their passions; instead, they should be allowing their God-given passion to clarify their vision. Ken Hemphill wrote, "Passion fuels vision and vision is the focus of passion. Leaders who are passionate about their work create vision."[8]

So passion should precede vision, not flow from vision. When your heart decides the path it wants to travel and the destination it wants to reach, your mind will follow by drawing a map to get there and your body will start packing for the trip. Of course, there will always be a certain "tension" between what you want and the current realities on the ground that stand between you and your destiny. This gap between what your heart desires and what your hands are currently holding will present you with two options: You can either hold to the vision until you eventually achieve it, or you can lower your expectations in order to force your dreams to match up with your current realities. If you choose the second option, as the vast majority of people do, the things that excite and move you will be pushed farther and farther into the back of your mind as you subconsciously seek to relieve the tension that exists between "what is" and "what can be."

It is human nature to trade momentary comfort for a lifetime of regret and frustration. It is commonplace to trade temporary feelings of security for years of "what if." This tendency of the human condition to make our realities match up with our dreams is the root cause of mediocrity and, indirectly, the root cause of most of the world's biggest problems (domestic violence, crime, drug addiction, etc.).

A man with a vision and a woman with a passion are too busy chasing their dreams to waste their precious time on stupid things. They are focused. They are immovable. They know who they are and they know where they are going. They won't allow anyone else to define them, because their passion and visions define them, so the hateful words of friends and family members roll off them like water off a duck's back and their own natural tendencies to develop bad habits and to take the path of least resistance in life never find expression.

Your vision definitely determines your actions in life, because we, as humans, always react to what we see. For instance, imagine a jogger going through the park in the early morning hours while the mist is still thick and heavy. Suddenly, he runs through a large, sticky spider web that was spun across the trail sometime during the night. The jogger, like most of us would do, starts squirming around, frantically brushing himself in an effort to get that sticky web off himself and to avoid an encounter with the spider. Depending on his personality, the jogger might even yell a little as he desperately tries to free himself from the discomfort of the web.

In life, you are going to have to risk looking like a fool in order to free yourself from the web of mediocrity that ensnares the average person.

The jogger knows exactly what he is doing and why he is doing it, but to those watching from a distance, this guy probably appears to have lost his mind. He's yelling something, but there's obviously nobody around to listen to him. He is squirming, dancing, jumping, brushing his hair, running his hands all over his body, and wiggling like somebody put ants in his jogging shorts, but there's no apparent reason for such behavior. In most parks in America, the bystanders would be calling 911 so somebody could come get this crazy man. But these observers don't see what the jogger sees. They don't feel what he feels.

In life, you are going to have to risk looking like a fool in order to free yourself from the web of mediocrity that ensnares the average person. At first, your passion won't make sense to others. Just as Joseph's brothers retaliated against him because of his dreams, most people will actually mock your dreams, mock you for believing in them, or try to convince you to give them up because they are atypical. But always remember this: Living your life by "common sense" will always make you common. When you go for what is in your heart, others may ridicule you or even ostracize you, but deep in their hearts they will admire you and eventually brag about knowing you, because passion is the fuel that drives us to greatness.

Nelson Mandela once said, "As we are liberated from our own fear, our presence automatically liberates others."[9] So whether they know it or not, the bystanders in your life are depending on you to make it. Consequently, you need to swim against the tide and run against the wind as you tenaciously, persistently, and methodically pursue your dreams. No matter what, refuse to let go of your vision and allow your passions to steer you through the maze of life. The greatest visionaries of all time were people who were passionate about their calling. In order to reach their individual destinations, each one was forced to overcome the common destroyers of passion that all of us face in life. But they were up for the battle, and they overcame the hypnotic lure of the voices of mediocrity.

We, too, if we intend to be successful, must take inventory of our lives in order to identify these same negative influences that exist all around us, and then we must protect ourselves from their effects. But what exactly are these destroyers of passion? What exactly breeds mediocrity? What are the things that these voices of "common sense" are planting in our minds each day to deter us from the purpose for which we were created?

As Mandela noted, fear is the primary deterrent to passion. Fear keeps people from moving forward. It keeps people in jobs they hate and relationships that are bad for them. Because we are afraid of being alone, making a mistake, or admitting to ourselves that we are doing the wrong thing with our lives, we "settle" for what we have and we abandon the dreams that really make our hearts quiver.

The second deterrent to passion is self-doubt. We humans tend to believe in others, but not in ourselves. Meanwhile, most of the people in whom we place our trust doubt themselves. They're just better than us at hiding it. But the fact remains that self-doubt, a specific type of fear, is the cause of many ambitions dying on the vine. In a cemetery, there are far too many unwritten songs, too many unwritten books, and too many dreams that never came to be. Too many people tragically live their whole lives doubting the abilities God gave them!

A sense of unworthiness is another deterrent to passion. It's amazing how many people feel guilty for their success and undeserving of their happiness. They feel guilty about even pursuing their passions, much less fulfilling them. Nobody knows the heights and depths of your faults and failures quite like you do. For this reason, you can easily allow your occasional mistakes or your minor character flaws to blind you to all the potential that lies within you. The irony is that there is nothing that can help you rise above your faults quite like immersing yourself in that thing which most excites you. Nevertheless, many people focus on what they used to be rather than what they were created to be.

Another killer of dreams is disbelief. All my life, I have noticed a strange phenomenon about belief and disbelief. I have noticed that people can believe in others; they just can't believe in themselves. Think about that for a moment. What makes another person better than you? Or what makes you inferior to someone else? Aren't both of you created in the image of God? Doesn't God love both of you equally? Don't both of you have a complicated mixture of past failures and future potential? Then what makes the successful man greater than you? Nothing! The only distinction between the person of mediocrity and the person of exceptionalism is the exceptional person's ability to believe that he can actually give birth to the dream that is within him. Greatness is not reserved for a tiny group of privileged people; greatness is a possibility for all who believe.

An additional negative thought process that snuffs out passion is a limited view of life. I personally know people with this problem, and it's difficult to help them see beyond today and the immediate circumstances of their lives. Over time, these people have fallen into a rut of "sameness" and predictability and they cannot see any way to get out of that rut, so they have simply accepted the path they are traveling and they can imagine no way to steer their lives in a different direction. It's as if their lives are running on automatic and the wheels of their locomotive are set on immovable tracks. In their minds, everything is predetermined and the course is established. The train is moving forward at full steam, and there's no way to even steer the thing in an alternative direction, because the rails they are riding are their only option. This sense of hopelessness is birthed in the negative belief that things are the way they always have been and that things will always remain the way they are. But just as your decisions and actions slowly created the world in which you live, new decisions and new actions can incrementally change the world of your future. A small decision today or a new relationship can dramatically change the direction of your life.

A final contributor to lost passion is an addiction to personal comfort. This is perhaps the most dangerous dream killing emotion of all, because a lot of people have already achieved some measure of success and a good reputation in an arena of life that is not really their passion. So why would these people want to risk what they have in order to chase something that might never become a reality? In their case, it's not so much a matter of fear as it is a matter of security and public respect. But those who are focused on the pursuit of money and public praise are those who are more concerned with others thinking they are successful than they are with actually being successful. Unfortunately, these people fail to understand that the greatest contribution they could ever make to the world is the gift of the "real them." They fail to comprehend that the most truthful measure of their lives is not what others think of them, but in the end, what God thinks of them and what they think of themselves. Henri Nouwen, a Catholic priest and popular spiritual writer, said, "In order to be of service to others we have to die to them; that is, we have to give up measuring our meaning and value with the yardstick of others."

Over time, people often allow other people and their own negative emotions to steal their dreams. They allow temporary circumstances to steal their dreams. When they were children, these people would dream every day. They wanted to be astronauts and explorers. They wanted to be mommies and daddies, and they wanted to live in big houses with white picket fences. They wanted to be stars and they knew they could change the world. In fact, when their teachers asked them, "What do you want to be when you grow up?" they always had an answer. But as time marched on and these children grew up, they allowed the realities of life to slowly rob them of their dreams. They stopped listening to the inner voice of their own uniqueness and they started listening instead to the advice of those around them who were already living lives of mediocrity. They started listening to the taunts of fear, self-doubt, unworthiness, disbelief, a limited view of life, and personal comfort. So, one by one, they slowly abandoned their dreams. Unfortunately, abandoned dreams never quite abandon us. They always linger around, haunting us with thoughts of "what if," tugging at our heartstrings every day, making us miserable.

Living your passion essentially means living the truth, but I have come to realize that most people are living a lie. The one who lies to you the most is yourself. You persuade yourself every day that you are happy, and, for the most part, you are. But there's still that lingering feeling that there's something more to life, that there's something you need to do, that there's a whole world out there that you aren't engaging, and that your life is rapidly slipping through your fingers.

Remember, truth always appears extreme at first. As philosopher Arthur Schopenhauer says, all truth passes through three stages. First, it is ridiculed. Second, it is violently opposed. And third, it is accepted as being self-evident.[10] Living the truth will require unusual courage and a willingness to face strong opposition, both from within and without. Every story of accomplishment includes some type of setback or rejection from people who are important in one's life. But eventually, that which is conceived through personal passion will give birth to something people will recognize as genuine and admire as genius.

Take a lesson from the turtle: You can only advance when you stick your neck out. Pursuing what you want will mean risking what you have. Actress Geena Davis put it quite well when she said, "If you risk nothing, then you risk everything."[11] By far, the leading cause of death for personal passion is comfort. Moving toward something significant always means moving away from something familiar, and most people just aren't willing to take that risk.

Passion also has a powerful magnetic effect on others; it draws people. Pretentiousness drives people away, but authentic passion attracts them. It is the root of what many people call charisma, that special "something" that makes certain people stand out from the crowd. Charisma is communicated through the eyes, the posture, and the voice, but it issues from a life of passion. According to Roger Ailes, a top media consultant and president of the Fox News Channel, "The essence of charisma is showing your commitment to an idea or a goal." So commit to following your heart by discovering your passion, living it, and giving it back to the world.

There are four paths to discovering your passion. You can discover your passion through experience. Gradually, you become aware of your passion through the day-to-day experiences of life. You also can discover your passion through change. Many people come to realize their primary passion in life through a major life adjustment, such as a birth, marriage, divorce, or death of a friend or loved one. You can discover your passion through intuition. Anything that is inborn, undeniable, and enduring is often the thing you should be doing with your life. Finally, you can discover your passion through an epiphany. Sometimes, a pivotal, life-altering event can suddenly and intensely make you aware of an underlying passion that deserves your full attention.

Of the four ways to discover your destiny, the most unusual way is through an epiphany, an unexpected and often catastrophic jolt that radically changes one's paradigm and priorities. Yet that is exactly what most people are waiting for before they will wake up to the passion that lies dormant within them. But you should not have to wait for an earthquake or a nuclear explosion before you connect with the real you. Instead, you should realize that your primary passion in life is already there and that it will probably come to the forefront through an internal whisper or through a deep, abiding impression that just won't leave you alone. Have you been listening to the internal whispers of your own soul? Have you been paying attention to the abiding motivations of your own heart?

Consider the following questions:

- Which section of the newspaper stands out to you? The Life section? The Money section? Style? National? International? Sports?

73

- What catalogs or periodicals do you read and collect? *People? Forbes?*

- What is the first section of the bookstore you visit? If all the sections of your favorite bookstore were removed except one, which section would you want them to keep?

- What part of nature moves you? The ocean? The mountains? Flowers? Wildlife?

- What are your three favorite movies? What is the common thread running through those movies that appeals to you?

- Who do you most admire? Why?

- If you had to live someone else's life instead of your own, whose life would you like to live?

- If you were allowed to make one powerful change in the world, what would it be?

- When was the last time you felt strongly about something? What was it that fired you up?

- What type of conversation draws you in? What subject gets you animated when you talk about it?

Usually, you will identify your passion in life by simply paying attention to your own tendencies, your own motivations, and your own penchants. That thing which constantly and irresistibly attracts you is probably that thing which also can give you purpose. It is the arena of life where you can make a difference, leave a mark, and create a legacy.

Perhaps one of the reasons people have such a difficult time seeing the obvious is because they misunderstand the nature of a God-given passion. A God-given passion is about others; it's not about you. It was given to you to benefit other people, and that is why

others can typically identify your calling in life while you are grop-
ing about aimlessly in search of it. If you are seeking your passion in
life merely to feel better about yourself, you might have a hard time
defining it. If you are seeking your passion because you want to live
a nicer life, you might search forever without satisfaction. But when
you finally realize that your God-given passion is actually given to
you because it impacts other people while gratifying your own created needs, you will probably be able to narrow your search and finally
recognize the passion that has been there all along.

You are here on this earth to bring glory to God and to benefit
others. It's not about you. It's about Him, and it's about them. True
passion always produces fruit: passion fruit. And fruit is never intended for the tree that bears it. Fruit always exists to benefit those
who wander beneath its branches. Passions that are pursued with
selfish motives only have a limited impact and a limited existence,
but passions that are pursued because they benefit others are passions that are limitless in their scope.

A God-given passion is about others; it's not about you.

You are blessed to be a blessing, because love is a giving thing.
Success is not as much about being driven as it is about being given.
When you are doing what you truly love to do, you will be compelled
to give yourself to that passion without reservation and your passion
will, in turn, enrich others. Love compels people to give of themselves. As Calvin Coolidge so eloquently put it, "No person was ever
honored for what he received. Honor has been the reward for what
he gave."[12] Never forget this.

What do you think when you hear these names: Jesus Christ? Adolph Hitler? Martin Luther King, Jr.? Princess Diana? Osama bin Laden? Mother Teresa? Some of these names invoke positive emotional feelings, and some of them evoke negative emotional feelings. The thing they have in common, however, is that each name moves you in some way. These were not "beige" people. They have been either bright figures of hope or dark figures of despair in human history. The mere mention of their names does something to incite your emotions. Why? Because each of them was passionate!

People feel passionate about passionate people. And people feel passionate about those who are passionate, because you can literally "feel" a person who has passion in his life. Actors and musicians are slightly below god status in Western society simply because they know how to emit strong emotions and how to stir emotional reactions in others. Have you ever watched the behavior of people at a Michael Jackson concert? Have you ever heard people sobbing during a movie? Have you ever seen the physical animation of the spectators at a college football game? Enough said!

Scientists have proven that emotions are contagious; they do something to us that logical thought cannot do. That is why it is edifying to watch people do what they love to do. When you are doing what you love, other people can actually feel the emotional energy that you give off and it affects them deeply on a subconscious level. Emotionally intense experiences have a way of imprinting themselves on our consciousness because our emotional memory is far deeper and far more enduring than our logical memory. So to make one's life an intense experience of living out personal passion is to make a permanent impression on others, to leave a legacy for all those who know you, and to positively and permanently inspire those who cross your path.

But while the fruit of passion is emotion, the signpost of passion is creativity. People who are passionate about their life's work are creative, regardless of their profession. In fact, creativity is nothing more than passion made visible. Agnes George DeMille, an early 20th-century dancer and choreographer, boldly stated, "It takes great passion and great energy to do anything creative." Creativity, therefore, is the thing that will set a passionate person apart from the crowd, even from those who are more skilled and more experienced.

Michael Jordan was arguably the greatest basketball player of all time, certainly one of the greatest. But while Michael Jordan's physical abilities made him a tremendous athlete and while his skills on the court made him famous, his creativity made him great, placing him in a class all his own. Jordan could create the most amazing shots at the most crucial moments in a game, and that's what made his name synonymous with greatness.

A man's creativity is a source of limitless potential. It is the door out of his present situation and the catalyst for all his future opportunities. God is introduced to us in the opening sentence of the Bible as "Creator," and since God's image is imbedded within each of us, we also should be creative by nature. It is our creativity that gives expression to our passion, and it is our passion that gives purpose to our lives. Bill Gates built the Microsoft Corporation and became one of the wealthiest men in the world, but it was his passion for technology as expressed through his creativity that set him apart and propelled him toward this notable achievement.

Not only does passion breed success; passion also breeds leadership. In fact, your passion for something automatically qualifies you as a leader in that arena, be it cooking, writing, speaking, or fishing. No matter what it is, passion gives you the ability to see farther and to work longer and to extract more out of yourself than the typical person. Passion pushes you ahead of your time and frees you from conventional thinking. Conventional thinking is comfortable. While comfort never produces progress in our lives, passion pushes us out of our comfort zones. Ideas that come from passion are, by nature, "hot" and original. They set the trends and create the future that the rest of the world eventually steps into. Passion is the catalyst for action and innovation. It is the force that is behind those people who seem to always make things happen.

Since passionate people produce passionate followers, passionate people are, by nature, leaders of others. They utilize their passions to inspire people on an individual level and to galvanize people on a massive scale. Great leaders know that in order to move large masses of people, you must connect with the emotions of those people. Emotions are created by one of two things: by someone who exudes passion or by one's own internal passion.

But passion, in order to be fruitful, must be directed. In other words, it must be structured. Just as electrical power must be channeled through the physical structure of cables and wires and just as ink must be channeled through the physical structure of a pen, so passion must be structured in order to find its expression and to produce something positive and lasting. Everything in life that is associated with power—whether electrical power, nuclear power, solar power, or wind power—must be converted, harnessed, directed, and channeled into a useful state. Otherwise, the power is wasted and the source of power becomes either impotent or destructive. But if the flow of that power is channeled through the form of structure, it becomes a thing of beauty and a thing of blessing.

It will take time and discipline to build your passion into full expression. Just as athletes, singers, and musicians are forced to work hard and to "train" the passion that is within them, so you must nurture your God-given passion in order to make it appealing to those who will be impacted by it. Even though you must not procrastinate in developing your passion, you also must resist the temptation to be in too big of a hurry, because things of substance take time to develop and mature.

Just as there is a gestation period between the time that an animal is impregnated and the time that she gives birth, so there is a gestation period between the time when you discover your passion and the time when that passion is fully mature, and that gestation period is the time when you must bring your passion to a full and healthy maturity. But the gestation period for great things is longer than the gestation period of little things. The gestation period for an elephant, for instance, is about twenty-two months while the gestation period for a hamster is about sixteen days. The bigger the dream and the greater the passion, the more time it will take to bring that dream to birth. Don't despise that precious time. Instead, use it to the fullest.

Everything great in life begins small, but it becomes great if it is genuine. Even God refuses to despise small things. Although God does despise "little" things—like "little" faith and "little" thinking—He refuses to despise small things. He himself asked, *"Who despises the day of small things?"* (Zechariah 4:10 NIV). God knows that, while "little" things are pathetic and hopeless, small things are merely the first stage of development for great things. Jesus himself changed the world through the lives of only eleven men.

Your investment in your passion—investment in time, investment in resources, investment in hard work—will determine your level of commitment to it, and your level of commitment to your passion will determine what becomes of it. The more you invest in fulfilling your passion, the more you will do that which is necessary to give it life. But the less you pour into it, the less likely you will be to fight for it when it is threatened or to maintain it when the going gets tough or the journey gets lonely. Big investment equals big commitment; little investment equals little commitment. It's that simple. Don't put it off for another minute. The pursuit of your passion begins with a simple decision you can make right now.

Before I conclude this discussion on passion, I want to ask you to commit to doing five specific and tangible things that can help you discover your passion and get started on the journey of bringing it to life. First, for the next thirty days, I want you to keep a "passion journal." I want you to record and catalog those things that move you, those things that "ring your bell" and give you joy and fulfillment. Pay attention to things you hate doing, but also note those things you love to do. Pay attention to what you regard as beautiful or worthwhile, but also pay attention to those things that disgust or repulse you. Consciously observe and note what attracts you, what brings you satisfaction, and what stirs your creative juices.

Second, I want you to take ten minutes and write down the names of at least six people whom you admire or detest. These are people you are passionate about! Then write one word beside that individual's name that best describes him or her. This will be the person's "brand" and it will help you put the name with the driving impetus of that person's life. It will also help you to better understand the powerful simplicity of the concept of passion. As you do this, the negative words that you write will give you a clearer understanding of those behaviors you resent and a clearer understanding of those positive values that are latent within you.

Next, ask your friends and family what they think you are passionate about. Sometimes, the people around you can see passions you don't see in yourself, and they can definitely feel the fire of the emotions you exude when you are engaging certain things. To see yourself through the eyes of those who truly know you can be embarrassing, but it also can be revelatory. So please do this exercise with honesty and sincerity.

Fourth, rent movies that move you and watch them again. Then ask yourself what they have in common. The common thread running through movies that move you is a thread that is inextricably linked to the God-given passion within you. Since nothing can move you unless it makes direct contact with a sensitive place within your deepest self, this can be a great way to start identifying your foundational passions.

Finally, list three watershed moments in your life, moments that have defined you. Then think about those experiences. What was it about them that so impacted you? Which negative experiences conditioned what you now hate? Which positive experiences brought to light what you now love?

Remember, you can't change your life
without changing your life.

Once you are finally awakened to the passion that is resident within you, feed that passion by investing time into it. Whether we are talking about human relationships or passionate pursuits, the proof of love is found in the investment of time. Build your life and build your environment to nurture your passion. Make sure that your surroundings are affirming your driving impetus and your destiny. Get books and audio recordings that stir your heart. Put up pictures and play music that motivate you to keep pursuing your dreams. Rent or buy movies that inspire you as you invest the necessary time to achieve your goals. But most importantly, spend your time with those people who are living their own lives of passion, a team of like-minded individuals who can challenge you to be your best.

If you want to be great, take these simple steps so you don't succumb to the common tendency of abandoning your passion in exchange for a life of comfort, familiarity, and mediocrity. Remember, you can't change your life without changing your life. But if you will do the right things instead of the common things that are modeled by most of the people around you, the rest of your life will be the best of your life.

CHAPTER 4

IMAGINATION

BRINGING YOUR DREAMS TO LIFE

Most people know the Christmas story. They know that Joseph and Mary traveled to Bethlehem and that Mary gave birth to Jesus in a stable. They also know that Mary was a virgin at the time when Jesus was born and that Jesus was a miraculous product of the Holy Spirit. But what a lot of people may not know is that, after the birth of Jesus, Joseph and Mary had several other children the good old fashioned way. Jesus, therefore, grew up with a house full of brothers and sisters.

On a few occasions in the gospel accounts, these brothers and sisters are mentioned and they are even named. But none of these young men and women actually accepted Jesus as their Savior until after the resurrection— a testimony to the reality of the resurrection itself. After the resurrection, however, at least two of Jesus' siblings not only became believers, but leading figures in the early Church as well. James was one of these leaders and Jude was the other. These two half-brothers of Jesus also authored books in the New Testament, books that bear their names.

James, who was known for his wisdom and his power of observation, wrote, "*A double minded man is unstable in all his ways*" (James 1:8). Writing further about this same man of indecision, James also said, "*...For he that wavereth is like a wave of the sea driven with the wind and tossed*" (James 1:6). James knew that it is impossible for a man to achieve what he wants until he first knows what he wants. But regardless of this sound biblical principle, too many people today have no idea what they want out of life and no idea where they are going. Like this unstable man that James describes, they are driven by the winds of whatever might be happening in their lives at any given moment, and they are tossed from one crisis to another. They have no purpose. They have no direction. And thus, they have no satisfaction.

I am convinced that one of the main reasons people fail to get what they want out of life is because they haven't decided what they want out of life.

I am convinced that one of the main reasons people fail to get what they want out of life is because they haven't decided what they want out of life. In other words, they haven't defined their desires in detail. I have learned that it is impossible for a man to leave where he is until he first decides where he would rather be. That's where vision and imagination come into play. No ship ever picks up anchor and sets sail on the high seas until the captain has a destination clearly in mind, and no person will ever pick up and move on with his life until he has a firm picture in his own mind of where he wants to be when the journey is finally concluded. The tragedy is that too many people have no destination in mind for their lives. They simply stay in port or they drift aimlessly on the high seas, tossed about by every breeze, every wave, and every circumstance that confronts them. In fact, it is the preponderance of the circumstances in their lives, rather than a clear destination, that defines their lives.

Whether you like it or not, you are going to have to live in the future. So I propose that it might as well be a future you have planned for yourself rather than a future that someone else or your own life's circumstances have planned for you. But before you can live your own future, you are going to have to become a dreamer and a planner. You are going to have to learn to imagine the place you want to be. All the greats did that.

In fact, Jesus himself was a tremendous visionary and planner. He was one who was driven by an internal picture of what He wanted the future to look like. Oh, I understand that Jesus told His followers, "...*Do not worry about your life, what you will eat or drink; or about your body, what you will wear...*" (Matthew 6:25 NIV). But Jesus was not trying to tell people to stop planning their lives. He was not telling them to drift aimlessly through life without purpose. In the Sermon on the Mount, Jesus was simply trying to tell people to stop worrying and fretting over those things that God would provide for them on the journey.

In fact, Jesus openly encouraged people to plan for the future. He planned for the future and spoke about things He was going to do in the days to come. He spoke about His pending crucifixion, about His ensuing resurrection, and about His second coming. He also spoke about heaven, which demonstrates that He had a clear destination in mind for His life and for ours. Believe me, anybody who can plan a marriage feast thousands of years ahead of time is a world-class planner. So Jesus wasn't telling people to give up their motivations and ambitions. To the contrary, He was telling them to keep pushing forward with purpose, but to stop sweating over the daily details along the way.

The great achievers in life clearly have a refined sense of both who they are and where they are going. They understand what their lives are all about and they have a clear sense of purpose and direction that cannot be changed by a breeze or a wave. To successful men and women, life is all about setting and achieving their heart's goals; everything else is merely commentary. They have the ability to set specific goals because they understand that goal setting will do more to guarantee their future success than any other mental activity they can engage. They understand that a present clarity of their decision is the essential starting point on their journey toward greatness. They also understand that the more focused they are through specific goals, the less likely they will be to drift away from their passions or to waste precious time and resources as they pursue them.

When you know where you are going in life, it is much easier to establish priorities and stick with them. It is much easier to redeem the time and to make the most of every day. It is much easier to make decisions and to define relationships. It is much easier to say "yes" to those things that can enrich your life and "no" to those things that can steal your destiny or condemn you to a lifestyle of habitual mediocrity. The God-given imaginations of the heart and the life-changing visions of the soul can completely alter the outcome of your life and the path you will travel to get to that destination. The more time and energy you spend on the important goals of your life, the more you will achieve during your life. But no man will ever get anywhere until he first knows where he is going.

Eleanor Roosevelt said, "The future belongs to those who believe in the beauty of their dreams."[14] Nothing is truer. These kinds of dreams—the beautiful kind that come from God and are deeply imbedded in what He made us to be—are the stuff that make life worth living and give us a starting point from which to do truly amazing things. But these kinds of dreams are not the typical "pipedreams" or "daydreams" that so many people confuse with vision. These are the dreams that have their substance in one's passions, not in one's fantasies. They are the first fruits of one's future, not an escape from the present. And they are the first glimpses into one's tomorrow, not a distraction from today's difficulties. The world's highest achievers are not those men and women who sit on the dock, watching the tide roll away while they waste time daydreaming about silly things. The world's most successful people are those who, deep inside their souls, can begin to see what they want their lives to look like in the weeks, months, and years to come. The highest achievers dream the biggest dreams.

You must dare to dream. In spite of how tenaciously the world may try to steal your dreams or discourage you from dreaming, you will never go anywhere in life until you can first see your destination in your own heart and mind. So dream. Napoleon Hill said, "All achievement and all earthly riches have their beginnings in an idea or a dream."[15] Therefore, if you want to extract a lot from life and if you want to give a lot to life, you need to learn how to imagine your life as it should be and then make your imaginations come true.

Marc Mero, a former champion with World Wrestling Entertainment (WWE), is a personal friend of mine. Marc travels all over the world, teaching principles of success and sharing the story of his meager beginnings and his ensuing achievements. For most of his life, Marc has had an admirable habit of writing down his dreams in a special notebook that he carries with him wherever he goes. Since he was a child, Marc has recorded all the deeper things that have resonated in his heart, and it is amazing how many of his dreams have come true over the course of his life due to his strong habit of capturing and recording the imaginations of his heart.

Marc's favorite little phrase is, "Think poz!" Obviously, he is a really positive person, and he is a real possibility thinker. Marc thinks this way and lives this way because his discovery of the power of imagination has really changed his life. When Marc was a young man, he used to dig swimming pools for a living. I must commend my friend because he has always been a hard worker and he always produced a quality product when he built those pools. But as Marc labored every day to put food on his table and a roof over his head, bigger dreams began to resonate in his soul and he started writing them down. Over time, this practice of recording his dreams turned his life around, and Marc eventually became one of the most accomplished wrestlers in the history of the WWE. Marc's dreams carried him from a blue-collar job to the status of a multi-millionaire and from insignificance to the top of his profession. And all this happened because Marc had dreams that he refused to let go, and he believed deep in his heart that he could accomplish those dreams.

Whether they think about it consciously or not, all the greats walk through three stages of dreaming. They start by imagining their dreams, then they visualize their dreams, and finally they plan their dreams. All dreams start with inspired imagination, but imagination alone will not make a dream come true. After the dream is born in one's heart, it must be transformed into a vision that consumes the soul and captivates the heart. Such a vision will then consume the one who gave it birth, and it will attach itself to the passion that is buried inside that person's soul as it slowly grows from an idea into a reality. But even vision and passion cannot make a dream come true without some realistic planning and hard work. Eventually, the genuine visionary learns how to go about the long, arduous process of realizing his dream by setting goals and by working the dream slowly into reality.

Every person with a legitimate dream and every company with a clearly defined vision will go through these three necessary processes. A dream is a blueprint for your ultimate destiny, but no blueprint becomes a standing structure without a lot of planning, execution, and good old-fashioned work.

IMAGINING YOUR DREAMS

As I explained earlier, the difference between a pipedream and a real dream is where we go with that idea. A pipedream is so fantastic, we typically use it to escape reality rather than to engage the future. But an actual God-given dream will burn in one's heart for so long, it becomes inescapable. It will imbed itself in one's mind so deeply, it becomes part of one's being. This is why it is important to capture that dream and to give it definition before time and the harsh realities of circumstance cause it to rust, rot, or evaporate.

The prophet Habakkuk said, "*Write the vision and make it plain on tablets, that he may run who reads it*" (Habakkuk 2:2 NKJV). Consequently, I encourage all people to take some time every day to write down their dreams. Over time, if a dream isn't real, it will diminish and die of natural causes. But by writing it down, a real dream will begin to take shape and definition. It will almost become tangible. So write down your dreams. In fact, start now to write down anything you may want to achieve with the rest of your life. Find some time occasionally, daily if possible, to write down your family dreams, your health dreams, your financial dreams, your spiritual dreams, and even dreams that involve your physical goals, the vacations you want to take, and the things you want to own. Write it all down. Record it, and let your imagination run free without limitation.

If you get stuck and you need to jump-start your imagination, just ask yourself, "What if?" What if everybody got paid the same salary? What would I do with my life if the salary didn't matter? What if I could have any job that I wanted? What would I do with my life? What if money were no object? What kind of house would I own? Where would I live? What would I do with my time? How would I spend my days?

Marc Mero wrote down his dreams so he could remember them. You, too, should write down your dreams, starting today. As you do, you will discover some amazing things. For instance, you will discover your passion. You also will discover your character. Over time, you will discover the difference between your real dreams and your daydreams. And you will discover how to develop your dreams into incredibly precise pictures of what you want to do, where you want to go, and how you want to get there.

VISUALIZING YOUR DREAMS
After you record your dreams, you need to learn to visualize them. King Solomon, that really wise leader of men, said, "*Where there is no vision, the people perish...*" (Proverbs 29:18). This is true, not only spiritually, but practically as well.

One of the main reasons people lose their dreams is because they fail to write them down, and one of the main reasons people fail to achieve their dreams is because they fail to visualize them. Perhaps the primary reason people fail to visualize their dreams is because the process of visualization takes time and effort. While the process of writing and recording dreams separates the man with a real dream from the man with a pipedream, the process of visualizing a dream separates the man with a wish list from a man with a real to-do list.

Visualizing a dream is a little bit like taking a photograph with one of those old Polaroid cameras and waiting for it to develop. After you snap the picture and pull the film out of the cartridge, you have to wait a while before you start seeing the blurry edges of the images in the shot. As time passes, the picture begins to slowly take form. At first, you can barely make out the shapes of people and things. But

---

One of the main reasons people lose their dreams is because they fail to write them down, and one of the main reasons people fail to achieve their dreams is because they fail to visualize them.

---

as the seconds tick away, you begin to recognize the landscape, the faces, and the various images in the scene. Eventually, you can see every detail of every subject in the photographic field.

A vision is a dream that gradually becomes so clear, nobody can take it away from you and nothing can discourage you from pursuing it. It becomes as real in your heart today as that thing will be when you actually hold it in your hand. You can see it, taste it, touch it, hear it, and smell it. As it takes further shape by means of additional visualization, your vision of your future becomes an all-consuming fire and the heart motivation that can propel you from where you are to where you want to be. And because of visualization, your dreams move beyond the realm of thoughts and words and they began to take shape in your soul as you truly begin to understand just how they can become realities.

Visualization is not a new thing or a man-made thing. It is not a New Age thing either. God is the author of the power of visualization, and He has sanctioned the visualization process in His own

Word. In the Old Testament, for instance, you will notice that God brought clarity to Abraham's dream through the use of visualization. God had told Abraham to leave his kindred and his home and to travel to a new land that God would give to him and his descendants forever. Abraham had done what God told him to do; he had traveled to the land of Canaan. Like all people, however, Abraham grew discouraged and impatient with his dream, because he was not seeing the provision of God's promise fast enough in his life. At that time, since Abraham didn't have a single descendant, he couldn't possibly see how God's promise could become a reality.

Empathizing with the tension between Abraham's faith in the promise and Abraham's difficulties with the present realities on the ground, God took Abraham outside his tent one night and asked him to look up at the heavens. You can read the story in Genesis 15, if you like. "Look up at the heavens and count the stars—if indeed you can count them," God told Abraham. "So shall your offspring be. Like the stars of the heavens and the grains of sand on the seashore, they will be too numerous to count." God used the imagery of stars and sand to help Abraham strengthen a vision within his heart that was growing weak due to the negative impact of temporary circumstances.

It's obvious to me that Abraham had already written down the dream. He had already recorded the promise God had made to him. Who else could have passed down to subsequent generations the information about Abraham's private life that is recorded in the book of Genesis? But with this amazing encounter with God, Abraham's dream transcended the writing process and took root in his heart as a developing and emerging photograph of what it could actually become. With the Lord's help, Abraham got a clear picture of his future.

In the New Testament, Jesus constantly used visualization to help His disciples grasp new concepts. Understanding that most of His followers were simple men and women without religious training, Jesus would help them visualize spiritual concepts that could change their lives by speaking to them in parables and with comparisons. Jesus told parables about sheep and coins, servants and sons, harvests and clouds, fish and wine—things His followers could relate to and understand, things they could "see" in their mind's eye. When Jesus taught, He constantly used the words "like" and "as." For example, in Matthew 13:31 (NIV), He said, "... *The kingdom of heaven is like a mustard seed.*" Another instance is found in Matthew 10:16 (NIV) when Jesus said, "... *Therefore be as shrewd as snakes and as innocent as doves.*"

Do you recall the Old Testament story of David? David was indeed one of the central figures in the Word of God and a mountain peak among the great men of God in human history. But like all of us, David's destiny hinged on two or three pivotal decisions that he made during the course of his life, the first of those being his decision as a young man to engage the Philistine champion, Goliath. If David had not challenged Goliath and if David had not successfully defeated him in hand-to-hand combat, the rest of David's story would probably never have happened.

David's encounter with Goliath was a defining moment for him. But what was it that caused this young shepherd boy to pick up five smooth stones and go out to do battle with a giant, who was an experienced warrior to boot? It was visualization. The circumstances around that situation actually helped David paint a solid mental picture of what a victory against Goliath could mean for him and his future.

David was actually too young to fight in the war between the Israelites and the Philistines. While his five older brothers fought in that war, David stayed home with his father and tended the family's sheep in his brothers' absence. The prophet Samuel had already anointed David as Israel's next king, but up to this point, nothing had really changed in David's life. Providentially, however, Jesse sent his youngest son, David, to the front lines to carry some food and supplies to his brothers. (In those days, soldiers were typically supplied by their families.) While David was there, visiting his brothers, he heard Goliath taunting the armies of Israel. Then he heard the Israelite soldiers talking about the incredible gifts King Saul had promised to the Israelite who would do battle with Goliath and kill him.

"The king will give great wealth to the man who kills him," the soldiers told David. "He will also give him his daughter in marriage and will exempt his father's family from taxes in Israel" (see 1 Samuel 17:25). So the idea of that royal promise took root in David's heart and David began to visualize what his life might look like should he actually step forward and accept the challenge. In fact, that promise impacted David so forcefully, he asked the soldiers to repeat it to him. "This is what will be done for the man who kills him," they said (see 1 Samuel 17:27).

So David started seeing these things in his future. He saw the money, and he saw the "honey." He captured in his mind's eye a picture of how his future could look and how the rest of his life could be if he could fulfill this request of the king. He could be wealthy, he could be married to the king's daughter, and his family could be exempt from taxes for a very long time. That visualization gave David the motivation he needed to actually go out and fight a giant that nobody else would fight.

David used visualization to get ahead in life. Jesus also used visualization to help His disciples understand deep spiritual truths. Abraham used visualization to sustain his faith. You, too, should appreciate the power of visualization. You should understand the divine origins of creative genius and you should embrace the mental power of imagination and its ability to move you beyond the realm of mere thought into the realm of positive action. The Bible shows us the sheer force of this concept. Modern celebrities and athletes also grasp its effectiveness, because, in recent years, most of the world-class achievers in athletics and the performing arts have surrounded themselves with professional psychologists who have helped them with attitudes, positive thought processes, and visualization. These great achievers, like the great achievers of faith, have finally come to realize that you cannot really travel from where you are to where you want to be until you can first define where you want to be and then visualize yourself as being there.

Vision is nothing more than a mental photograph of where you want to go in life or what you want to achieve. But the key to having a vision is to first possess an accurate appraisal of where you are right now and then to possess a genuine vision of where you hope to be at a specific date in the future. Vision, therefore, should encompass all the meaningful areas of your life, because each area impacts another area. No young minister can hope to build a mega-church, for instance, unless that minister has the health to sustain him in his work and a family that supports him in his pursuits. No would-be singer can hope to become accomplished at her art unless that singer has the finances to launch her career and the relationships that will provide her with open doors of opportunity.

I encourage every person to formulate a comprehensive vision for his or her life. A comprehensive vision will incorporate one's work and career. It also will incorporate one's finances and health. It will incorporate one's relationships, giving strategy, recreation, and free time. All these things are important and all of them are interrelated, but all of them also are essential to a balanced, happy, and healthy life. And each of them impacts one's quality of life. The common thread that runs through all these meaningful aspects of life is the thread of vision. Without a vision for each of these important aspects of life, mediocrity will set in and rob you of your potential for greatness.

In the visualization stage of imagination, it's not important to see all the details clearly. At this stage, it's important simply to know the general direction in which you should travel and to start planning for the various legs of the journey. Over time, the precise destination will become clearer and clearer. As you more accurately pinpoint precisely "what" you should be doing in the future, the "how" will begin to take care of itself. Mike Murdock, a noted writer and Christian teacher, says, "When your heart decides a destination, your mind will design a map to reach it."[16] So you must begin to formulate a picture of where you want to end up before you can develop a plan for getting there.

Jim Carrey is one of the most beloved and successful comedians of my time. He has made a lot of successful movies and has earned a great deal of money in the process. But you may not know that Jim Carrey began his career in stand-up comedy, landing his first broadcasting job in 1990 on a television program called *In Living Color*. Yet during those early days of modest success and career building, Jim Carrey saw himself doing so much more. He was happy to be earning a full-time living at his craft. Nevertheless, Jim Carrey wanted to be in films and his vision was to play lead roles in highly successful movies. He wanted to earn eight-digit paychecks and receive awards for his performances.

But Jim Carrey was more than a daydreamer; Carrey actually wrote down his dreams and he actually visualized his dreams. In fact, Carrey went so far as to write himself a check for several million dollars. He postdated that check and he put it in his wallet, carrying it with him everywhere he went for the next several years.[17] As time passed and as the due date for the check grew closer, Carrey's vision helped ease the wait and his passion helped him work hard every day in anticipation of his big payoff. Between the time when he wrote that check to himself and the date the check would become due, Jim Carrey's passion and work ethic helped him become a big star, and his popularity at the box office was rising rapidly. He starred in movies like *Ace Ventura: Pet Detective*, *The Mask*, and *Dumb and Dumber*. A few days before Carrey's postdated check to himself became due, he was offered the lead role in a movie that would pay him an amount equal to the check he had been carrying in his wallet for the past five years. And to make his success sweeter, Jim Carrey would be nominated for a Golden Globe Award for his performance in *The Mask*.

So daring to dream wasn't a waste of time for Jim Carrey, and daring to visualize his dreams wasn't a waste either. In fact, it isn't a waste of time for anybody to write checks or to count stars or to do anything else that can help them give mental substance to the dreams their hearts have produced.

Walt Disney is another great example of one who turned his dreams into reality through the power of visualization. Disney, of course, holds a special place in my heart because I live in the Orlando area, and I have seen firsthand what his personal dreams have done to an entire region of the country. But it wasn't always that way. Today, millions of people visit Walt Disney World and the various resorts and attractions associated with it, and millions more watch Disney movies at the theater and at home. But once upon a time, all this wonderful stuff was nothing more than a dream beating inside a young man's heart.

Walt Disney was a dreamer, and, through imagination and visualization, he eventually turned his dream into an empire. It all started with a cartoon mouse. Then it evolved into a couple of world-class family playgrounds. Now it has become a multi-billion-dollar conglomerate. In fact, Walt Disney's vision was so strong, so powerful, and so enduring that his vision has continued to grow after his death.

A former Disney executive shared with me the story of the day Walt Disney World was dedicated on October 1, 1971. Unfortunately, Walt Disney himself was not alive to attend that momentous ceremony. Nevertheless, Walt's nephew, Roy, was there to celebrate that day and to represent the Disney family at the festive occasion. After the dedicatory activities had ended, a reporter interviewed Roy Disney, and, in the course of the interview, the reporter commented on how sad it was that Walt Disney, the architect of the dream, could not be there to see his dream come to life. At that, Roy Disney spoke up and let the reporter know that he was wrong in his conclusion. Roy Disney smiled and explained to the reporter that Disney World was part of Walt's grand vision. "Believe me," Roy said, "Walt saw all this finished long before any of us did."

Disney saw the vision completed, because he was an exceptional visionary. He had an extraordinary ability to see the invisible and to imagine things that could be. Disney knew that the process of visualization was gradual, not once and for all. In fact, the visualization process is a lot like a GPS system. All you have to know is two things: where you are right now and where you want to be when the journey is over. If you can type in your present location and if you can enter the place you want to be, the GPS system will take over and get you there. It will plot your course and tell you where to turn. It will look out for you and guide you along the way. It will keep you from taking rabbit trails and keep you from going in circles. All you have to do is enter the coordinates, execute the plan, and follow the instructions. Then, as you get closer to your destination, it will become more and more clear that you are getting close to the place you wanted to be all along. In the beginning, your destination may not be absolutely clear in your mind; it may be just a vague idea. But as you actually work the plan and start traveling in the right direction, your final destination will get closer and closer, clearer and clearer.

Bishop I.V. Hilliard, pastor of the New Light Christian Center Church in Houston, shared in one of his sermons, "If you see what you want, you'll get what you see." Albert Einstein said, "Imagination is everything. It is the preview of life's coming attractions."[18] Why not be the first to see your future by getting a mental picture of what you want it to look like? You're going to have to live in the future anyway, so it might as well be the future you are picturing for yourself, rather than a future that somebody else is designing for you. But unless you draw that picture in your own mind, program the destination into your own internal GPS system, and start traveling the prescribed path to get there, you won't ever go anywhere meaningful in life. Worse yet, you will be carried along in somebody else's bus to a destination that somebody else has chosen for you, and your life will never be the unique thing that God destined it to be when He created you.

Visualization is one of the most powerful tools in your success toolbox. In fact, researchers have found that whenever you perform any task, your brain uses the same processes and mechanisms that it uses when you visualize yourself performing that task. So chemically and mechanically, the brain doesn't know the difference between the real thing and the imagined thing. This is why it is healthy to practice positive visualization. It stimulates the mind and brings satisfaction to the soul. It also sustains us while we wait for the realization of our dreams and while we work toward them.

One of these studies, conducted by Harvard University, proved that students who visualize their tasks in advance of performing them have nearly a 100-percent success rate when it comes to the actual fulfillment of the task. At the same time, those students who do not visualize their tasks ahead of time have about a 55-percent rate of achievement. Your brain can achieve a lot more when you effectively use the power of visualization. That is why performance experts have become so popular since the 1980's. These experts have helped high-level performers, Olympic and professional athletes, and even coaches squeeze a lot more productivity out of themselves and those they lead.

Stanford University also conducted a study of visualization and its impact on performance, specifically athletic performance. Using basketball players as their subjects, the architects of this study had half the players lie on the bleachers every day, visualizing themselves shooting free throws, while the other half of the squad went about their daily free throw shooting drills as usual, without advance visualization. Because both groups shot free throws consistently, the practice paid off and both groups of players improved their free throw shooting capabilities. But the squad that spent time visualizing their free throws prior to shooting them actually saw their averages rise higher than those of the control group.

When you visualize your goals as already complete, your brain creates a conflict with your subconscious mind between what you actually have and what you're just hoping for. But if you continue to feed vivid, colorful, and specific pictures to your brain through visualization, your brain will begin to capture that information and will begin to do the things that are necessary to bring that picture to life. In other words, your brain will go to work achieving the things you are imagining and actuating the pictures you are sending it. Be careful, though, because this process also works in reverse. The person who dwells on negative thoughts and negative images stimulates his brain to give life to his worst nightmares.

So the process is easy: Close your eyes and picture those things you have written in your dream book, just as if they were already complete. And be precise. Remember, the pictures need to be specific, colorful, and vivid. Vague outlines of misty things hidden in the fog of uncertainty won't do the trick and won't stimulate your brain.

Consequently, if one of your objectives in life is to own a nice house, you need to learn how to close your eyes and actually start walking through that house. You need to learn how to see every detail of every little thing in that house. You need to be able to picture the living room, the bedroom, and the landscaping all the way around the house. You need to be able, in your mind, to sit on your back patio and look out over the view. Can you see it? You need to be able to picture your neighborhood, the traffic on the street, and the various pieces of furniture in your house. In your mind, go from room to room and formulate exact details so that the image of your future house becomes as real in your mind as those things that are taking place in your life right now.

This process should be the same for every dream in your life: your finances, your marriage, your career, and even the special vacations you want to take and personal things you want to do. Write down your dreams, and then learn to visualize your dreams with increasing clarity. Make the images as sharp as possible in your mind, because you will achieve few significant things in life that you did not visualize in advance.

Dr. David Yonggi Cho, senior pastor of the world's largest congregation, wrote an excellent book about the importance of visualization, *The Fourth Dimension* (Alachua, FL: Bridge-Logos Publishers, 1979). In his book, Cho suggests a daily ritual of visualization, particularly in the mornings immediately following prayer. At this time, Cho explains, energy is at its peak and creativity is flowing. So it would be advantageous to seize these opportunities and to utilize this quiet time to start giving details to the mental pictures that your dreams have created. If you have difficulty picturing your dreams in detail, or if you want to enhance your ability to visualize the things buried within your heart, you can start a "vision board" or a "dream wall" to help you with the process.

I have a dream wall myself, and I know lots of people who have dream walls in one form or another. A dream wall is simply a place where you display pictures and images of those things you want to have or those things you want to do in your future. Photographs, keepsakes, and other tangible representations of your goals and ambitions can help you focus your mind on those pursuits, thus increasing the chances that you will actually do those things that will bring your dreams to life.

For instance, if there is a specific type of car I am hoping to drive in the future, I could go down to the dealership and pick up one of those promotional booklets with a full-page, full-color picture of the car I want to drive. Then I could cut that picture out of the booklet and post it on my dream wall. Better yet, I could go down to the dealership with a friend and let him take a picture of me sitting in the driver's seat of that car.

Similarly, if I wanted to travel to France, I could post a picture of the Eiffel Tower on my dream wall. I could even make this picture more personal by taking a small photograph of myself and mounting it beside the picture of the Eiffel Tower, so it looks like I'm standing right there. I could do the same with the Sydney Opera House or the Grand Canyon or the Great Wall of China.

If I am hoping to be a millionaire one day, I might follow Jim Carrey's lead and write myself a check for $1 million, posting it on my dream wall. Or I could create a computer-generated bank statement that shows a couple of million dollars in my checking account. When I get an idea for a new book, the first thing I could do is design a cover for the book, then wrap that cover around an existing book so I could look at it and see my new book as if it were already finished. In fact, this is what I typically do before I start writing a book.

In a sense, I guess a dream wall is a little self-deceiving. These things don't actually exist in the real world. But that's my point: They may not exist in the real world right now, but they do already exist in my heart and mind. If I have written them down and visualized them, they are as real in my heart right now as they will be in the physical world on a specific day in the future. Since they are not yet tangible, my dream wall helps me keep them fresh in my mind, so I can see them and feel them and experience them on a daily basis. This keeps me focused on my dreams and keeps me motivated to work toward them. In other words, my dream wall helps me visualize these things as if they were already a reality, and I need to do that every day of my life if I honestly hope to make my dreams come true.

In fact, whether you have a dream wall or not, you need to take the time to dream and to visualize. Many of the world's highest achievers do. I heard of one high-level executive who started each day by lying in his bed for thirty minutes after waking. To the average person, it seems like a waste of precious time to wake up and then lie in the bed for another half hour before starting the workday. But this executive used that time— the most mentally active portion of his day— to think, to dream, and to visualize what he wanted to achieve. Those 30 minutes each day made him what he was and set him apart from those around him.

Another great idea I have heard over the years is the concept of an "hour of power." There is no better way to start the day than with twenty minutes of reading, followed by twenty minutes of visualization, followed by twenty minutes of physical exercise. Starting your day this way could truly change your life. Just imagine twenty minutes of strong inspiration every day, followed by twenty minutes of concentrated visualization, followed by twenty minutes of intense physical exercise. In a short period of time, you could be a totally different person, especially when you consider that the first part of your day is the most productive part of your day.

My early morning regimen and my dream wall have given birth to many ambitions in my life. In fact, one of the first little dreams that came true in my life came true as a direct result of these processes. Early in my marriage, there was a particular resort that my wife and I wanted to visit. This place was beautiful, and we really liked it. So we

The individual who will work hard for his dreams and sacrifice for his dreams is the individual who is serious about his dreams.

collected pictures of the resort, cutting them out of brochures and other promotional items we had collected or received in the mail. We posted those pictures on our dream wall, including photographs of the swimming pool and all the lounge chairs surrounding that pool. Then, about four years later, we actually found ourselves lying in those very same lounge chairs beside that very same pool, and we realized just how potent visualization can be. Visualizing that goal helped us stay focused and helped us do what was necessary to keep that dream alive and to turn it into a reality. And that brings me to my final point in this chapter.

PLANNING YOUR DREAMS

I would never minimize the importance of writing down one's dreams and visualizing one's dreams, because the person who never dreams, never sees his dreams come true. Nevertheless, it's just as bad to dream great dreams and then allow those dreams to die on the vine from lack of direct attention. The cold, hard truth is that you have to work your dreams after you capture them in written form and after you give them substance through the power of visualization.

This stage of creative thinking— the work stage— is the stage that separates the men from the boys, the participants from the spectators, and the daydreamers from the "imagineers." The individual who will work hard for his dreams and sacrifice for his dreams is the individual who is serious about his dreams. He is the person who will possess his dreams too, because nothing really happens without a realistic plan to make it happen and without a lot of hard work and sacrifice to give substance to the idea.

From time to time, I like to advise young entrepreneurs on the businesses they are trying to launch, and sometimes I personally invest in those new start-ups. But whenever someone approaches me with an idea for a new business, seeking my advice or my participation, the first thing I request is a copy of that person's business plan. Bank executives feel the same way. Whenever a would-be entrepreneur walks into a bank requesting a $100,000 loan to start a new business, the very first question the loan officer will ask him is, "Where is your business plan?" Why is this the first question when somebody is seeking support for his dream? Because a person who is serious about something will have a plan for achieving it! When you have taken the time to plan how you will actually achieve something, that effort shows that you have committed to walking the walk, not just talking the talk.

There are lots of books and software programs out there that can help you develop a business plan for your new venture. These same books and computer programs can also be utilized in planning your life in general. So whether you want to build a new microchip conglomerate or launch a new church, the process of getting from here to there is pretty much the same. You start with a mission statement. Then you define your primary goals and you break those goals down into bite-sized, measurable pieces. Finally, you put the little pieces in some kind of logical sequence and you start the process.

The key element of success I have noticed in this final stage of creative thinking—the implementation phase—is the motivation to do something every day to move the dream forward, regardless of how insignificant that daily task might seem. Nothing kills a dream faster than telling yourself, "I'll get to that one of these days." In the real world, "one of these days" is self-talk for "never." So I make it a habit to do something tangible every day to push my dreams forward. Even if I advance my dreams just one inch each day, that means that my dreams will be 30 feet farther along a year from now than they are today. That's a lot better than just looking at the same old picture on my dream wall for twelve months, telling myself that I will try to get to that dream "one of these days."

If you intend to be great at what you do, you need to start a habit of creating a daily to-do list. I have been doing this for years, and I make sure that my daily list contains all the things I need to do in order to function and survive. I also include a few of those things that I just want to do in order to move closer to the destination I have determined for myself in life.

The proper method for achieving goals is really not that complicated. Like the process for achieving one's dreams, the process for completing the various tasks that will get from your present situation to your final destination is a deliberate and methodical process.

First, decide exactly what it is you want to do and where it is you want to end up. Believe it or not, most people never do this much. Most people just wish their lives away and talk boringly about those things they are going to do "one of these days." One of these days, they are going to write a book. One of these days, they are going to learn to fly an airplane. One of these days, they are going to buy a fishing boat. One of these days, they are going to go back to school or start a business or learn a foreign language or get married. But the person of greatness who is discontented with where he is will determine exactly where he wants to go and will not lie to himself about the necessary things he must do to get there.

Second, write it down. Specifically, you need to write down exactly what you are trying to achieve, in as much detail as possible at this early stage of implementation. I know this sounds familiar, because the imagination process itself started with the recording of dreams and ambitions. But now that the process of dreaming has moved you beyond the idea phase to the actual implementation phase, the same rules apply. You need to write down what you have decided to do. If you don't, you will lose the thought, or worse, you will procrastinate and never take your dream seriously. So just as the serious dreamer needs to record his dreams, so the serious dreamer needs to record the specific steps he intends to take to achieve his dreams.

Third, set a deadline. In the same way that Jim Carrey post-dated his $10-million check for a specific date, you should have a target date in mind for the achievement of your dream. To tell yourself that you will reach your goal "some day" or "one of these days" is really a subtle way of convincing yourself that you won't achieve your dream at all. Set a deadline. Even if you miss your deadline, at least the existence of a deadline will get you moving in a forward direction and will give you some tangible way of measuring your progress.

Fourth, develop a list of everything you can think of doing to achieve the dream you have written down by the deadline you have established. By working to achieve all the various processes associated with the pursuit of your dream, the dream itself will begin to take shape in the real world. The closer your ultimate dream becomes to reality, the more encouraged you will be and the harder you will work to finish the remaining processes for completing your dream. At this point, while you are developing your list of things to do, don't worry about the order of your thoughts. Just write them down before you forget them and before they escape you. Then let them lie around for a while and grow on you as they take shape in your heart and mind. Keep adding to your list as new thoughts and new ideas come to you. In time, you will be amazed at how many pieces of the puzzle you begin to see in your mind.

Fifth, organize all the little processes into some sort of logical sequence. Sometimes this is easy, because it doesn't take a lot of brainpower to figure out that you need to build the birdhouse before you can paint it. But most of the time, the formulation of this sequence takes some genuine contemplation because the order of things won't be quite so obvious. If you get stuck, I recommend working backward. Write each thing to do on its own separate little piece of paper, and then find a big table where you can arrange all the little pieces in a long, straight line. As you place at the end of the table the piece of paper which you believe denotes the final task, ask yourself which task needs to be performed before you can start this final task. Then, after you place that task in front of the final task, ask yourself which task needs to be performed before you can start this one. Pick up each piece of paper, hold it in your hand, and ask yourself where that specific task needs to be placed in the "timeline" of tasks. Each task will come before certain tasks, and each task will come after certain other tasks. In time, you will have a long sequence of little processes that will take you from where you are to where you want to be. This timeline creation activity isn't complicated, but it is time consuming and it will require some serious concentration on your part. But like all the stages in the planning process of bringing your dreams to life, this stage of creative thinking will separate the professionals from the amateurs.

Some timelines that emerge from this process will be based on the obvious flow of mechanical operations. Like the building of a birdhouse, one activity will obviously precede a subsequent activity and will follow a prerequisite activity. Other timelines will be based on priority rather than mechanics. For instance, you may need to know the legal ramifications of a particular decision before you actually sign the documents and write the check, and you may need to file paperwork with your particular state government after the documents are signed. Still other timelines will be based on necessity. For example, you won't be able to become a brain surgeon— no matter how hard you work at it— until you first graduate from medical school, and you won't be able to get into medical school until you first graduate college. The point I'm trying to make is that your list of things to do needs to be organized into a step-by-step sequence that you can check off as you complete one process and move on to the next one. One process builds upon another.

Sequence is important. One guy can get up in the morning, take a shower, get dressed, eat breakfast, and drive to work. His next-door neighbor can get up at the same time, take a shower, eat breakfast, drive to work, and then get dressed. While the first guy may get a promotion for being early, the second man will probably get arrested for indecent exposure. Both men did the same things, but they did those things in a different sequence. So think through the sequential progression of the things you need to do and then manipulate that list into its logical order.

Sixth, take action immediately on your plan. Don't procrastinate. Get going. Since time is the most precious commodity you possess, don't waste it. The apostle Paul encouraged his converts to "...*walk circumspectly, not as fools, but as wise, redeeming the time, because the days are evil*" (Ephesians 5:15-16). The New International Version translates that same exhortation this way: "*Be very careful, then, how you live—not as unwise, but as wise, making the most of every opportunity, because the days are evil*" (Ephesians 5:15-16 NIV). Make sure you follow this ancient, yet wise advice. Redeem the time, and make the most of the opportunities you have before you now. Do something today to move your ideals forward. Dreams are a little like muscle. If you allow your muscles to go too long without exercise, they can deteriorate and turn to flab. They can stiffen and lose their flexibility. So don't delay. Get busy now implementing your plan of action.

Finally, do something every day to move your dreams forward. Remember, the journey to greatness is not a journey of a few miles; it is a journey of thousands of inches. The journey to success is not a journey of a few giant leaps; it is a journey of hundreds of baby steps. Like the tortoise, you will defeat the hare by continuous and deliberate action, not by intermittent bursts of mania. So make it a personal habit to move your goals forward a little bit each day, and, in time, you will travel the whole nine yards. Make a daily to-do list that will enable you to advance the next process on your timeline, and rejoice in the progress you see yourself making. Believe me, it is much more gratifying and much more motivating to stop and look back at the distance you have already traveled than it is to constantly look ahead at what you need to do.

Here's a promise I can make to you: If you regularly practice goal setting and planning in your life and if you combine this practice with the other principles I expound in this book, you will be encouraged by how much you can accomplish in a relatively short period of time. In just a year or two, you can do things that might take other people five to ten years to achieve. And you will be utterly amazed at how much you can achieve over the course of your lifetime. The more I study the lives of successful people and the more I rub shoulders with these people personally, the more I am convinced that most of the world has it wrong. Success is not about skill, and it's not about being smarter than other people. Success is one-third passion, one-third work, and one-third inspiration and organization. I've seen a lot of people with less ability do far greater things with their lives than their counterparts, because these people had dreams and workable plans for making their dreams come true.

Success is not about talent alone, because every individual has talent in some area of life. Success is not about experience alone, because experience is nothing more than habits and perspectives one has accumulated as a result of things done in the past. And success is not about education alone, because education is the collection of facts that other people think you need to know. All these things have their place and all these things are important when they are combined with the other elements of successful living. I highly recommend that people get a good education, build experience in various aspects of life, and hone their talents to their optimum level. But genuine success—success that sets people apart and makes their lives memorable and impactful—is something that flows from a different fountain. While success is strengthened by talent, tempered by experience, and refined by education, it is conceived by the heart and driven by something that is intangible and unlearned. Unlike talent, it is not refined in a public forum. Unlike experience, it is not attained through public interaction. Unlike education, it not acquired in a public classroom. Rather, it is discovered in the deep recesses of one's most private thoughts and it is brought to life, little by little, in the mind's eye through visualization and planning.

Your dreams are precious and unique,
and they were given to you by God.

Let your imagination take control. Your imagination is that part of you that makes you different from everybody else, and the thing that makes you different is the thing that will make you great. To ignore your imaginative nature and to listen instead to all the voices that are vying for your attention is to buy into the safe and predictable, yet unfulfilling kind of life that most of your advisors secretly want to escape. So don't go down that pathway of mediocrity. Don't fall into that trap of common thinking. Your dreams are precious and unique, and they were given to you by God. God can help you move your dreams from the realm of ideas into the realm of reality, but you must become His partner in the effort. And in that effort, your imagination is your greatest ally.

CHAPTER 5

RELATIONSHIPS

NO MAN IS AN ISLAND

Throughout our nation's history, we Americans have celebrated the individualist. We love any story about the man who defies the odds and goes it alone, fighting the bad guys with one hand and the authorities with the other. We like the rebellious tough guy and the one-man police force, like John McClane in *Die Hard*. We embrace the maverick and the one-man defense force, like Rambo or the Terminator. We admire the overcomer and the one-man championship team, like Rocky or Forrest Gump.

But our cultural love affair with the army of one doesn't stop at the box office; we carry it into the real world. In 2008, John McCain and Sarah Palin ran for President and Vice-President respectively by portraying themselves as "mavericks." They wanted the world to know that they didn't need anybody else. They didn't need anyone's approval. They didn't need anyone's acceptance. They were tough, they were focused, they were undaunted, and they were more interested in doing the right thing than being "cool" or popular.

All that's fine, and there's certainly nothing wrong with being principled and resilient. There's also nothing wrong with being unique in your thinking when the masses are traveling in the wrong direction. In fact, this book is very much about defying the status quo and marching to the beat of your own drum. Nevertheless, life requires a necessary balance. Extremism rarely works. So in spite of the fact that individualism can be a good thing, the love of individualism must be balanced with the harsh realization that nobody can live life alone. Nobody is completely self-sufficient or self-made. And nobody can achieve success without the help of others.

Here's the truth: You can only reach your goals with the assistance of others. No individual is a stand-alone entity and no individual is completely self-reliant. All of us, in one way or another, need others, especially if we intend to do great things. The "greats" learn this fact early and make it a central part of their strategy for success.

I learned this principle in a harsh, yet somewhat humorous way when I was a young boy. I've already told you the story about the time I tried to run away from home. I was angry with the key people in my life, especially my family. I was hurt, and I was so bitter and so upset, I finally reached a place where I wanted to live alone. I didn't need my parents. I didn't want my friends anymore. I hated my school. So I decided to leave and to build a new life without all these "unnecessary" people.

When I told my mother about my intentions to run away, she asked me if I needed her to get the suitcase out for me. When I told her "yes," she asked, "So you need my help?" Of course, that redundant question just provoked me more and made me more determined to run away. My mom waited a little while and then asked me what I intended to do. I told her I was going to go to the airport and travel far away and start my life over. Since I had saved a little money as a young man, I thought I could afford an airline ticket. She then asked me if I would like her to call a taxi to take me to the airport. Realizing where she was heading with her questioning, I declined. I told her I would walk. But she still made her point: Even if I walked all the way to the airport, I would still need the services of the airline and the pilot of the aircraft to get me where I wanted to go. She was making her point rather poignantly. No matter where I went and no matter what I did, I was going to need other people in order to reach my destination. I couldn't live life by myself.

No man is an island. You've heard this statement all your life, and it's true. Joint ventures are necessary for sustaining and advancing life. Cooperative efforts are necessary for greatness. King Solomon, that wise leader whom we have quoted copiously in this book, said, *"Two are better than one; because they have a good reward for their labour"* (Ecclesiastes 4:9). That's a concept all of us need to "get," a concept we need to apply to our lives in order to climb the ladder of success and conquer the giants that stand between us and our goals. Every other chapter in this book deals with individual traits and qualities and the need to search oneself and make personal adjustments. In some ways, this chapter does too. But what makes this chapter different is its emphasis on the role that others play in your destiny. The lesson you should glean from this chapter is that it is your responsibility to grasp this power of relationship and learn how to utilize relationships to benefit yourself in your ascent to greatness.

For starters, you can understand that relationships exist on multiple levels. Some relationships are intense; others are casual. Some are close; others are more distant. In fact, psychologists tell us that relationships exist on at least five levels, as demonstrated through our conversation. The lowest level of communication is the cliché level, where we give people the programmed questions and statements that others expect regarding the weather, sports, and so forth. The next level is the gossip level, where we talk about more substantive issues, especially people. The third level of relationship building is the "testing the waters" stage, where we actually put forth ideas, including dreams and goals, to see how the other person reacts to them. The fourth level is the "passionate" level, where we reveal true thoughts and feelings and where we share the passions and emotions that really make us tick, realizing that the relationship in question has advanced to the point that we won't be rejected if we say something unusual or "wrong." And the ultimate level of relationship and communication is the level where we connect spiritually, actually becoming "one" in mind, heart, and motivation.

All of us have relationships on every one of these levels. We have family and friends, of course. But we also have coworkers and clients. Farther down the food chain, we have suppliers and vendors, the mailman, the delivery guy, and the lawn care people. We rarely think about it, but we all know a lot of people on a lot of different levels. The point I am making here is that this is healthy. This is good. We should have many relationships on many different levels, and we should embrace relationships at all levels, learning to appreciate the value they add to our lives and learning to harness the benefits that other people afford us by their involvement in our lives.

Jesus had relationships on multiple levels. On the lowest level, there were the "masses," those people who came to hear Him preach or watch Him work miracles, yet who stayed far in the background. They never stepped up to get involved in His life or ministry, they never engaged Jesus personally, and they never abandoned their fishing nets to follow Christ.

On the next level were those 500 people who were close enough to Jesus to be permitted to see Him with their own eyes during the forty days He walked the earth after His resurrection. Jesus obviously trusted these men and women enough to at least allow them one encounter with Him during those forty days.

On the third level were the 120 men and women who were committed strongly enough to Jesus to obey the one command He gave to them before He ascended into heaven. They went back to Jerusalem and prayed, as the Lord told them to do. And, ten days later, they experienced the mighty outpouring of the Holy Spirit on the Day of Pentecost.

The fourth level of relationship for Jesus was that level where the people were actually willing to get involved in His vision and His work. These were the seventy disciples He sent out to preach, to heal, and to set people free from the power of Satan. These men traveled in two's and they returned to Jesus after completing their various assignments in order to report on their experiences and successes.

The fifth level of relationship for Jesus was His relationship with His twelve disciples. These men lived with Him. They abandoned their occupations, bid farewell to their families, and walked with Jesus night and day during His entire earthly ministry. They were the men to whom Jesus would hand the torch of leadership in His Church. They were the cream of the crop spiritually.

On the sixth level were the three very close disciples, Peter, James, and John. Jesus would often talk with them about very deep things and would allow these three men to share experiences with Him that the other disciples were not privileged to share.

Then at the top of the pyramid was the apostle John, the "disciple whom Jesus loved," who actually stood at the foot of the cross when all the rest of the disciples had fled and who accepted the responsibility of caring for Jesus' mother after His death and ascension into heaven.

I hope you can see from this detailed account that even the Son of God accepted people on different levels, and those people accepted Him on different levels, depending on the extent to which they desired to be involved in His life and His work. It's interesting to note that Jesus never challenged people for landing where they chose to land on His relationship scale. He loved the masses as much as He loved the apostle John, and He accepted people, no matter which level of relationship they felt comfortable pursuing with Him.

In life, you and I also experience relationships on multiple levels, and, if we're smart like Jesus, we learn to accept a person on the level that makes him feel most comfortable. There are those who will be very close to you, because they will want to be close and you will want them to be close. There are others who will have no desire to fill an intimate place in your life. These people will be more comfortable with short, passing conversations about today's chances for rain or the current football standings.

The point is that you should recognize your many relationships, value them, and learn to recognize and appreciate what they add to your life. If you really ponder the role that all these people play in your life, you will soon realize that all of them add something and that their individual contributions combine to make your life what it is. Your mailman brings you the bills and the checks you are expecting from those who owe you money. The grocery clerk who knows your name also orders the salmon every week that you like to broil on your gas grill. The teacher at the nearby elementary school doesn't teach any of your children personally, but she does create part of the curriculum that your child's teacher utilizes in his classroom. And your boss provides you with both a paycheck and opportunities for growth and advancement. Only your husband (or wife) sleeps with you at night and only your kids sit in your lap, but there are literally thousands of people out there who make your life what it is. And you know what? You wouldn't have the life you have without them.

Social intelligence and the recognition of the role of others in your life is a key component to personal success and happiness. In fact, these qualities are big contributors to the survival of many people who might otherwise fail professionally. Those who get the importance of people are those who have the support of others during corporate upheavals, even though their performance might not be the best in the company. And those who learn to build friendships in the pursuit of the brass ring are those who will have the help of others when they make mistakes or need to recover from some sort of setback.

Truly successful people are socially aggressive. They grasp the absolute necessity of creating relationships in the workplace and nurturing relationships on various levels in the marketplace. They

---

Social intelligence and the recognition of the role of others in your life is a key component to personal success and happiness.

---

are sensitive in their dealings with others, and though they may not always be close to everyone with whom they associate, they seem to always be liked and respected. They have a way of making other people want to help them. They understand human behavior and what makes people tick as well as what bonds people to one another. And perhaps most importantly, they work smoothly with those around them, even those who are different from them or those who grate on them a little.

John D. Rockefeller said, "The ability to deal with people is as purchasable a commodity as sugar or coffee, and it is worth more than any other commodity under the sun."[19] Rockefeller realized that his own success depended on those who worked with him and around him, and he realized that their success depended on their ability to formulate and develop relationships on many levels. Rockefeller also realized that, in order to thrive in almost any endeavor, a man or woman needs strong contacts, friends, and relationships of all types. So Rockefeller consciously and deliberately sought out and surrounded himself with people who possessed the talent to appreciate, develop, and nurture relationships.

If you think about it, all the successful people you know have that talent. They know large numbers of people. They remember names. They have a large database of email addresses and phone numbers and a bottomless list of contacts for almost any situation that could possibly arise. They know somebody somewhere who can do just about anything your heart could imagine. They are great at staying in touch with people—old friends from school, former teachers and colleagues, old mentors and Army buddies—and they can name about a million people who owe them favors. Their friends, contacts, and business associates span many ages, backgrounds, and fields of expertise, and their network seems to grow by the day. They always have time to talk to people and their phones ring continuously.

These people understand the value of relationships and the centrality of relationships to their own personal pursuits. You need to follow their example. If you want to be great at all you do, you need to hone those friendships that will provide you with the resources and support you are going to need to make that journey. You need to build your own database, and you need to formulate your own professional and personal associations. In fact, by the time you are forty, you should have a pretty good circle of friends in the arena of professional achievement that interests you. If you don't, you need to get busy building relationships with people you can rely on and turn to! Find colleagues who will do you favors and support your projects (as you, in turn, support theirs). You need an army of supporters who can supply you with the thousands of nuts and bolts necessary to construct your dream! You also need respected mentors who can serve as a reality check for your new ideas and as a sounding board for your plans.

The man or woman who would be great must have many relationships on many different levels that span many different fields and many different personalities. Some relationships are intimate and personal and lifelong; others are casual, professional, or perhaps temporary. All relationships are important on the journey to excellence. But in the professional arena (and perhaps the personal arena too), no relationship is more important than the relationship you will have with one or more mentors, people who can inspire and teach you throughout life. In fact, all great people have mentors. The "greats" surround themselves with people who are great achievers, people who can help them grow and with whom they can grow together. These mentors usually become instrumental in helping them get where they want to go.

Too many people in the professional world fail to grasp this concept. They fail to understand the importance of relationships on the professional level. Instead, they live their entire lives never understanding the principle of combined effort, and they suffer as a result. They assume that their failures and struggles have been the result of bad "luck" or bad decisions. But what they fail to understand is that they could have avoided most of their setbacks while succeeding in most of their ventures if they only had created a network of people who supported their undertakings and who were involved in their lives.

I am part of a couple of professional networks, and I deliberately make the time for these associations because I understand their absolute necessity to my personal growth, professional development, and financial success. What I have learned over the years is that although I need the advice and help of others, I am helped more by the inspiration and motivation derived simply by being around other people who are achieving great things with their lives. Just being around accomplished people raises me to a higher level. Just being in an environment that is saturated with mental energy and ambition inspires me. Just knowing what other people are doing makes me want to do more.

I have personally watched pastors of small churches get involved in networks with high achievers, and I have watched the churches where these pastors serve grow as a direct result of the changes that took place in these men. I have watched men and women with talent and viable ideas get involved in circles where most of the people around them have already done what they want to do, and I have seen these men and women blossom like a flower and rise like a powerful rocket because the relationships forged in these environments, though shallow in the beginning, became catalysts that inspired them and urged them on.

In fact, let me tell you about three such people, because I am personally acquainted with their story. These three men came to know each other about twenty-six years ago and became highly instrumental in helping each other achieve success. You would recognize these men if you saw them or heard their names, because today all three of them are well known and successful. But twenty-six years ago, when they were just getting started in their respective pursuits, these men became good friends. Realizing at this early stage in their lives that their friendships were providential and that together they possessed all the creativity and faith that was necessary for all of them to succeed, they decided to spend some significant time together. They also decided to vacation together at least once a year so they could pour into each other's lives and draw from one another. They gave birth to a tradition of vacationing together in Hawaii for one week each year. One of these men was a businessman, one was a pastor, and one was an evangelist. Today, one of these men runs a major publishing company, another one serves as senior pastor at one of America's great mega-churches, and the third one operates a thriving television ministry. These men grew together by utilizing their relationship to catapult them to success. At times, they drew from one another. At other times, they contributed to each other. Consistently, one man helped the other. And all profited from the three-way relationship.

Your ability to survive and prosper in a competitive marketplace depends on your ability to develop those strong partnerships and alliances necessary for broadening your talents and multiplying your opportunities. There is great benefit in simply being around people who can draw out your potential and inspire you to greater achievement. These same people can also become the missing link you need for forward movement and problem solving. You need people in your life who believe in you, who can advise and educate you, who see potential solutions to your problems, who have walked where you desire to walk, who possess the resources you need to make things happen, and who can encourage you and stand behind you to double all of life's pleasure and divide all of life's sorrow.

I love the story of Steven Spielberg. When Spielberg was a young boy, he was like a lot of little boys, somewhat rejected by his little friends. According to Spielberg himself, he was usually the last one picked to play football, baseball, and even badminton. But Spielberg's mother saw promise in her young son. She saw his potential and the latent vestiges of destiny, because Steven was a highly creative boy, even at a young age. His imagination was noticeable, at least to his mother.

So Steven's mom encouraged his natural interests and even helped him develop them. When Steven got his first camera, his mother would pick him up after school and take him places where he could shoot footage and begin developing his talents as a filmmaker. She saw things in him that he didn't even see in himself. She believed in him. She helped draw his potential out of him. Most importantly, she became part of his solution instead of being part of his problem like everybody else. Now look at what Steven Spielberg has accomplished with his life. A great deal of those achievements can be traced back to those formative years when somebody else became instrumental in catapulting him to success.

It is vital that you have people who recognize your true capabilities and believe in you.

It is vital that you have people who recognize your true capabilities and believe in you. If those people aren't there at all, either you have failed to formulate your professional network, or nobody else sees the potential in you that you see in yourself. Leaders are always developing a large network of other highly successful and self-motivated people who can be instrumental in the development of their dream. Leaders also are straightforward and unapologetic in asking these key people for help when they need it along the way.

Why are people so hesitant to ask for help? I don't know. There could be several reasons. Perhaps they are afraid of exposing their weaknesses. Perhaps they think that other people wouldn't want to help them. Maybe they don't want to feel indebted. I don't know why people hesitate to ask for help. More than likely, the reasons are too numerous to count. But I do know this: Great people ask for help all the time, and great people give help all the time. Virtually every day of their lives, people of achievement seek the advice, input, or direct assistance of people who are part of their circle of trust. They also gladly give those same things back to the others who are members of that circle.

Asking for help, especially from someone who views you as capable and gifted, is a surefire way to strengthen and solidify your friendship and burgeoning relationship with that person. It "cements" them to you in a very lasting way and makes them feel personally integrated into your professional advancement and success.

Understand the power and the importance of the mentoring process. Understand that you need to draw from others, because it will move you along at a much faster rate. And understand that you need to pour into others too, because it will satisfy your God-given need to help others and will increase your own sense of self-worth and significance. When others want something you've got, that says a lot about you, especially when the person asking for your help is a strong, capable individual. And when you share the most personal parts of yourself, that provides you with a sense of purpose like nothing else can.

In a survey of nearly 4,000 successful executives, approximately two-thirds said they had at least one personal "mentor" in their lives. Obviously, the word mentor means different things to different people, but the basic premise behind the word is that two-thirds of these executives readily confessed that they regularly seek the help of somebody else in their climb up the corporate ladder. Those professionals who openly seek the counsel and direct assistance of others end up better educated, earning more at their professions, and are happier in life. Everybody finds fulfillment in taking another person under his wing and teaching him. Likewise, everybody finds personal worth in being helped along by somebody else who sees potential and worth in him.

A good athlete has two things: talent and drive. But a world-class athlete has something in addition to those two elements: a coach. Jack Nicklaus, for instance, had a golf teacher by the name of Jack Grout. Nicklaus was the greatest golfer who ever lived. With eighteen major championships over three separate decades, Nicklaus' records are still unparalleled. Interestingly, Nicklaus would begin every golf season by visiting his coach, Jack Grout, for lessons. In fact, Nicklaus would go back to the basics and start over from scratch as if he was a novice golfer. He would learn to hold the club properly. He would learn a proper stance. Then he would work on the mechanics of his swing. Jack Grout was his coach until Grout died in 1989.

Sometimes it's not easy to find the best teachers in your field. But when a world-class athlete finds someone who can help him ratchet up his performance and draw the very best out of him on a consistent basis, that athlete will spend almost any amount of money and travel almost any distance to spend time with that mentor and coach. The athlete knows the value of that coach in his life, and he will tell you the contributions of that coach are worth almost anything it takes.

Great achievers seek help, and great achievers know the value of other key people in their lives. Wise leaders and accomplished people, therefore, promote the mentoring system, whether they do it systematically and purposely or whether they do it casually and accidentally. When you have a mentor of your own, you naturally become a mentor to someone else. The "hidden system" of group support that exists in the business world, political world, church world, and elsewhere is the real support system that holds up the structures of American life. In every endeavor, there is an elaborate network of souls who pour into one another and draw out of one another all that is needed to propel the enterprise forward. Each individual, no matter his title or status, has people "above" him in the pyramid and "below" him. In effect, professional relationships were the very first network marketing model, and professional relationships will continue long after the last network marketing business closes its doors.

The mentoring process has been around for a long time, and it will continue to be around for a lot longer, because it is the most successful method for advancing oneself and building future generations simultaneously, no matter what the pursuit may be. The concept was even sanctioned by God himself as the preferred method of leadership and was exhibited through the lives of both Moses and Jesus. Moses used leadership through mentoring when he led the Israelites through the wilderness for forty years, and Jesus employed the mentoring approach to leadership when He was preparing His disciples to lead the Early Church. Moses led through relationship by personally finding and preparing the next generation of leaders for Israel and by gradually handing off his authority to those who would succeed him. Jesus led through relationship by focusing the majority of His ministry efforts on twelve men rather than the hoards of people who pursued Him to see a miracle.

Obviously, Moses and Jesus understood what great people still understand thousands of years later. They understood there are only a finite number of hours in a day and that a lone wolf is limited in what he can do by himself during that limited span of time. They also understood that if they would choose and train a select number of promising people, pull those people close to them, pour into them, and then utilize them to help carry the burden of the work and propel the vision forward, they could achieve far more than they could ever hope to achieve by themselves. Besides, the vision would survive them and could actually become larger in subsequent years. So Jesus often passed up opportunities to preach and to heal and, instead, trained a dozen men who could change the world on His behalf. In them, He saw growth, potential, and faith. So he focused on building relationships with those men as Moses did with Joshua and others.

People who head up organizations in the modern era realize they have the same time restraints as Moses and Jesus, and they realize their vision is bigger than they can accommodate with their own two hands. So they help themselves out by drawing people around them and helping those people grow. They carefully select men and women with unproven, yet noticeable potential, faithfully sow into these promising protégés, and then release to them the responsibility and authority for the work. Then they watch them soar.

Andrew Carnegie, commonly regarded as the second richest man in history, built his financial empire through steel. In fact, he was one of the pioneers of the American steel industry and was largely responsible for propelling this country to the forefront of the industrial revolution. Carnegie died in 1911 and was buried in North Tarrytown, New York. The epitaph on his tombstone, which he wrote himself, tells his story of success in a single phrase: "A man who knew how to enlist in his service better men than himself."[20]

Whether we are talking about mentoring younger and less experienced people in order to achieve your dream or networking with peers and more accomplished people of achievement to provide yourself with counsel, support, and help along the way, relationship building is an essential activity in anyone's pursuit of excellence and greatness. One recent historical figure who perhaps understood and applied this principle better than anyone else was President Dwight D. Eisenhower.

Before Eisenhower became the 34th president of the United States, he was the Supreme Commander of the Allied Forces in Europe during World War II. His claim to fame was the successful invasion of Normandy on D-Day in 1944, a brilliant military maneuver that is still remembered and memorialized to this day. Eisenhower was the architect and director of that invasion, which liberated the continent from German occupation and led to the rapid conclusion of the war in Europe.

But on June 5, 1944, the night before the invasion, Eisenhower wasn't so sure his plan would work. Like many of us, he had done his best to plan for the big event. But so many things could have gone wrong, so he sat down at his portable table and scribbled out a press release in long hand so he would have something to share with the press the next day in the event of the invasion's failure. He wrote, "My decision to attack at this time and place was based upon the best information available. The troops, the air, and the Navy did all that bravery and devotion to duty could do. If any blame or fault attaches to the attempt, it is mine alone." After writing this depressing statement, Eisenhower folded the paper, placed it in his wallet, and went to dinner. Obviously, the press release became unnecessary, and it was never released. As the invasion became a complete success, Eisenhower was thrust into the national spotlight as a war hero and was propelled to the presidency as a result of his unprecedented popularity with the American people.

What was it that caused Eisenhower to succeed at this ambitious assignment? If you know anything about him, he was probably the most unlikely candidate to lead the Allies in that crucial invasion. Eisenhower was from Kansas, not one of the major cities of the East or West Coasts. He did attend West Point, but he was certainly not a standout there. Although he was well liked as a student, he was not exceptional in any measurable way. Within his class of 164 students, Eisenhower ranked 61st in academics and 125th in discipline. In 1940, just one year before the United States was thrust into the war, Eisenhower was an obscure lieutenant colonel. In his twenty-eight years of military service, he had never experienced a single day of combat. Providentially, however, Eisenhower was noticed and was rapidly promoted until he eventually assumed command of all the Allied Forces in Europe. Nevertheless, the task before him was daunting, to say the least.

To win the war against Germany, Eisenhower would have to co-ordinate the military forces of multiple nations. This meant he would have to bridge various languages, cultures, traditions, and objectives in order to unify these sometimes-contradictory elements into a single, focused, fighting force. In addition, Eisenhower would have to build a consensus among some of the most diverse and eccentric personalities ever to join in a single endeavor—men like Winston Churchill, George Patton, Charles de Gaulle, and Bernard Montgomery. No wonder war-weary England was unimpressed with him when he set foot in their country to lead the war effort against the formidable Third Reich.

But on D-Day, less than two-and-a-half years after arriving in England, Eisenhower, in spite of his lack of experience and lack of support, became the mastermind and architect behind one of the greatest military triumphs in world history. What was it that made him a success in spite of his obvious handicaps? Despite his modest military record and lack of previous achievements and despite the fact that most of his generals were smarter and more experienced, Eisenhower knew how to formulate the most unlikely coalition of great people and guide them toward a magnificent goal that was greater than any of them could possibly achieve alone. He pushed on some people; he gently persuaded others. He massaged the in-flated ego of one; he threatened another. But he managed to create a well-oiled machine of the world's most brilliant strategists, politi-cians, warriors, and common people. He knew the power of relation-ships, and he mastered the art of developing and nurturing them to achieve his objectives.

Every incredible opportunity will come into your life disguised as a relationship. Although a lot of people will be blind to this real-ity their entire lives, you need to understand that your life will go nowhere slowly until you learn to value and pursue relationships of all kinds, those that benefit you immediately as well as those that are

Every incredible opportunity will come into your life disguised as a relationship.

difficult and trying. A lot of times, people overlook the value of re-lationships in their lives and especially in their professional pursuits because they prefer the familiar, the comfortable, and the safe things of life. But relationships are the insurance policy of success. If you know enough people in enough places, if you have enough friends in enough nooks and crannies of the world, you cannot possibly fail. You might have a setback or two, but your support system of friends and associates won't let you totally collapse. They will consider it their responsibility and their privilege to assist you in your efforts.

By yourself, you will have limitations, no matter who you are. But if you can learn to invest time in people and in developing relationships on various levels with others, the people in your life will fill in the gaps that God has given you to keep you humble and dependent upon Him. You see, according to the Bible, God gives each individual certain gifts and strengths. Just as He gives the rabbit the gift of speed and the bird the gift of flight, so He gives each man and woman certain qualities that can give them an edge in life. But the Bible also makes it abundantly clear that God doesn't give everything to any one individual. Romans 12 and 1 Corinthians 12 both teach us that God gives a person one or two specific strengths so that person can share his strengths with others. God gives another person one or two different strengths so the first person will be encouraged to nurture a strong relationship with him in order to utilize the strengths he has. So we are designed by God to give and take at the same time in order to improve the quality of one another's lives.

If you really think about it, everything that operates in our culture is a picture of relationship. The economy, for example, is a picture of relationship. If you were suddenly the last person in the world, you could literally go from bank to bank, cleaning the cash out of all the vaults. But what good would that money do you? You cannot buy what other people aren't producing and providing. So connection is a natural state. We all need each other. You don't own your own cow; you get your milk by visiting your local grocer, who obtained the milk from his local distributor, who purchased the milk from a regional manufacturer, who acquired the original product from local farmers. You don't have an oil rig in your back yard. When you need gasoline to fuel your car, you drive to the nearest gas station, which obtained the fuel from a distributor, who purchased the fuel from a national refinery, etc. You didn't build your own house. You don't make your own clothes or grow the cotton or sheer the sheep that provide the wool. You don't grow your own food, not all of it anyway. Economically, we are intertwined. We are intertwined in every area of life.

So whether we recognize it or not, whether we like it or not, the world operates through connection and relationship. I need what other people provide, and they, in turn, need what I provide. I guess if I had to, I could survive without operating in this system. I could go to a deserted island somewhere in the South Pacific and learn to live off berries and water, make my home in a cave, and wrap palm leaves around myself to keep me warm and block the burning rays of the sun. But my quality of life would suffer immensely, and I would be all alone in the world (literally). The truth is I need people, and you do too.

In modern pop culture, we celebrate individuality. On some levels, I think this celebration is good and healthy, because each of us needs to discover and harness those distinctions that make us unique and give us purpose and direction in life. But we must be careful not to overlook the multiple unseen relationships behind every successful individual, the relationships that helped make that man or woman who they are. Nobody can do it alone, and that fact is undeniable. We are individuals in community, and most aspects of our lives are intimately connected with the lives and efforts of others.

Tiger Woods is perhaps the greatest golfer playing the game today. He hasn't yet equaled the achievements of Jack Nicklaus, but he is well on his way to matching or surpassing Nicklaus' many records.

Yet even Tiger Woods needs other people. His father taught him the game of golf and spent countless hours with him when he was a small boy, showing him the fundamental principles of the game and instilling in him a love for the sport. Today, Woods draws more attention on a golf course than any other golfer, in spite of his recent divorce and moral issues. But Woods' trainer helps keep him fit so he can play at his highest level. His coach works continuously on his putting stroke and swing to make sure he doesn't pick up any bad habits. His caddie scouts and charts every blade of grass and every tree and undulation on the course so he doesn't find himself in a situation where he doesn't know what to do. Tiger Woods, like all other successful people, is a cooperative venture.

If you like movies, you appreciate the acting abilities of the men and women of the silver screen. If you like movies a lot, you probably have your own favorite actors and actresses. But behind every actor who claims an Academy Award and behind every actress who makes you cry at the theater, there are screenwriters who created the words and the characters, makeup artists who made the actors look their very best, directors who made everything come together, an unseen host of other people who made the movie successful, thus making the actors and actresses successful. In fact, if you want to know exactly how many people contributed to the success of a particular movie, just stick around for a few minutes after the movie is over and watch the closing credits. All actresses like Angelina Jolie are a cooperative venture.

It takes a lot of people to pull off something great in the theater or on the golf course. It takes a lot of people to pull off something great in business, politics, or research. And it takes a lot of people to pull off something great in your life. Every success story is a joint venture. Thomas Edison, for instance, acquired an astounding 400 patents in a six-year period of time. But what few people know is that "Thomas Edison" was actually a fifteen-man team with a common goal. As one of his team members so aptly put it, "Edison is, in reality, a collective noun." His work was the result of the efforts of many men.

New relationships can introduce you to a new world. Whenever you meet a new person or make a new friend, you have no idea how significant that person might become in the months and years that follow. Likewise, old relationships can become your springboard to success, providing you with the necessary resources, wisdom, and support while you traverse the dangerous waters and currents of worthwhile pursuits. Good old King Solomon reminds us that *"where there is no vision, the people perish"* (Proverbs 29:18). The inverse is true, as well: Without people, the vision perishes. A vision requires the input and contributions of many people. Without those people, a vision cannot succeed.

Just as you invest time in your education and career, invest time in people.

My advice to you, therefore, is to recognize the immense value of the people in your life, not simply for what they provide you emotionally and relationally, but also for what they can provide you professionally, academically, and in every other arena of life. Just as you invest time in your education and career, invest time in people. Meet somebody new every chance you get and stay in touch with the people you know. Nurture and develop new relationships, but never let old friendships die. Keep your contact information up to date. Answer your phone, return your messages, and have lunch as often as possible with people in your network. No man is an island. Whatever you hope to become and whatever you hope to achieve, you will achieve largely with the help of others. Besides, the journey is a lot more fun when there are others around to share it with you and to applaud your efforts when you finally arrive.

CHAPTER 6

FOCUS

MORE BANG FOR YOUR BUCK

Have you ever fired a rifle? Better yet, have you ever fired a shotgun? I have a friend who lives near me in Florida, and he told me an interesting story recently about a childhood experience with a rifle and a shotgun that is well worth passing along to you.

Nick was born and raised in rural North Carolina during the 1950s and 1960s. His father, a veteran of World War II, was an avid hunter, and, when Nick was a child, he used to take Nick hunting with him. Typically, Nick's father would join several other men and hunt for quail on Saturday mornings. Each man would pack a 12-gauge shotgun, and, with trained hunting dogs leading the way, the men would set out in search of quail. Little Nick would tag along to watch.

"There's nothing quite as frightening as the first time you jump a covey of quail," Nick told me. "The birds make a tremendous noise when you come upon them, and the shotguns make an even louder noise. For a young boy, it can be a real adrenaline rush."

Intrigued with the camaraderie of the men and eager to follow in his father's footsteps, Nick would often ask his dad if he could hold his gun. And sometimes, after the day of hunting was over, Nick would ask his father if he could fire his gun.

"I'll let you hold it," his dad would say to him, "but you're too young right now to shoot that gun." So Nick would hold the 12-gauge shotgun with pride, thinking anxiously about the day when his father would allow him to load the chamber and pull the trigger.

Finally, the day came when Nick's dad told him he could fire the gun. At the end of the hunting session, when all the men had returned to their automobiles, Nick's father placed a rusted tin can about thirty feet away and told Nick that he would allow him to shoot the can. All the men stood around and cheered Nick on. This was a rite of passage for a young man in the Deep South, and all the men wanted to participate in this momentous event.

Nick's father loaded the chamber with a single 12-gauge cartridge, placed the shotgun in Nick's small hands, and carefully walked him through the processes he would need to follow. As Nick placed the gun against his right shoulder, his father warned him to keep the stock of the gun snugly in place. "The gun is going to kick back hard," he told Nick, "so you need to make sure you hold it firmly against your shoulder."

Nick is almost sixty years old now, but he can vividly recall every detail of that life-changing experience. He remembers placing the stock of the gun snugly against his right shoulder. He remembers raising the barrel and pointing the gun at the tin can, doing his best with his small arms to hold the barrel of the heavy gun still as he aimed at his target. Finally, when he felt that he was ready, Nick pulled the trigger.

It all happened in the blink of an eye. The noise was overwhelming and the tin can had been completely demolished. But the thing that Nick remembers most is the powerful jolt he felt and the ringing in his ears. His father was right. There had been a powerful kick. In fact, the kick was so strong, Nick declined an offer to fire the gun again. He was shaken, but he did his best to hide the trauma from the men around him. Of course, as Nick grew, he overcame the fear of the gun's kick as he continued hunting with his father. But Nick never forgot the unbelievable power of that weapon and the sheer force of the recoil of that gun when he fired it for the very first time.

When Nick's twelfth birthday rolled around (Nick was born on Christmas Day), he sat down under the tree, like all children his age, and proceeded to open his gifts. One box was extremely large and particularly long, and, when he opened it, he found his very own gun. This gun, however, was not a shotgun. This gun was a .22-calibre rifle, complete with a case and a bountiful supply of ammunition. You won't be surprised to learn that Nick was anxious to take the gun outside and fire it. So later in the day, Nick's father took him to a place where it was safe to shoot the gun.

Before Nick fired his new gun, Nick's father explained to him that this gun was more dangerous than the shotguns he had fired over the past couple of years. Nick's father told him that this new gun had a tremendous range and that Nick must always be aware of those things that might lie in the bullet's flight path as far as a mile away.

Keeping this new information in mind, Nick raised the gun and fired it at a paper target his father had mounted on a tree about 100 feet away. As always, Nick secured the stock of the gun firmly against his right shoulder, he steadied the gun until the sight was set on the target, and he pulled the trigger. But Nick was surprised at the lack of recoil. He was surprised at the lack of noise. In addition, Nick was surprised that the cartridges for his new gun were so tiny when compared to the larger cartridges he was accustomed to loading in his father's 12-gauge shotgun. Nick asked his father why his new rifle, in spite of its lack of punch and power, was more dangerous than the shotguns he had fired previously. His dad told him something he remembers to this day. As a twelve-year-old boy, Nick learned the power of focus.

A shotgun cartridge contains hundreds of tiny pellets. All these pellets are packed tightly into a large casing, and, when fired, the casing opens and the pellets are propelled in multiple directions in a powerful explosion created by a large amount of gunpowder. The opening of the barrel of a shotgun is huge in order to allow all these little pellets to "spray" outward as they exit the barrel of the gun, giving at least one of those pellets a high probability of striking a moving target at a close range. The large amount of gunpowder causes the shotgun to make an extremely loud noise, and the powerful kick is the simple result of the law of physics: Great energy is created in order to spray all these pellets outward with force, and the energy creates a recoil that is quite strong.

The shotgun is designed this way in order to give the hunter the maximum possibility of striking a moving target. He doesn't even need to aim that accurately in order to be successful. But the shotgun has an obvious disadvantage: The farther the pellets travel, the farther they spread apart, and the farther they travel, the slower they travel. Consequently, the shotgun is very effective at close range, but its range is very limited. As soon as the pellets travel a few feet, they completely lose their velocity and they actually fall harmlessly to the ground.

The rifle, on the other hand, has a much smaller cartridge with a much smaller load of gunpowder. The rifle makes very little noise when it is fired, and it has virtually no recoil because it expends very little energy. Nevertheless, the tiny cartridge that is fired from a rifle has a range of about 1 mile and is very deadly. Why? Because a rifle cartridge fires a single piece of lead, not a large number of pellets. The single cartridge exits the rifle through a tiny hole in the end of the gun, giving it precise direction as it spins out of the end of the barrel. The lead pellet follows a straight path from the barrel of the gun to its target, and it impacts its target at a high velocity and with incredible accuracy. As Nick puts it, "A rifle, properly aimed, can pick a housefly off a fence post at 50 yards."

The energy created by the rifle is not consumed by spreading pellets all over the place; the energy of the rifle is reserved for propelling a single piece of lead at a precise target. The power of the rifle is not consumed in the first instant it is fired; the rifle is constructed to be effective at greater distances, to be much more accurate, and to concentrate its undiluted force on one stationery object.

Thus is the power of focus. Because of the lack of focus, the powerful force of a shotgun is severely limited at greater distances. Because of the principle of focus, the less powerful force of a rifle is intensified at greater distances. The rifle is more deadly and more accurate from long distances because the rifle was designed to be focused on a specific target. The shotgun is less deadly and less accurate from long distances because the shotgun was not designed for focus. Instead, the shotgun was designed for the hunter who is not aiming at any specific target.

I convey this true story to you, because, when I heard it, I thought it was an excellent illustration of the point I want to make in this chapter, the point that phenomenal success is the outcome of a focused life. Sure, if you're not aiming at anything in particular, if you're just shooting into the air, hoping to hit something like those hunters were hoping to hit a flying bird, then you want to scatter yourself in as many directions as possible with as much of a kick as possible. But if you are wanting instead to do something specific and enduring with your life, then you are going to have to learn what Nick learned from his father: A focused approach to a goal is much more powerful than a haphazard approach.

Successful people, like the rifle in our illustration, are not necessarily more powerful than unfocused people. In fact, they are often less powerful. But because they are focused, these people are able to squeeze more effectiveness from themselves than their counterparts who are not focused. In fact, for the most part, highly successful people are just average people with a focus. They have learned to hone in upon a single target and to expend all their internal "gunpowder" in an effort to propel their lives forward toward a single, defined target.

Focus equals direction. Focus also equals power and strength, because focus better harnesses the attributes that one has in hand and pools those limited resources in order to more effectively achieve a goal.

If you study the lives of accomplished people, you will soon learn that every great person has a focus. Focus equals direction. Focus also equals power and strength, because focus better harnesses the attributes that one has in hand and pools those limited resources in order to more effectively achieve a goal. Unfortunately, most people are not focused in their lives and particularly in their approach to the future. In fact, most people live totally frantic and scattered lives, and they feel like they are expending great amounts of energy while never striking a real target.

Have you ever worked nonstop all day long, but at the end of the day couldn't remember anything meaningful that you did? Have you ever felt exhausted at the end of a long day, but at the end of that day you really couldn't say that you had done anything significant to advance your dreams or push your passions forward? Feelings like this are typical because most people feel this way most of the time. The reason they feel this way is because their lives are devoted to what's urgent instead of what's important. Their lives are devoted to a daily series of emergencies rather than the execution of a plan. Day by day, the activities in their lives increase, but they walk around with an aching realization that they aren't really getting anything done. They feel like time is marching on but they're making no meaningful progress in life, and their lives are nothing more than physical existence. The problem is that their lives lack focus.

Everything significant that has ever been accomplished in this world was accomplished by a maniac on a mission. Whether with noble or evil intent, the real movers and shakers throughout history are individuals who have possessed a singular focus in life compelling them to expend every moment of their waking lives and every ounce of their intelligence and creativity to achieve one great goal. The person with focus is virtually an unstoppable force. The powers of nature, the realities of time, and the opposition of other people may slow him down, but in the end, he will prevail, because he will not relent until "that thing" which consumes him comes to life. In the same way, the person who desires to be great must bring his life into order. He or she must develop a focus. Jesus said, "…*When thine eye is single, thy whole body also is full of light…*" (Luke 11:34). The ability to focus on one primary and overriding objective without the blight of distraction is the ability to do great things and rise above the fray.

I am convinced the only reason people fail is not laziness or ignorance or lack of ambition or a lack of talent. I am convinced that the only reason people fail is a lack of focus in their lives. The best way to destroy a man's dream or potential is by breaking his focus, by giving him too many pursuits or too many mini-dreams in life that conflict with one another. It's kind of like a woman with a certain amount of money to spend on clothing. The woman with a finite amount of money can either buy one really nice dress or a dozen cheaper ones. The more she spreads out her money, however, the lower the quality of clothing she will bring home from the mall. If there's only so much money to spend and yet she wants the best quality possible, this woman is going to have to focus. She is going to have to spend the entire day shopping for that one perfect dress that makes her liver quiver when she sees it. In the same way, you and I possess a finite amount of time. God has given all of us twenty-four hours each day, and He has given us a certain number of years upon this earth. If we want to extract the highest quality from the time we have, we are going to have to learn to focus on "that thing" which is most important to us.

You can do anything in life you want to do, but you cannot do everything. I am convinced you can achieve anything, be anything, and build anything you put your mind to, but the harsh realities of life won't allow you to do them all. If you truly want to be great, you must focus your limited time and resources upon that sole passion that deserves your time and your life. In the Bible, James said, "*A double minded man is unstable in all his ways*" (James 1:8). He "*is like a wave of the sea, blown and tossed by the wind*" (James 1:6). This observation is still true today. If you divide your heart, you will divide your effectiveness. But if you focus your heart upon something specific, nothing can take it away from you.

I read somewhere that the average person has 2,400 thoughts each day. Some of these thoughts are unavoidable and they are controlled by what happens around us. But many of them are chosen. They are given birth by that which resonates in our hearts. The passions that are strongest in the heart become the thoughts that are most prevalent in the mind, and the thoughts that are most prevalent in the mind become the forces that dominate our lives. Consequently, you can see that too many thoughts scattered in too many directions can divide a person's time, attention, and resources. Too many thoughts scattered in too many directions can divide a person's energy, potential, and chances for success. The juggling of too many balls brings a greater likelihood of dropping them all. The pursuit of too many destinations brings greater confusion on the journey. In all aspects of life, focus is the prerequisite for success and the assurance for progress.

Whether you realize it or not, your habits of thought control your life. What you think about in those 2,400 daily episodes is what you will end up doing with your time and your talents. And since 90 percent of human behavior is based on the habits we develop over time, I am convinced that the development of good thinking habits is the best way to focus one's limited resources and thus improve the possibilities of a great life. By focusing our thoughts, we focus our lives. We learn to focus our thoughts by developing habits of focused thinking.

The writer Charles C. Noble said, "First we make our habits, then our habits make us."[21] Nowhere is this truer than in the arena of the thought life. The more often a thought is repeated, the more powerful that thought becomes and the more permanently it attaches itself to a person's soul. Then those replayed thoughts shape the person's destiny and the very outcome of his life. This is why so much has been written over the years about the thought life; it is the seedbed of all that life will become. This also is why the meditations of one's heart are extremely important.

Perhaps my favorite verse in the Bible is Joshua 1:8. Joshua was certainly a man of greatness and a man of focus, and he was the hand-picked successor to Moses, the greatest leader in the Old Testament. Although Joshua made some of the same mistakes that all human beings make, he never lost his focus. Thus, he became great in spite of his shortcomings. The reason for his undivided focus can be found in the opening sentences of the book that bears his name when God told him, *"Do not let this Book of the Law depart from your mouth; meditate on it day and night, so that you may be careful to do everything written in it. Then you will be prosperous and successful"* (Joshua 1:8, NIV).

God wants us to think His thoughts about every situation that confronts us in our lives, and He wants us to think those thoughts "day and night." In other words, God wants us to read the Bible and gradually learn how He thinks so we can think like He thinks all the time. No matter the situation, whether it is day or night, whether circumstances are good or bad, whether we are joyful or bewildered, whether we are alone or with others, God wants us to think about every situation in our lives the same way He thinks about it. God knows the thoughts we think are destined to become habits in our behavior. He knows the thoughts we think are bound to become either life (which follows good thoughts) or death (which follows bad thoughts). So God wants us to retrain our thinking by thinking correctly about everything all the time so we can learn to focus our lives on things that will produce greatness for us.

The apostle Paul wrote, "…*Whatsoever things are true, whatsoever things are honest, whatsoever things are just, whatsoever things are pure, whatsoever things are lovely, whatsoever things are of good report; if there be any virtue, and if there be any praise, think on these things*" (Philippians 4:8). Paul too, speaking for God, knew the thought life must be directed, and then life itself could be corrected. He knew that a man's mind had to be focused before a man's life could be focused.

God wants us to think His thoughts about every situation
that confronts us in our lives, and He wants us to
think those thoughts "day and night."

You can change the focus of your life and learn to focus on that for which you were created by simply changing the repetition of thoughts that your brain manufactures. You can change the way you see life and the way you see your own future; then those changes can actually reshape your future. All permanent change in the human realm is the result of repetition. By changing the soundtrack that your mind plays over and over, you can actually change your focus in life and eventually your life's direction.

I have another good friend in the South who is a professional NASCAR driver, and he once told me about the training process that new drivers undergo before they are allowed to drive in NASCAR events. He told me the primary concern of all new racecar drivers is the wall. Nobody wants to hit the wall, especially at 200 miles per hour. He also explained to me that the centrifugal force of the automobile tends to propel the car directly toward the wall as the car speeds around the track. So the wall is a constant problem for all drivers, and it is the primary fear for new drivers. Everything is pulling the driver toward the wall as he drives around the oval track, so an inexperienced driver tends to be very afraid of hitting the wall.

Consequently, he explained, the wall is all a new driver thinks about. As he drives faster and faster, he keeps telling himself, "Don't hit the wall. Don't hit the wall." The wall becomes his focus, and the avoidance of the wall—not winning the race—becomes his primary objective. As they are learning to function as NASCAR rookies, these drivers are actually trained to turn their thoughts away from the wall and onto the infield. Rookie drivers quickly learn that you are drawn toward that thing which dominates your thoughts, and so they are deliberately retrained in their thinking to direct their focus on the infield instead of the wall. Over time, their focus is drawn away from the wall and toward the infield, and as a result, the feeling that they are being pulled toward the wall as they speed around the track is drastically reduced and the crippling fear is completely disarmed. They become potential winners.

You are dominated by what you choose to think about, and perhaps that explains why advertisers spend millions upon millions of dollars telling you the same thing over and over and over again. These marketers want to get you in the habit of thinking about their products, and they develop that habit of thinking in you through repetition. Over and over, they show you the images. Over and over, they whisper the slogan. Then, as time marches on, you will think like they want you to think and you will go looking for their products when you find yourself in need of them. Focus is the natural result of what you think about, and what you think about is created by repetition. Through repetition, you can change your thinking, and by changing your thinking, you can change your focus. Focus is the key to success in everything you will ever set out to do.

Unfortunately, the average person is inclined to be busy rather than effective and to be stretched to the limits rather than focused. The fast pace of our modern culture seems to feed this natural tendency. We as a society are a people who worship at the shrine of busyness rather than the shrine of effectiveness. We are a society that is given to diversification of activity rather than specialization. We are a culture that lauds variety over similarity and multiplicity over simplicity. Somehow, we have conditioned ourselves to believe that focus is bad because it is restrictive. Our infatuation with being broad has caused us to become mediocre. Instead of being great at one or two things, we are now content to be mediocre at dozens of things.

On the surface, being busy may look the same as being focused. But being focused has nothing to do with being busy, and being busy has nothing to do with being focused. Focused people spend the majority of their productive time thinking about and participating in activities directly connected to their destinies, while busy people divide their productive energies among a multitude of activities that have nothing to do with their passions or dreams. Focused people expend their energy placing one brick upon another until their dream eventually begins to take shape, while busy people expend their energy putting out fires so they can rush off to the next fire. At the end of the day, both the focused person and the busy person are tired and sweaty, but only one of them can look back over his shoulder to see something he has accomplished and then look ahead to see a goal that is getting closer by the day.

For example, a focused person may select a business course as one of his semester electives, because he hopes to own his own business within five years and he wants to learn specifically about the inner workings of a small business. A busy person, on the other hand, may select the same course as one of his semester electives just because he wants to expose himself to something new and learn a little bit about a lot of different subjects. In other words, he wants to "broaden himself" and "expand his horizons" (socially acceptable euphemisms for "I'm not focused yet").

The logic of the busy person is wrapped around the fact that he doesn't want to put all his eggs in one basket. He wants to learn a little bit about everything so he can always have options and have something to fall back on if his initial pursuits don't work out. The outgrowth of this logic can be seen clearly in statistics related to occupation. According to Marketwire, 69 percent of today's students expect to change career paths at least once in their lives. In other words, 69 out of every 100 American students expect to completely change direction in life at least once. Why? Because these students have no consuming passion and no real direction in life! Like many of their parents, they will merely find jobs and then change jobs like they change a dirty pair of socks, because they will never identify and pursue "that thing" which God grafted within them to give them real purpose and significance.

When a person is focused upon something that truly stirs his soul and ignites his heart, he simply cannot think about anything else.

Greatness, unlike mediocrity, comes from an undeniable passion, and one's passion is more than just a job. Certainly, the ideal lifestyle would be to earn good money doing what you love to do. But money is the residue of passion, not the driving force behind it. The driving force behind passion is focus. When a person is focused upon something that truly stirs his soul and ignites his heart, he simply cannot think about anything else. He simply cannot do anything else. Nothing else interests him. Nothing else satisfies him. Nothing else gives him a sense of completion or a sense of purpose.

The idea that you should not put all your eggs in one basket is not a godly idea or a wise one. This idea, like many of the profundities of the world, is based upon ignorance and sustained by fear. It is not based upon faith and not founded upon true principles of greatness. Perhaps the most obvious truth of all is that greatness is rare; therefore, the man who would be great must do that which is contrary to the norm. He must "think outside the box" and paddle upstream. He must defy "common sense" and swim against the tide. He must also reject the "stinking thinking" that locks most of the people of this world into a corral of social behavior that provides them with a certain sense of commonality and safety, yet deprives them of their God-given originality and their ability to pursue their dreams.

Do what everyone else does and you will get what everyone else gets out of life. But if you want your life to look different, then it doesn't take a rocket scientist to figure out that you are going to have to do something different with your life. Here's a simple mathematical formula that will never fail you: Do what everyone else is doing and you will end up like everybody else, but do something different and you will end up differently. Simple, huh? Yet profound!

I suggest you get alone with God and follow the guidelines in the earlier chapters of this book until you clearly define your passion and your singular purpose in life. Then I suggest you pour yourself into that passion with uncompromising abandon, because no great person ever became great in his spare time. He became great by setting aside every other distraction and every other pursuit and devoting himself exclusively to the love of his life and the reason for which he was made.

Fear is one of the major reasons people fail to focus their lives. It is perhaps the primary reason people abandon their dreams. By nature, people are afraid they might miss out on something if they deny themselves all the variety life has to offer in order to focus their thoughts and energies upon a singular ambition. They are subconsciously fearful they might regret the opportunities they declined. It takes a certain amount of courage in order to focus, and it takes a certain amount of faith. You have to believe in yourself in order to focus. You have to believe in your passion and your dreams. You have to believe you are doing the right thing and that the sacrifices you are making today will give you a return on your investment tomorrow. You must have faith that, every time you subtract something from your life to make more room for your passion or every time you take something out of your schedule to create more time to pursue your destiny, these sacrifices will eventually pay off later in a significant way.

There is a principle of life that runs through every facet of human existence: It's the principle of delayed gratification. In order to reap benefits later, you must sacrifice something today. This is true in the arena of health. This is true in the arena of finances. This is true in education, business, agriculture, and love. The harvest comes after you have planted the seeds. The wealth comes after you have denied yourself in order to invest your money. The business grows and thrives after you have worked hard and denied yourself a salary so you could put that money back into the fledgling enterprise. Every joy, therefore, is preceded by a certain amount of pain, because tomorrow's abundance is always created by today's sacrifices. This principle holds true in the arena of focus, as well. The individual who ignores all the distractions that life hurls at him in order to focus on his future is the person who will reap the benefits of that focused approach later in life. He will have no regrets.

Focus will cost you in the short term, but focusing your time and your energies will eventually benefit you tremendously and bring fulfillment and success to your life. So make the decision: Would you prefer to feel good today, or would you prefer to resist the temporal distractions of the hour in favor of pursuing something greater?

Always remember your future is not something that is ahead of you. Your future is something that is inside of you. With this in mind, take careful inventory of your talents and gifts, and then determine to focus your time, your energy, and your resources on developing those talents and gifts. This is your future, because the talents God gave you are prophetic. They reveal who you were created to be, and they are your greatest potential for success.

I guess every earthly father treats his children differently, but when I got married and left home, my father gave me a certain amount of money to help me get started in life. It wasn't a lot, but it was enough to get started. It was enough to take care of some of my early household needs, and I could work hard and eventually turn that little investment into something substantial. Similarly, our heavenly Father gives us gifts and talents when He launches us into the world. Like the money our earthly fathers give to us, we can choose whether to squander those gifts and waste those talents, or we can choose to embrace them, sharpen them, develop them, and utilize them to make the future what God intended it to be. Your talents are your greatest strengths, but you must learn to see them as your key to the future and as your stepping-stone to greatness.

In the Bible, Joseph's ability to interpret dreams was the key to his destiny. Fortunately, Joseph recognized this talent, embraced it, refused to be distracted, and patiently developed his special gift under God's guidance. Following the example of Joseph who discovered his talent at an early age, Oprah Winfrey entered oratory contests as a child. Just as Joseph knew that his ability to interpret dreams was somehow linked to his future, so Oprah Winfrey knew that public speaking was somehow linked to hers. This also explains why Tiger Woods was hitting golf balls at the age of three.

When you finally discover and embrace that singular ability that God has given you—the ability that comes naturally, the ability that makes you feel significant and complete, the ability that rises above all your other skills and talents, the ability that causes people to sit up and take notice—then you have harnessed your best hope for the future God intended you to live. Focus your thinking, therefore, on "that thing" and begin structuring your activities around this singular area of strength. If you allow fear or temptation to pull you away from your greatest strength in favor of "diversification" or "well roundedness," you may end up okay in life, but you won't end up achieving your greatest potential. You may end up with a good job—perhaps several jobs—but you won't end up with a real purpose.

Begin now to remove from your life those things that distract you. Think of ways every day to use your strengths and develop them, because your future wealth, prosperity, and success depend on it. All the good things in life are directly linked to your dominant God-given gift.

Since people are paid exceptionally well for things they do exceptionally well, highly successful people always focus on the area of their greatest strength. It's as simple as that, yet as difficult as that. To illustrate, let me tell you about an interview I saw on television a couple of years ago. It was during the Olympic Games. As usual, the Chinese Ping-Pong team was an unshakable force. During an interview with the team's coach, a reporter asked, "How do work with your team members to help them overcome their individual weaknesses?" Surprisingly, yet understandably, the coach said, "We don't work on the individual player's weaknesses. We focus so much on his strengths, his weaknesses just disappear."

Focus on your strengths instead of your weaknesses. Focus on the infield instead of the wall. Focus on the specific target instead of the middle of the flock of flying birds. Focus on the one or two things that make you unique and limit those things that make you like everybody else. The biblical "law of difference" teaches us that it is "that thing" which makes you different that can also make you great.

God believes in you so much. He has entrusted you with a fingerprint that is unlike any other fingerprint in the world. He has blessed you with a DNA code that nobody else possesses. Your retina is so unique that it can be scanned in order to set you apart from every other individual on the planet. You are one-of-a-kind, and God has given you one-of-a-kind gifts and talents, as well.

Just take a thoughtful look at God's creation, and you can get a snapshot of how He thinks and how He operates. God has given each little creature its own major strength. He gave the squirrel claws that enable him to climb trees and to scale brick walls at lightning speed. He has given the fish gills and the ability to swim underwater. He has given birds the ability to fly. He has given rabbits speed. He has given tigers and lions very sharp teeth and powerful bodies.

You will never see an animal ignoring his point of strength in order to develop a point of weakness. Only humans can do something that insane. When the rabbit senses danger, he will run, not swim. When the fish senses danger, he will swim, not climb. And when the lion is hungry, he will wait patiently to pounce upon his prey and crush him, not fly in circles above him until he dies. Animals don't go to school to acquire skills they lack, and they do not pursue things that distract them from their primary strengths or "broaden their horizons." Perhaps because their very survival depends upon it, they hone the one great talent that God has given to them and they instinctively ignore any tendency to emulate the other animals.

Too many people despise their talents. They spend all their time trying to imitate other people rather than living the original life plan that God gave them. Envy is a terrible disease of the soul that is unique to human beings and destroys far too many dreams. But God did not create you to be somebody else. Just as He created the fish to be the fish and the bird to be the bird, so He created you to be you. Nobody else can be you. If you don't live out the life God created you to live, nobody else can. Yet the vast majority of people, if they would be honest, would tell you they would rather be somebody else. They would rather be Donald Trump, Angelina Jolie, Tiger Woods, or Oprah Winfrey. But the great irony is these people got to be who they are by dealing with their own tendencies to envy others and focusing instead upon their unique gifts and abilities. They all became "originals." It's sad to think that others would want to become mere "copies."

You are genetically perfect for the assignment God has given you in life.

You are genetically perfect for the assignment God has given you in life. That assignment, if pursued, will give you all the satisfaction and sense of completeness you could ever want. It also can give you all the "things" and pleasures you could ever want. Everything about you—from your looks, to your thinking, to the way you talk—is designed specifically and intentionally to equip you for that unique purpose God has for you in life. Unlike the animals, who are smarter than us in a lot of ways, we humans spend far too much time trying to put in what we believe God has left out. The fact of the matter is God hasn't left out anything. He has tried to help us focus by giving us only those abilities we will need in order to be successful. He expects us to embrace those abilities and nurture them.

"But I don't have any talents," you might say. Not true! According to Romans 12:6, God has given gifts, talents, and abilities to each individual. The apostle Paul explained to the believers in ancient Rome that *"we have different gifts, according to the grace given us..."* (Romans 12:6 NIV). God declares outright in His written Word that He has given at least one strength to each individual He has made. But God makes it equally clear that He has not given every gift to anybody.

"But how can I recognize my primary gift and any supporting talents I may have received from God?" you might ask. "I'm having difficulty identifying them. I just can't see them, I just can't put my finger on them, and I'm desperate to understand what I should be doing with my life."

Let me close this chapter by leaving you with a brief explanation of three specific things you can look for in yourself in order to discover the primary and secondary talents God has given you. First, look for passion. Wherever you find passion in yourself, you will find purpose. As I have explained extensively in previous sections of this book, passion reveals the presence of a God-given talent. This is especially true when you feel a particular passion early in life.

I have already told you about Oprah Winfrey's childhood passion for oratory, and I have explained to you about Tiger Wood's childhood passion for golf. But there are many other examples.

Many great musicians, athletes, actors, and even scientists found their great love for what they do at a very early age. Matt Damon and Ben Affleck, for instance, were already good friends when they were children, and they used to find quiet spots at school where they could slip away from the crowd to talk about their passion for acting. Similarly, Picasso attended an adult art school when he was a teenager, because he already had discovered his great passion in life. The presence of an undeniable passion usually indicates a God-given talent.

Second, look for a tendency for rapid learning. I have seen this many times in life: A person digests principles, concepts, and huge volumes of information almost immediately because of a latent talent in that particular field of study. A child with a God-given talent for art will rush home from school so he or she can paint or draw. That same child will spend large volumes of his time surfing the Internet to learn more about art and will spend weekends at the mall, rummaging through art supply stores. Every time you buy that child a new piece of art equipment or a book about art, he will have a slight look of disappointment on his face because the thing you bought him is no longer interesting. Faster than you could notice it, he moved beyond that level months ago. In fact, your son or daughter can tell you more about art than the special documentary playing on PBS tonight.

People absorb and retain that which strikes a chord of interest in their hearts. They hunger for and seek out information that feeds their appetite for the thing they most love. Therefore, the presence of rapid learning or an insatiable appetite for learning in any area of life is typically a solid indicator of the presence of a God-given talent.

Finally, look for the presence of personal fulfillment. Your Creator designed you so that you feel good when you use the talents

He placed within you. So take a quick inventory of your thoughts and feelings. What positive activities bring you the greatest pleasure? What activities do you most look forward to engaging? Are you ever searching your calendar or perusing your own mind, trying to schedule the next time you can participate in a particular activity you really love? If so, that's a strong sign the activity in question is bringing you a sense of significance and personal achievement. And the presence of such meaningful fulfillment is often a sign that you have tapped into a primary talent.

In the end, you can be like the shotgun or you can be like the rifle. Sure the shotgun has a lot of kick. It makes a lot of noise and gets an awful lot of attention. Nobody can ignore the impressive and powerful sound of a shotgun. But the shotgun is really more of a noisemaker than it is a powerful force. Sure, it makes a bang you cannot ignore. But it sprays itself in so many directions that its power is very quickly lost and its range is negligible. The rifle, on the other hand, doesn't make a lot of noise and doesn't draw a lot of attention. On the surface, it's not nearly as impressive as a shotgun. But while the shotgun energy quickly dissipates and its range is strictly "short-term," the rifle is effective and reliable at very great distances. It is extremely accurate and is an effective killing machine. Why? Because its force is focused and its target is always specific!

Use your God-given talent to create the future you were designed to live. Identify and embrace the unique ability that is yours, and then focus upon the development of that gift and its application in your life. Use your singular strength as God intended you to use it, to enrich the lives of others and to propel your own life from where it is right now to where you know it can go. Stop spreading yourself so thin and aim at the target. Remember: You can do anything you want to do, but you can't do everything. You need to focus.

CHAPTER 7

COURAGE

JUST DO IT

On November 16, 2010, President Barack Obama awarded the Congressional Medal of Honor to Army Staff Sergeant Salvatore Giunta, the first living recipient of the award since the Vietnam War. Giunta received the nation's highest award for valor due to actions he performed in Afghanistan on October 25, 2007.

In an interview conducted shortly after he was chosen to receive the award, Giunta said he felt like the award was actually a team effort, He was only doing his job and any soldier in his platoon would have done what he did that day as he risked his life in an effort to save a wounded comrade.[22]

Giunta's feelings about his actions were common for people who do heroic things. Whether they pull pedestrians from burning automobiles or perform acts of bravery on the battlefield, most modern-day heroes seem to share a belief that their actions were not exceptional and that they really had no choice in the matter. In the face of danger, they really didn't sit down and think through what they did before they did it. Almost instinctively, they were compelled to act by the circumstances. In their eyes, they did what any reasonable person would do in that situation.

Courage, therefore, seems to be more about action than forethought. It is not so much a character trait as it is a propensity to get involved. Those who are singled out for recognition as heroes are people who simply saw a situation that demanded action and, without really thinking about it, leaped into action. From there, adrenaline took over. So from our perspective, their actions are extraordinary. But from their perspective, their behaviors were simply those that any person would exhibit under the same conditions. They weren't being brave; they were just doing what needed to be done.

As a culture, we deeply admire and publicly applaud acts of heroism and lives of success, but what we rarely consider is that both courage and success are linked to action. They are linked to the simple activity of getting off the bleachers and getting involved in the game. Remarkable things can happen when a person actually does something, even though the action performed may not be perfectly planned out and may not be the perfect thing to do.

The Greek philosopher Sophocles said, "Heaven never helps the man who will not act."[23] It's amazing how some things have never changed. The key to success some 2,500 years ago when Sophocles wrote these words is the same key that brings success in today's world. Actions speak louder than words. At some point, a person has to stop planning, stop talking, stop thinking, and actually do something to move his life forward. In life, nothing happens until somebody pulls the trigger or presses the button, and nobody will actually do these kinds of things without the will to act and the courage that compels it.

If you have ever paid close attention, you may notice that most people will do just about anything to avoid taking action. They will talk, they will plan, they will prepare, and they will organize. They will think, they will pray, they will seek counsel, and they will investigate. But too many people spend their entire lives doing anything but taking action, because they lack the courage to act. They spend their years procrastinating because they are afraid to actually take the leap of faith.

Procrastination is the natural assassin of opportunity and the exact opposite of courage. You've heard it said that opportunity only knocks once. I don't necessarily agree with that assessment, but I do know that it knocks infrequently. I also know that when opportunity does finally knock at your door, it comes disguised as hard work and as risk. People fail to act, not because they are lazy or lack passion or drive, but because they are afraid. They are afraid to take a chance. They are afraid to jump off the diving board. Nevertheless, the reality of the world in which we live is that nothing happens until

---

Procrastination is the natural assassin of opportunity
and the exact opposite of courage.

---

somebody does something. Thinking, praying, and planning all have their place. But the ditch doesn't get dug until somebody picks up a shovel.

In their best-selling book, *In Search of Excellence* (New York: Harper Collins, 2004), Tom Peters and Robert Waterman expose the character traits of some of the greatest companies in the world in an effort to isolate those specific qualities that set those companies apart from all the mediocre businesses flooding the landscape. One of those qualities that Peters and Waterman recognize and describe is "a bias for action." The world's greatest companies don't just sit around, talking and planning themselves to death. When the fire is stoked and the metal is hot, they actually strike. In fact, if they make mistakes, they err on the side of moving too decisively, not too tentatively.

If you want to be great in all you do, you need that same motivation in your life. You need that "gotta do it now" mindset and that "need to do something today" attitude. One of the primary things separating the "greats" from common people is that the world's great achievers have an insatiable desire to get busy, to do something immediately, to fix something today, and to get going right now. God seemed to leave out the gene for procrastination when He made people of greatness, because these people have little tolerance for inactivity. They are action oriented, and they despise waiting. They want to get things done just as quickly as they can, sometimes faster.

You also need to stop procrastinating and do something right now to move your life forward, because today is the only day you have to get something done in your life. You have no guarantee of tomorrow. In fact, the only thing God has given you is today. Yesterday is gone, and you can't do anything to change it. Tomorrow will never come, because when tomorrow does get here, it won't be "tomorrow" anymore; you will just rename it "today." So today is the only opportunity God has given to you to move your life forward, to change directions, to turn things around, or to push your dreams ahead. There's no such thing as tomorrow. You only have today. So get busy right now. Do something. Try something. Start taking action before the sun goes down, because all the little actions that you do on this day and on subsequent days will add up to big results.

Have you ever noticed how fast children seem to grow when you don't see them every day? Like most people, I have relatives I only see during the holidays, at weddings, and at other special gatherings, and these relatives have children. They don't notice their own children growing. I don't notice my children growing from day to day either. But when I see my relatives' children after a few months or a couple of years, I am blown away by how much they have grown. The reason their growth impacts me and not their parents is because their parents fail to recognize the tiny daily advances that their children's bodies are making, while I get to see the accumulation of those microscopic advances in a single dramatic unveiling. That's exactly the way it is with dreams and goals. If we are always waiting to get started on them, they will never grow. But if we start doing something today, no matter how small and seemingly insignificant, those daily baby steps will add up to recognizable results in the not-too-distant future.

Years ago, the Toyota Motor Corporation started buying leather tool belts for all their employees who worked on their plant assembly lines. Because the company purchased these tool belts in bulk, they got them for about $20 each. Nevertheless, one plant manager spent about $100,000 each year just to buy tool belts for his assembly line workers. In an interview with a local reporter who was doing a story on the plant, the tool belts became a subject of some curiosity as the reporter delved into the company's logic behind the seemingly large expenditure.

"Have you ever considered how much money you could save by eliminating the tool belts?" the reporter asked.

The plant manager just smiled and did his best to persuade the reporter of the greater logic behind the expenditure. It seems that Toyota had done some extensive research, and they had discovered that the belts actually saved them money. If each assembly worker dropped his screwdriver just once during his shift, the amount of time lost by stopping the line and bending over to retrieve the screwdriver would cost Toyota more than $100 million per year in lost productivity. So Toyota came to realize that thousands of tiny actions can add up to something really significant, and they concluded that the $100,000 expenditure was actually a wise investment for them.

Abraham Lincoln, one of my favorite philosophers, once said, "Things may come to those who wait, but only the things left by those who hustle."[24] The world rewards action, not thought. And the world rewards implementation, not ideas. Yes, this book and others like it expound the virtues of contemplation, planning, soul-searching, and creative thinking. But the authors of all these books, myself included, assume that all these noble preliminaries will eventually lead to action. Unless you put action to your thoughts and deeds to your dreams, all your grand schemes will come up empty and will merely die along with you at the end of your life. You need to start doing something now. You need to take action today, no matter how slight, because all those tiny actions will pile up and enable you to reach the sky one day.

The cold, hard truth is that the world doesn't pay you for what you *know*. The world pays you for what you *do*. The world doesn't reward you for your *imagination*. The world rewards you for your *actions* and *achievements*. This is a simple principle, I know, but it is amazing to me how many people don't get this. The majority of people I know, even the brilliant ones, get so bogged down in the planning and the conceptualizing that they never get out of the starting gate. When one or two of them finally take action, they finally manage to set in motion all kinds of things that propel them to success.

Active people make things happen. They stir things up and set in motion a whole series of events that, like dominoes, impact each other in a chain reaction resulting in a lot of progress and change. People of action, for instance, draw to themselves other people with similar goals, talents, and dreams. Due to action, all the people with similar dreams and different resources for achieving their dreams find one another and pool their energies and resources to make things happen. They work, network, investigate, and explore new possibilities and new ways of doing things. Over time, they build an entire network of friends, associates, and resources. They also gain valuable experience and acquire priceless counsel that makes them better and more confident at what they do. Then these people attract even more people who will support and encourage them, as well as help them in their efforts, and the cycle continues. But all these things happen simply because one or two individuals get busy and get going, setting in motion the forces of cooperation and synergy that are often needed to create great results. Good things eventually begin to flow in their direction when they simply take action.

Of course, there is a place for vision, goal setting, and defining one's passion. There is a place for building character and a time for learning to focus on what's important. To skip these vital stepping-stones to greatness is to rush headlong into chaos and to invite failure and destruction. But once the preliminary processes have been completed, there eventually comes a time when a person needs to put the preliminaries behind him and actually begin his quest for significance and greatness.

The Chinese philosopher Lao-tzu said, "A journey of a thousand miles begins with a single step."[25] Your journey, too, must begin with a first step. Like any journey, you must know exactly where you are going before you start. Like any journey, you must plot your course, pack the appropriate accoutrements, fill your gas tank, and plan your finances. But when the day comes to depart, you won't get anywhere until you actually enter the car, start the engine, aim the vehicle, and press the accelerator. Action is the key to moving forward.

Consequently, the day must come when you finally start writing that book, draft your business plan, call your travel agent, enroll in classes, or file papers to open your business. The day must come when you finally get up off the sofa, slip on your shoes, and go do something tangible to set your dream in motion. Nothing will ever happen with your passion and vision for life until you take action.

Procrastinators say, "Ready! Aim! Fire!" Courageous winners say, "Ready, fire, aim!" Both procrastinators and winners do the same things; they just do those things in a different order. You see, it's the aiming part that delays the kill. Sure, you need to aim. But if you're not careful, you can spend so much time aiming that the opportunity eludes you. The wind shifts. The target moves. Too many people spend their whole lives aiming, and they never pull the trigger. They want to get everything perfect before they fire the gun. Unfortunately, things will never be perfect, and winners know this. They know you have to shoot first and then adjust your aim accordingly.

Before a successful person hits his target, he typically takes a lot of shots and misses. But he just keeps shooting and keeps adjusting his aim. He knows he is more likely to hit his target by shooting, even if the trajectory isn't perfect, than he is by simply aiming. He knows that if he pulls the trigger, he at least has a chance of striking the bull's eye. But if he just sits there aiming all the time, he has absolutely no hope of hitting anything.

As I explained earlier, most successful people have a low tolerance for talking and planning. They prefer action. They have a bias for action. During the necessary planning and visualizing stages of the dream, these people get "antsy" because they want to stop talking and start doing something. They often come across as impatient and impulsive. They typically shoot first and aim later. They typically move the ball forward, even if they aren't quite sure where the goal line is and which person is playing what position. They believe they can figure out all those things later. Right now, they just want the ball.

Two college students came home for the summer with plans to get full-time jobs and earn some spending money for the next semester. While one student sat down to work on her resume, the other one got on the phone and started calling some of the area's largest employers. At the end of the first week, the first young lady had quite an impressive resume. In fact, her resume was so impressive, that she knew it would blow away anything the employers in her small town had ever seen from somebody her age. But at the end of that same week, the second young lady was actually working. She found a job the second day and started working the third day. Her idea was to find a job first, before all the summer jobs were gone, and then create a simple resume if her employer actually asked her for one.

Don't get me wrong. Planning is important, and it definitely has its place. You shouldn't act before you know what you are doing. But there's a healthy "tension" that should exist between planning and activity, because while too much planning with no activity leads to nothing, too much activity with no planning leads to failure. So find a balance. Plan a little, then get off your bottom and do something. Then come back and refine your plan. Then do something about that. Amazingly, your activity will actually help you refine your plan more than planning will help you refine your plan. So put planning in perspective and do something today, no matter how small, to advance your dream. Refuse to spend your whole life waiting for the perfect time to act. Quit waiting for the right person to come along. Quit waiting for things to change. Quit waiting for the ideal inspiration. Quit waiting for a new administration in Washington. Quit waiting for perfection or permission. Just do it!

Ray Kroc, the founder of McDonald's, often said that there are three keys to success. The first key is being in the right place at the right time. The second key is knowing that you are there. The third key is taking action in the situation. Follow the advice of Ray Kroc and follow the advice of Nike, a great company. Just do it, and do it now!

Why do people procrastinate? I imagine some procrastination can be traced back to laziness or self-esteem issues. But most people procrastinate because they are afraid. Specifically, they are afraid of failure. While the average person takes great pains to avoid failure and consequently avoids his dream, people of greatness look at failure as simply one leg of the journey to success. They view it as a learning process, just something you have to deal with to get from here to there or from the known to the unknown. Failure doesn't frighten courageous people, because they know that as long as they are breathing, failure is temporary and the experience gained from it is invaluable.

I am convinced that the greatest obstacle to success is fear—
fear of criticism and the fear of failure.

People of courage set out on their life's pursuit even in the face of doubt and uncertainty and even though they know that failure is a real possibility. In fact, they have an amazing ability to make decisions and take action in spite of the risks and in spite of their past setbacks. They believe in themselves and in their dreams so much that they are willing to ignore the natural human tendency to avoid failure. Instead, they defiantly stare it in the face as they move forward.

Do you remember the NASCAR driver from the previous chapter? When you force yourself to do the opposite of what your natural tendencies are telling you to do, and when you turn toward your fear instead of away from it, your fear shrinks. It loses its grip on you and its power over your life. Just as the professional driver learns to focus on the infield instead of the wall, you need to focus on your dream instead of failure. As you do, your fears will dissipate and your aggressive pursuit of the finish line will intensify.

Of course, when you take action, failure is a distinct possibility. Actually, failure is a distinct *probability*, because the only way to really learn to do something right is to do it wrong the first time and then correct your mistakes. Michael Moncur, a freelance writer and consultant, said, "Good judgment comes from experience, and experience comes from bad judgment."[26] Thomas J. Watson, a self-made industrialist and the founder of IBM, said, "The way to succeed is to double your error rate."[27] So if you want to be successful faster, it seems like you actually need to fail first, because success lies on the far side of failure. Of course, it's always great when you can succeed without experiencing any failure first. But you shouldn't fear failure, because most successful people taste some measure of failure before they actually taste success.

I am convinced the greatest obstacle to success is fear—fear of criticism and the fear of failure. But the man who can confront his fear of both criticism and failure by actually doing something in spite of it is the man who will far surpass his fellows. Have you ever noticed how leaders emerge from within a group? At first, everybody is equal and everybody is viewed the same by the other members of the group. But as problems arise and as situations develop that demand immediate action, the leaders are those who rise up to face the challenge, and in spite of the fear of possible failure and criticism, they confront the issues on behalf of the group. This is true in government. This is true in religion. This is true in business. In fact, Peter Drucker, a noted writer and management consultant, said, "Whenever you see a successful business, someone once made a courageous decision."[28]

Great success comes only from taking risks, from going where no man has gone before. No matter how much you plan, you will always face difficulties, disappointments, setbacks, and defeats. So you might as well forge ahead. You might as well push it all to the middle of the table and start doing something today.

Just as the NASCAR driver works on his thinking until he changes his perspective of the wall, you need to work on your thinking and change your perspective of risk. Risk is not your enemy, and risk is not that bad. In fact, any investment is a risk. The investment of your money is a risk, because there's no guarantee you will make more money and you may actually lose your money. The investment of your time is a risk, because there's no guarantee your time will produce anything lasting or meaningful. The investment you make in your marriage and your relationships is risky, because there is no guarantee that the people you love will love you back or that they will remain faithful or consistent in their love for you. And the investment you make emotionally in people, places, and things will always be risky, because people move, places change, and things rust and tarnish.

Risk, therefore, is all around you. It is an inevitable fact of life. This is why manufacturers sell warranties on almost everything they make and why insurance companies make enough money to buy skyscrapers in Manhattan. People are willing to pay huge premiums in order to minimize the risk in their lives. Behind any worthwhile venture, including life itself, there are tremendous risks. The best way to confront risk is by facing it head-on and by dealing with the natural fear of failure accompanying it. The fear of making a mistake and failing is definitely the biggest obstacle to action in people's lives. If you intend to be great or to be a leader among men, you need to push through that fear. The ability to overcome the fear of failure is one of the undeniable marks of greatness.

Henry Ford said, "Failure is simply the opportunity to begin again, this time more intelligently."[29] Like so many of the "greats," Ford experienced failure in his own life, yet he had the ability to get back on his feet, brush himself off, face his fears head-on, and begin again. Eventually, experience wins out, wisdom acquired through failure prevails, and things turn around. So you must allow your setbacks and your fear of more setbacks to propel you to greater resolve and stronger action, not take you out of the game.

Life is a learning process, not a one-time performance. Richard Buckminster Fuller, an American engineer and inventor, who was expelled twice from Harvard, said, "You can never learn less; you can only learn more."[30] Obviously, the reason he knew so much is because he made so many mistakes when he was younger.

Courage is one of the key ingredients for success. The capability to get back up when you've been knocked down, or the aptitude to take decisive action when everything is telling you to wait for things to be perfect is definitely a character trait that separates the men from the boys and the "greats" from the "wannabes."

Warren Buffet is renowned for his ability to make a decision. He has stated that with all the relevant information in hand, he can make a decision on whether to buy a company in a matter of minutes. Now that's courage and confidence. This courage is derived from a deeply imbedded quality of the soul that won't allow him to sit idle on the sidelines while life passes him by. Life is not a spectator sport. You must participate in order to win. But in order to participate, you must overcome your fear of getting knocked down.

Someone once described the game of football as 60,000 people who desperately need exercise watching twenty-two men who desperately need rest. But the game of football is highly indicative of life itself. Most people watch from the sidelines; few ever really get off the bleachers and get in the game. Sure, there's a risk you might lose. Sure, there's a risk you might fumble the ball, sprain an ankle, miss a tackle, or slip on the wet grass. But nobody scores a touchdown or celebrates in the locker room until somebody faces fear, suits up, and runs onto the field.

The goal posts are standing there for the world to see. Sure, the broadcasters and reporters are nestled in their skyboxes waiting to criticize your every move, and the opposing team is warming up waiting to destroy your game plan. But the band is playing on your behalf, and the crowd is waiting to cheer you on when you do something truly amazing. So get up, get going, and just do it!

CHAPTER 8

PERSISTENCE

WINNING BY STICKING AROUND

John Osteen was the founding pastor of Lakewood Church, the largest church in the United States and one of the great churches serving my generation. But Lakewood Church was not always a large church. Starting the church in 1959 in an abandoned feed store in a predominantly black neighborhood, Osteen was faithful to give his best every day to the small group of people who initially attended his church. His passion and his zeal then attracted many more people, and by the time Osteen died in 1999, he had built a thriving congregation that exceeds more than 43,000 people under his son and successor, Joel Osteen.

Toward the end of his life, Osteen was being questioned by a writer about the great church he had built. And, of course, the writer wanted to know Osteen's "secret" for success, what rare and mysterious quality he possessed that enabled him to do what few church leaders had ever done in the history of Christendom. When con-

175

fronted with this question, Osteen simply said that he had been successful because he had been in Houston longer than any other pastor. The other pastors who were there when he first arrived in 1959 had died, retired, or accepted positions in other communities. They were no longer at their posts in Houston. Osteen attributed his success, therefore, to the fact that he had simply been around longer than his peers. While others had packed up and moved away over the years, he stuck things through, and he stayed in Houston so long that he basically outlasted all the other pastors of all the other churches.

Great achievers often achieve great things
simply because they refuse to give up.

Persistence is one of the most common qualities of great achievers. Great achievers often achieve great things simply because they refuse to give up. Sure, other qualities play a role, perhaps a more important role. But when all other things are equal, when all those vying for success are basically on the same level in other regards, persistence will usually cause one person to rise above the rest. As the others give up and quit the race, one by one, the guy who simply refuses to go away will eventually prevail. He will inevitably be the one who breaks the ribbon and takes home the first-place trophy.

The longer you stay in the race, even if you aren't the fastest or the most highly conditioned, the more likely you are to prevail. The more times you swing at the ball, even if you aren't the most powerful hitter in the game, the more likely you are to eventually hit one out of the park. Success often comes, not through skill or ambition or even ingenuity, but through simple, old-fashioned guts.

I don't have to tell you that your climb to the top of the ladder won't always be easy. You already know that. But what you may not always consider is that persistence pays off. Sometimes you just have to plant your feet, dig in, and refuse to be moved. No matter how much you may have planned, things are going to happen along the way that you could never have envisioned and which will throw you off stride. No matter how much passion you may possess, people and circumstances will cause your passion to rise and fall. No matter how strong your vision may be, distractions will raise their ugly heads. In the end, you just need to stick around, no matter how hard it gets and no matter how long it takes.

The "greats" are committed to their goals, and that commitment is not built upon emotion or circumstances. Knowing in advance they will have difficult days on their ascent to the top, they simply refuse to give up. Along the way, they learn lessons they didn't know when they started out. Along the way, they develop new attitudes they didn't have in the beginning. Along the way, they face setbacks and defeats that force them to make difficult decisions and to reevaluate their priorities and methods. Nevertheless, the one thing that sustains them through all the changes in life and in the marketplace is their stubborn refusal to back down or go away. They just won't forfeit the game.

Ross Perot, the well-known billionaire who ran for president in 1992 and 1996, says that most people give up when they are just about to achieve success. That's true. People will get to the one-yard line and then walk away just when they're about to score the winning touchdown. Sadly, people will fight hard the entire game and then give up during the last minute of the game when they have the ball.

Gary is a friend of mine who is the founding pastor of one of the largest churches in central Florida. Gary grew up in rural Alabama in the 1950s in a Pentecostal home where he learned about the Lord from his father and mother. Gary's mom and dad, who had very little formal education, were pioneer pastors before Gary was even born.

Gary's parents are deceased now, but Gary once shared a true story with me about an experience his mother had when she was a young girl. When Edith was in high school, she was an impressive long-distance runner. She was fast. She had endurance. Nobody could compete with her. Edith attended a tiny school in the middle of nowhere, and in those days when she was growing up, she rarely had the opportunity to travel to a large town, much less a city. But when Edith was running track for her small rural high school, her track team actually won the regional championships, and Edith had a once-in-a-lifetime opportunity to run in the state championships in Birmingham.

When the time came for Edith's event, she ran her typically strong race. Coming around the last corner of the final lap, Edith had her typically commanding lead over the rest of the field. The second-place runner was many yards behind her. But as Edith approached the finish line, she encountered an obstacle she didn't know how to confront. Astonishingly, Elizabeth came to a screeching halt and just stood there and stared at this strange sight. It was a tape, stretched across the track at the finish line, and Edith had never seen a tape before. She didn't know what she was supposed to do. Was she supposed to crawl under it? Was she supposed to jump over it? Had the race been stopped? What was going on?

Never having seen a tape stretched across the finish line, Edith just stood there and stared at it until the second-place runner finally caught up with her and broke through the tape to take the gold medal. Edith lost. She was definitely the fastest runner in the state of Alabama, but just one foot short of the finish line, she failed to take her rightful prize. She gave up just inches short of her greatest achievement because an unexpected obstacle caused her to quit running.

I heard another story years ago about a group of coal miners who were trapped in a cave-in in West Virginia back in the days before they had sophisticated search and rescue equipment. As they were prone to do in those days, these miners used their own tools to begin digging toward the surface. They knew their chances of survival were less than good, but they continued to dig anyway with the hope they might beat the odds and break through to freedom.

Eventually, the miners lost their battle. They had dug for days, and they had made commendable progress, but they died before they were able to break through to the fresh air and sunshine. When the search and rescue people finally found the dead miners, they were alarmed to learn that the miners were only a couple of inches from the surface. If they could have just slung the pick a couple of more times, they would have broken through. They would have survived. But the miners lost their lives just one or two inches from safety.

In the Bible, few people were as tenacious as the apostle Paul. That poor man went through beatings, imprisonments, false accusations, loneliness, sickness, persecution, rejection, and a whole host of other things that would have caused the most committed among us to give up. But Paul refused to give up, and he became one of the greatest leaders in the early Church. He established countless churches around the Mediterranean, mentored strong young men to succeed him in his ministry, and wrote most of the New Testament epistles.

Paul used the analogy of a race to describe his own approach to his vision and life's work. And, at the end of his life, when his work was finished and his journey was complete, Paul told his young protégé, Timothy, "*I have fought a good fight, I have finished my course, I have kept the faith*" (2 Timothy 4:7). Paul knew that, in the end, we are judged by what we finish, not by what we start. So Paul's tenacity and stubborn refusal to quit were foundational ingredients in his formula for spiritual greatness and success. They were key ingredients in his legacy. Perhaps that's why, at an earlier point in his life, the great apostle told one of his churches, "*Watch ye, stand fast in the faith, quit you like men, be strong*" (1 Corinthians 16:13).

Obviously, Paul got this "holy stubbornness" from Jesus himself and from the disciples Jesus mentored. For instance, early in His ministry, Jesus had a profound effect on these unlearned fishermen. He taught them how to stop running and how to start sticking with those things that needed to be done. One of the places where we see this developing quality of persistence in the disciples is in Mark 6. In this New Testament chapter, Jesus told His disciples to travel by boat across the Sea of Galilee (a large fresh-water lake where many of the disciples had previously worked as fishermen) and to meet up with Him again on the other side. On the way, the disciples ran into a storm. Although their small boat was being hammered by the winds and waves and their lives were in peril, the disciples persisted in their efforts and continued to row against the contrary winds. Eventually, they rowed to shore.

This is a far different scene from Mark 4, just a couple of pages prior to this scene. In Mark 4, Jesus also had commanded His disciples to travel by boat across the great lake. In Mark 4, the disciples also had encountered a severe, life-threatening storm. But on this initial bout with high winds, the disciples had panicked. The storm had overwhelmed them, and their fear had overcome them. Jesus was forced to save them from the storm and from themselves. But apparently, the disciples learned their lesson (that's what disciples are supposed to do). By the time the events of Mark 6 rolled around, the disciples had learned some resolve. They had learned some tenacity. They had learned the value and benefits of persistence. And they refused to let any storm stand between them and their goals.

These illustrations from the Bible are real pictures of persistence and diligence. In these memorable accounts, the people involved

---

No matter how severe it might be,
your storm can't last forever.

---

continued to press toward their objectives, and their determination paid off. They showed through real-life situations that disciplined consistency can often win in the end and that the ability to hold one's course even in the midst of a troubling storm can pay big dividends.

So whatever you choose to do with your life, don't give up. If you encounter winds and waves, you have the power to ride out the storm. No matter how severe it might be, your storm can't last forever. You also have the ability to change course and make on-the-spot decisions that can help you evade the storm or minimize its impact. Don't quit paddling your boat. Don't succumb to the natural human tendency to throw up your hands and forfeit the game. Yes, failure will come along the way. You won't hit a homerun every time. But you don't have to fail at your ultimate goal. You don't have to quit. You don't have to be a prisoner of your shifting circumstances. With persistence and patience, you can actually become the creator of new circumstances.

Your ability to stay on target in the face of setbacks and disappointments is really a measuring rod you and others can use to determine your level of belief in yourself. Your persistence and desire also serve as barometers of your long-range potential for success. Nobody can predict what will happen along the way, and certainly nobody can predict the long-term circumstances of the marketplace or of life. But the man with an unrelenting desire and the woman with tenacity of spirit will always be able to ride the shifting waves of change and adjust to the unpredictable headwinds that toss their little boat around on the open seas. They will prevail, and while most of those who started the journey with them may turn around at the first sign of trouble, these great individuals will arrive safely on the other side.

Persistence, therefore, is one of the key traits that separate those who just get by from those who are truly remarkable. Those whom I would categorize as "good" achieve most of their limited success through the sheer force of talent, charm, and hard work. But those who are "great," those who do remarkable things with their lives, just stick around longer than anybody else and wait for the competition to give up. They don't retreat in the face of setbacks. They don't shirk in the face of disappointment. They don't quiver in the face of delay. And they never capitulate in the face of the unknown. In fact, persistent people seem to move forward in spite of these things. They are willing to stand still for a while, even move backward a little bit if necessary, in order to wait for the storm to pass and the crisis to die down. They know persistence is a habit, a quality of self-discipline. They choose to exercise the self-discipline of patient, persistent strength, because the harder they choose to run with endurance, the harder it is for them to quit.

My grandmother used to tell me, "I'm never down. I'm either up or I'm giving up. But I'm never down." And she was right. The person who is perpetually down is really in the process of giving up. The person who is a winner is always up or, if he has suffered a setback, is on his way back up. Quitting is just a permanent solution for a temporary problem, because a man who is down can always get back up, but a man who quits will never take another step forward.

There's an old Japanese proverb that says, "Fall down seven times; get up eight." And the Bible declares, "*For though a righteous man falls seven times, he rises again…*" (Proverbs 24:16 NIV). The secret is to not quit.

If God expects you to stumble once in a while, how can you expect your life to be a continuous carousel of colossal achievement? The key to long-term success is to keep getting back on your feet and keep trudging forward. If you can just do that, you will be amazed how far you can go in life.

Terry Fox lost his right leg to cancer. In 1980, Terry embarked on a cross-country run in Canada to draw attention to the plight of those suffering with cancer and to raise money for cancer research. Terry had to run nearly twenty-four miles per day, just shy of a twenty-six-mile marathon. Nevertheless, Terry wouldn't quit. Obviously, running on an artificial leg wasn't something that was easy or enjoyable. But Terry had a unique way of shuffling and hobbling along in order to accommodate his disability. As if his challenge wasn't hard enough, there was the terrain— sometimes mountainous— and the wind, the heat, and the rain. But Terry ran every single day for 143 days, eventually traveling 3,339 miles before he was forced to quit. The doctors discovered that Terry's cancer had spread into his lungs.

Terry Fox died as a result of his spreading cancer, but as long as his ailing body would allow him to do anything at all, he wouldn't give up on his passion for finding a cure for cancer. He became a model of persistence, inspiring many and leaving a legacy that endures to this day. Because of Terry's insatiable desire to finish what he started, annual runs for cancer research are held in his honor in more than sixty nations of the world. Those runs have netted hundreds of millions of dollars for cancer research.

Immediately after he was forced to terminate his run across North America, a reporter asked Terry how he had done what he did. "How did you keep going?" the reporter asked.

"I just kept running," Terry replied. "I didn't think about the distance I had to go. I just focused on the next telephone pole. I refused to give up. I figured if I could run to the next telephone pole, that would be enough. But as soon as I reached that pole, I immediately focused on the next one and the next one and the next one. I just didn't quit."[31]

Winston Churchill was one of the greatest leaders of the 20th century. He may very well have been the primary force that saved Western civilization from tyranny and oppression. Churchill was forced to lead Great Britain and to balance his country's delicate political alliances with the United States and the Soviet Union during one of the darkest eras in the history of his nation. He was successful primarily because of his persistence and tenacity. He just wouldn't quit, and his tenacity became his trademark. In the midst of his darkest days and at a time when the war was going very badly for his side, he gave one of the most famous speeches of his life. At the famed Harrow School in London, he said, "Never give in. Never, never, never, never, in nothing great or small, large or petty, never give in except to convictions of honor and good sense."

Churchill was known among the Brits for his "bulldog" spirit because he believed in unyielding determination and the willingness to endure hardship and remain committed to a cause even in the midst of indescribable opposition. He understood that, even in the face of almost certain defeat and failure, the man or woman who can persist can often triumph because of a sanctified stubbornness that just won't let them give up.

Churchill liked the label he received from the British people because he understood that the bulldog was specially designed by God with unique physical abilities that allowed it to prevail through tenacity. According to Churchill, the bulldog's nose is slanted backward. And that is not an accident or a coincidence. The bulldog's nose is backward for a reason. Because the slant of the bulldog's nose is toward his own body instead of outward, the bulldog can latch on to his opponent and continue breathing without letting go. This uncommon design, Churchill believed, is nature's way of showing us both the necessity and the incredible advantage of sheer persistence.

Life is filled with examples of great men and women who prevailed in life simply because they refused to quit. If you watch any of the old black-and-white movies about the lives of people like Lou Gehrig, Benny Goodman, or any other person of achievement, you will see that these people persisted through disappointment, rejection, and outright resistance in order to climb to the top of their respective fields. The Bible echoes the same theme of persistence before success. People like Abraham, Moses, and David were well known for their persistent faith and enduring patience. The annals of history also bear out the fact that greatness is preceded by tenacity. Ross Perot, who eventually became a billionaire, was rejected seventy-eight times before he made his first sale. And Thomas Edison made over 10,000 attempts before he felt he had finally crafted a viable light bulb.

Perhaps my favorite example of persistence is Abraham Lincoln. Lincoln is regarded by many Americans as our nation's greatest president. But how many Americans also know that he persisted through more failures than any other president? Abraham Lincoln had a very difficult childhood and less than one year of formal schooling. Then, at the age of twenty-two, he suffered a business failure. At the age of twenty-three, he was defeated for the state legislature. At the age of twenty-four, he again failed at business. At the age of twenty-five, he was finally elected to the legislature. At twenty-six, his wife-to-be died. At twenty-nine, he was defeated in his bid for Speaker of the House. At thirty-one, he was defeated in his bid as an elector. At the age of thirty-three, he finally married, but he endured a difficult marriage and family life. Only one of his four sons would live past the age of eighteen. At the age of thirty-four, he was defeated in his run for the United States Congress. At the age of thirty-seven, he was elected to Congress. At thirty-nine, he was defeated in his bid for reelection. At forty-six, he was defeated for the United States Senate. At forty-seven, he was defeated as a candidate for vice-president. At forty-nine, he was again defeated for the Senate. But at the age of fifty-one, Abraham Lincoln was elected as the sixteenth

---

If at first you don't succeed, then you are among the world's greatest achievers.

---

president of the United States. Perhaps Lincoln's acquaintance with temporary failure prepared him providentially to guide the United States through the difficult trials of the Civil War, because in the initial stages of that war, the Union suffered defeat after defeat and setback after setback before they finally prevailed under Lincoln's persistent leadership.

So don't quit! Don't give up. And never, never give in. You never know whether success may be just around the corner or whether light and fresh air may be one shovel full of dirt away. If at first you don't succeed, then you're about average. If at first you don't succeed, then you are among most of the world's greatest achievers. Hang in there, and refuse to walk away from your dreams. The next thing you try could be the filament that lights up the bulb.

I would never consider myself to be among the likes of Lincoln or Edison, but I am a living testimony to this principle. I could have quit a lot of times in my life. There were many occasions over the course of the years when it would have been easier for me to walk away and abandon my dreams than to continue pursuing them. But the obstacles and difficulties and outright defeats that have plagued me throughout my life didn't make me who I am; they merely revealed who I am. Something within me just wouldn't let me quit. It wouldn't let me give up and walk away. My trials revealed persistence, and that persistence saw me through.

When you face difficulties, avoid the natural tendency to retreat. Avoid the tendency to throw up your hands and walk away. Instead, when you run into a roadblock on your journey to greatness, stop and think for a moment before you turn around. First, think about the fact that this highway of achievement needs to be riddled with potholes and barriers. That's so the half-hearted and the wannabes will get off the road and go home. That's why those who don't belong there will eventually quit along the way. The roadblocks are there to separate the strong from the weak and the truly great people from those who just think they're great. Believe me, nobody has ever traveled this highway without suffering a lot of difficulties. Knowing the roadblocks are purposely built into the journey should help you continue because you will then have realistic expectations. The trip to the top isn't supposed to be easy.

Second, think about the specific obstacle you are encountering at the moment. There is a way around it. Perhaps you need to dig underneath it. Perhaps you can go around it to the right or the left. Perhaps you can climb over it. There's always more than one way to scale a mountain. So instead of giving up and crawling back home with your tail between your legs, take a few minutes and brainstorm with yourself. Think of three ways you can overcome this challenge. Sometimes the best strategy won't always be the obvious one or the first one.

I believe there's no such thing as a problem without a solution. No matter what the problem may be, there is a solution to that problem. The bigger problem, however, lies with our thinking, not with the problem at hand. We don't want to do the hard work or pay the bitter price to implement the solution. We don't want to face the consequences of our decision, so we tend to tell ourselves there is no solution to the problem we face. Nevertheless, the solution is there. We just have to find it and then take the necessary risks to put it to work. Always be solution-oriented in your thinking, because the answer to your problem is always right in front of you. Be willing to pay the price to implement your decision, because wishful thinking never moved any mountain. Only unrelenting faith and a really big shovel can successfully move a mountain.

For centuries, Mount Everest, the world's tallest mountain, loomed insurmountable to the world's best climbers. The climate, the altitude, and the terrain all made it seemingly impossible for any human being to successfully scale the peak of that monstrous edifice of nature. But in 1953, Sir Edmund Hillary successfully ascended the summit of the world's tallest mountain. Since then, almost 3,000 people have made the journey. Building on the knowledge that Sir Edmund provided for them, the successive climbers have become quite innovative, finding two distinct ways to conquer that peak and utilizing modern equipment and technology to aid them in the quest.

The 1969 moon landing is another example of human tenacity. For centuries, men could only stare at the moon or study it through the lens of a telescope. But over time and with much faith and persistence, people came together and mapped out a plan for actually traveling there and returning safely to earth.

There is no such thing as a problem without a solution. You just have to find the solution and pay the price to implement it. But the unwillingness of millions of people to do those two things causes them to give up their dreams just as soon as they encounter the first pothole in the road or the first collapsed bridge on the highway. If you want to eventually stand in the winner's circle along with all the other greats of human history, you must face the fact that your journey will be riddled with challenges. But a solution awaits each of those challenges for the one who is courageous enough to confront them. Never give in. Never, never, never, never, in nothing great or small, large or petty, never give in.

Dr. Norman Vincent Peale, one of the pioneers of possibility thinking, said, "It's always too early to quit."[32] And he was right. As long as there is breath in your lungs and a head on your shoulders, you don't have to accept the way things are. You can always keep pushing on that door until it opens or keep twisting that lid on the jar until it eventually comes off. You can keep looking for that needle in the haystack. You can keep fighting the good fight of faith and running the marathon of life. If you just don't quit, you will eventually "inch" your way to the finish line and wear the victor's crown. Glory awaits the persistent.

CHAPTER 9

INTEGRITY

GUARDING WHO YOU ARE INSIDE

When you were a kid, did you ever play "king of the mountain"? Over the years, I've come to realize that this child's game is played everywhere. It's universal. But it goes by different names in different parts of the country. Some people call it "king of the mountain" while others call it "king of the hill".

Whatever it's called, the object of the game is the same. A group of children find a big pile of dirt or sand somewhere, particularly in a construction area (where they shouldn't be playing in the first place). They all start running to see who can be the first to climb to the top of the dirt pile. Literally crawling and fighting their way to the top, they strive to achieve their goal of temporary dominance by pushing their little friends out of their way, trampling them underfoot, grabbing them from behind, and shoving them back down the hill they just climbed. Whoever manages to reach the summit of the dirt pile first is declared "king of the mountain."

Unfortunately, reaching the summit of the dirt pile is just the beginning of the victor's challenges. Now he must fight off all the rest of the children who continually come after him in an effort to dethrone him from his supreme position and take the summit from him. It's an all-out brawl, though friendly, as all the children band together out of necessity in order to overthrow the current "king of the hill" and take his place at the top of the world. As one king is overthrown, another one arises. Then the children have a new target, a new "king" to take down. And the game goes on and on, finally ending when everybody gets tired. Mothers definitely hate this game because of the dirty clothes, the dirt-smudged faces, and the minor injuries this game produces.

Nevertheless, this little game for children serves as an excellent analogy for our next trait of greatness, because integrity is a quality that keeps us at the pinnacle of greatness throughout our lives. While talent and personality might take us to the top of our respective fields of endeavor, character will actually keep us there. But unlike the "king of the hill" in our little competition, the man of character will never fall.

In modern America, talent, appearance, and personality have become far more important than they used to be in previous generations, primarily because of the advent of television, motion pictures, and "instant media" like the Internet. Don't get me wrong—talent is something to be admired and good looks are commendable. After all, everybody likes a nice-looking person, and I'd much rather have a stellar personality than an objectionable one. But all these qualities are surface things, and all of them can be purchased or faked for the few moments that a person might stand in front of a camera or in the spotlight in front of an audience or at a job interview. Character, on the other hand, is what's inside you. Character cannot be contrived.

Character should be more highly admired than talent, and character should be more highly sought than attractiveness or personality. Why? Because far too often, those with talent or good looks end up disappointing us after life eventually uncovers their lack of character. While good looks can be artificially created with a makeup brush and a surgeon's scalpel, character is created over the course of one's life through the many experiences one encounters and the many decisions one makes. Character and integrity are developed as one learns responsibility and accountability through the growth process of life. And God honors integrity. In the Bible, the apostle Paul writes that *"suffering produces perseverance; perseverance, character; and character, hope"* (Romans 5:3-4 NIV).

If you have ever climbed an extremely tall ladder, you know that these special ladders typically start out wide at the bottom and then become narrower as you ascend them. They start out roomy, but they get tight. Life is a little bit like one of these tall ladders— the higher you climb in business, the higher you climb in ministry, the higher

---

Character should be more highly admired than talent, and character should be more highly sought than attractiveness or personality.

---

you climb in life, the more your responsibilities increase (the height of the ladder) and the more your options decrease (the width of the ladder). On the ladder of success, there's not much room at the top to move around, because the increase in authority has been offset by the increase in visibility and accountability. By the time you get to the top of your ladder, more people are able to see you. They're watching you a lot more closely than they used to because you are easier to see. That's why it is important to develop character as you ascend the ladder of success. At the pinnacle of your life, it will become a lot more about "being" than "doing."

Sooner or later, every man will be forced to ask himself three very important questions that will tell him everything he needs to know about himself and his character: Did I do what I said I would

---

When all is said and done, leadership is really nothing more than the ability to inspire other people to follow you towards your desination.

---

do? Did I do it when I said I would do it? Did I stand behind it after I did it? As time progresses, the answers to these questions will become obvious to those observing you from afar as you sit atop the ladder of success. But unless you also know the answers to these critical questions, your "success" will be meaningless and empty and all your achievements will leave you disappointed. Life won't bring you any real satisfaction or significance unless you also know you did the right things for the right reasons as you worked toward your goals. Ralph Waldo Emerson put it this way: "Guard your integrity as a sacred thing."

Integrity lies at the very heart of greatness and leadership, because everything you will ever do revolves around who you are on the inside. Who you are on the inside is demonstrated every day by your actions, the things you do and the words you speak. Therefore, successful people, and particularly great leaders are characterized by honesty, trustworthiness, and dealing straight with every person they encounter, no matter the situation.

When all is said and done, leadership is really nothing more than the ability to inspire other people to follow you towards your destination. But this definition, by nature, means that people must be "sold" on two things before they will forsake their own pursuits and get in line behind you and your dream. First, they must be "sold" on the destination. They must believe in the objective you are pursuing. Second, they must believe in you as a person. They must believe you can indeed take them to this defined destination and that you are worthy of their sacrifice. They must be "sold out," not just to the journey, but to the individual who will be leading them on this journey.

By nature, people want to follow. But by nature, people aren't inclined to follow. By nature, people are skeptical, especially of other people. So people have to be inspired before they will lay down their individual agendas in order to take up yours. They have to believe in the person they are being asked to emulate. If you are a leader—whether in the political sense, the spiritual sense, or in business—you are asking people to sacrifice their own priorities in order to adopt yours, and you are asking people to sacrifice all that is precious to them for the pursuit of a common objective that is bigger than their own. But of equal importance, you are asking them to believe you are the person who can take them there and you are the person who is worthy of their sacrifices. You won't use them and throw them away. You won't mislead them or deceive them. You are the man or the woman who knows how to get to the Promised Land, and all the things you have told them about the Promised Land will be found true upon their eventual arrival there.

But why would people—especially people who have been burned and disappointed more times than you can imagine—want to trust you? The fact is they won't trust you unless you can inspire them to do so. Their trust must be earned. As a leader, you must do something that is rare in the world, yet something which the people know is possible and for which they have been searching all their lives. You must show them integrity. You must speak the truth, and then you must live the truth you speak. You must mean what you preach, and then you must practice what you preach. You must stay true to your message and your vision, but more importantly, you must stay true to yourself. Only by living privately the way you live publicly can you ever hope to possess the spiritual authority that is so genuine it can truly impact lives, defeat skepticism, and motivate people to lay down their individual agendas and take up yours. And you must do this over and over, in every situation of life, continually and without fail to make your followers truly believe in you.

As a leader, you must be a good role model. You must always conduct your life as if everybody is watching you, even when nobody is watching you. You must keep your word always. You must be consistent in the way you treat people, never regarding one person as more important than another and always respecting those around you, regardless of their status in life.

A great and successful person does not lump other people into categories or treat "lesser" people with prejudice. He does not see black and white. He does not care about gender, age, or social status. He does not treat an important client one way while treating his employees another way. He does not favor the individual who can do something in return for him. People of mediocrity, of course, will view others through a paradigm that is conditioned by the immediate circumstances and by the prospects of acquiring an immediate return on investment. If an isolated act of integrity can be advantageous, a person of poor character will treat others favorably in any given situation. But a person like this can never be an enduring leader, because a person like this can only motivate others through manipulation or compensation. The person who desires to legitimately inspire others to fight alongside him for a lifetime must be consistent in all situations and with all people. He must be a man of predictable integrity.

Thomas Carlyle, the Scottish writer, said, "A great man shows his greatness by the way he treats little men."[33] "Great men," by nature, treat all other men kindly, honestly, and respectfully, because "great men" are always looking ahead. While "little men" have a short-term view of life, focusing on those actions and behaviors that can benefit them today, the truly great men of this world refuse to sacrifice the meaningful things in life, like honor and integrity, for short-term profit or short-term gain. Because they have a long-term view of life, they won't jeopardize the substance of their lives in order to get out of a tight or uncomfortable situation Instead, they will always look at the bigger picture of how today's actions might affect tomorrow's circumstances. They are men of integrity.

When you are a man or woman of integrity, little things can easily turn into big things. The way you treat "little men" today can definitely impact your future, because many of those "little men" will become "great men" in the future. Surprisingly, many of the people who appear "great" today will become "little" in a rapidly changing world. In the same way, the accumulation of the "little" things you do will have a lasting impact on those around you, and the "little" words you say will leave enduring impressions and mold an unshakable reputation.

I think I can drive home this principle by sharing with you a true story about something that happened to me when I was in high school. In my junior year of high school, I got a new car for my birthday, and I told a bunch of my friends that I just got a Vette. Wow!

Can you imagine a high school boy with a Vette? That news really made an impact on a lot of my friends, especially the guys, who were just consumed with jealousy and envy. There were two brothers in particular who seemed enthralled by the fact that Dave Martin had a Vette. They were so excited, and of course, they wanted to see it. I managed, however, to "hem haw" around and avoid letting them see my new car for a while. Then eventually they moved out of town.

Over the years, I kept in touch with these two brothers, and they continued to be impressed by the fact they had a friend who owned a Vette. I did everything in my power to perpetuate their image of me as the "big man on campus." A few years later, however, I saw them again at my ten-year high school reunion. Sure enough, the subject came up once again. They wanted to know everything about my Vette. Did I still own it? What kind of condition was it in? Did I have it with me at the reunion? Could they see it and perhaps drive it?

After more than a decade, I was finally forced to confess to these two brothers that my Vette was actually a Chevette, not a Corvette. I hadn't actually told them a lie, because I did own a Vette. But it was a Chevette, not a Corvette as they supposed. I was so embarrassed, because I had allowed this little white lie to go way too far and drag out way too long. I was humiliated because my reputation took a nosedive that day in the presence of some of my closest friends in the world.

But that's the way it is with "little" things. Little things become big things. In the life of the man with integrity, the little things he says and the little things he does over time build his image and opens to him new opportunities. Likewise, in the life of the man without integrity, the little things he says and the little things he does pile up and come back to haunt him. He reaps a bitter harvest of broken hopes, broken dreams, and broken relationships.

As a young man, I learned a valuable lesson from that little episode with my Chevette. I learned that dishonesty has a long tail that never seems to end. I learned that once you start being dishonest in any area of your life, the need to be dishonest never ends. Lies just keep stretching out farther and farther.

I also learned that it is always best to be honest about everything, the big things and the little things. I learned that it is best to be honest when you file your tax returns in April, to be honest when you take a test at school, and to be honest when you fill out an application for a job. But I've also learned that it is best to be honest when you realize that you are driving over the speed limit and to be honest when you get a phone call from somebody you really don't want to talk to. Instead of "fudging" the speed limit, it's best to submit to the law, even when you are alone And instead of asking your staff or your children to tell the annoying caller that you aren't there, it's best to do the right thing by being truthful with the caller.

In the biblical parable of the talents, the master said to his servant, "...*Well done, good and faithful servant! You have been faithful with a few things; I will put you in charge of many things...*" (Matthew 25:21 NIV). There's a spiritual principle at work here. Whenever you are faithful with the "little" things in life, you will be entrusted with greater things. And whenever you are faithful with the simple things, you will build a reputation among others as one who is trustworthy in all things.

Telling the truth, especially in an uncomfortable situation, is to pass a test of sorts, a character test. The thing about life is that it will throw all kinds of "tests" at you every day, and it will be up to you how you will handle these tests and whether you will pass them. These tests will take on different forms and will come at you in different ways and at different times. But it is the tests or challenges of life that are necessary for molding character.

Character is shaped by the challenges of life, including both the victories and the defeats that result from life's challenges. But character is more than the challenges themselves and it is more than the outcome of the challenges. Character is the sum total of the mental and ethical traits that a man develops as a result of walking through life's difficulties. While the events and circumstances associated with life are beyond one's control, the development of good character is a choice, because character is shaped by the decisions we make while we are walking through our challenges. Consequently, character is a growing and evolving part of our being that results from the way we respond to the myriad of temptations, trials, and disappointments that confront us. The setbacks themselves are not character, and the sheer number of problems we have faced are not character. But the genuine life lessons we learn from such things and the wisdom we glean and apply from them are the true building blocks of integrity.

Character development is a choice, or, better stated, a series of choices. Unless we choose to learn from our experiences and then apply the wisdom we have learned, we are doomed to mediocrity and a less than stellar life. We also are doomed to continually repeat the mistakes we have made in the past. However, if we choose to have an attitude that will allow our experiences to shape us into better people and if we will accumulate knowledge and wisdom from each experience, our problems and even our failures can become the launching pads for true greatness. In *The Golden Gems of Life*, written 130 years ago, S.C. Gerguson and E.A. Allen said, "By repetition of acts the character becomes slowly but decidedly formed."

No man is free from testing, but every man is free to respond to that testing differently. All of us walk through a daily maze of conflicts, confrontations, and moral decisions. Although each of us will make a poor choice now and then, the preponderance of our choices will determine the kind of character we develop, and character will determine the outcome of our lives. Those who make mostly good choices in life will develop good character, and those who make mostly bad choices will develop bad character. The trials of life, therefore, do not make your character. Instead, they reveal your character and present you with watershed moments along the journey to alter your character or to refine it. In other words, life's problems treat you a little like a tube of toothpaste. They squeeze you until what's buried deep inside you eventually comes out.

Under pressure, a tube of toothpaste reveals its true contents. What's in there comes out for the world to see. And the primary reason God allows things to go wrong in your life is so you can see clearly what's inside you and deal with it. God already knows what's in there, but you and I have a tendency to lie to ourselves about our true natures. So God permits the storms of life to toss us around enough so we can see the wide gap that exists between the way He pictures us in our completed perfection and the way we are actually

The primary reason God allows things to go wrong in your life is so you can see clearly what's inside you and deal with it.

walking out or refusing to walk out that picture He has of us. Problems, therefore, give us opportunities to grow.

To truly grasp this concept, let's go back to Joseph for a moment. You remember Joseph from the previous chapter. He's the man in the Old Testament who had a dream that his father, mother, and eleven brothers would all bow down to him. Then, over the course of time and through a strange series of events, Joseph actually became second-in-command within the nation of Egypt and his family did come and bow down to him. But Joseph first went through many years of testing. Being sold into slavery by his brothers, he served for many years as a slave in the household of Potiphar. Then he became an inmate in prison. But the thing that landed Joseph in prison was a false accusation made against him while he was Potiphar's slave. It seems that Joseph was a good-looking guy, and Potiphar's wife apparently made advances toward Joseph in an effort to initiate a sexual relationship with him. But Joseph refused the continuous opportunities to betray Potiphar, his master. So, with a rage born out of rejection, Potiphar's wife accused Joseph of sexually assaulting her, and Joseph was thrown into prison.

When Potiphar's wife expressed to Joseph her interests in having a sexual relationship with him, Joseph could have surrendered to the temptation. Not only would he have derived the temporary pleasure associated with the physical intimacy, but he also could have saved himself a lot of trouble and false accusations. He could have kept the wife of his master happy, and he could have maintained his position as head servant of the estate, with all its comforts and amenities. But Joseph chose instead to do the right thing when nobody was looking. He chose to run away from the temptation and to stay true to his moral convictions. In time, Joseph's character and integrity took him from the prison to the palace.

God made a promise to Joseph through the dream He gave him as a young man, and eventually there was provision for that dream. But between the promise and the provision, there were a lot of problems for Joseph. In fact, his strict adherence to high moral principles actually caused some of those problems. That's the way it will always be for the man or woman of character. Whether we do right or do wrong in life, we will encounter problems simply because life is problematic. But the way in which we deal with the problems of life, especially when nobody is watching us, will determine the extent to which God's promises will actually be provided for us. Our problems, therefore, can become little opportunities to develop character. They can prepare us to realize and fully enjoy the dreams for which we strive, if we will remain faithful to our own internal code of morality and do the right things in the midst of our problems. But if we choose to despise our problems and to let our problems harden us instead of molding us, we will become hard and bitter. Eventually we will be broken by the problems God permitted in our lives to build us and shape us.

In *The Golden Gems of Life*, Gerguson and Allen also write, "Character is to a man what the flywheel is to the engine. By the force of its momentum it carries him through times of temptation and trial; it steadies him in times of popular excitement and tumult, and exerts a guiding and controlling influence over his life.... It is a strong and sure staff of support when everything else fails." Life's problems don't make our character; they reveal our character and give us ample opportunities to grow and change as human beings.

Have you ever seen a person do something under pressure that is completely "out of character" for that person? Or have you ever heard a person under pressure say something that is completely "out of character"? Perhaps the person who would never lie might tell a little white lie when his job is at stake. Or perhaps an individual who would never use foul language might cuss a little when his car is rammed from behind at a traffic light.

I contend that people like this aren't actually acting "out of character" when they are under pressure. I contend that the pressure is actually revealing exactly what's hidden deep down inside that person. I contend there is a latent problem out there just waiting to happen that has the power to reveal a moral weakness or character flaw that everyday life might never expose. I contend that the problematic nature of life is designed to expose, piece by piece, the true nature of one's character.

All of us have accidentally turned over a cup of coffee or a glass of water. What happens when you knock over a cup of coffee? Coffee spills out all over the table and all over the floor. You don't knock over a cup of coffee and then clean up a puddle of Kool-Aid. You don't spill a glass of milk and then clean cola stains out of the carpeting. What spills out of a glass when it is turned upside down is what was in the glass in the first place, and what spills out of you when you are turned upside down by life is what was inside you all along. The beauty of life, however, is that life affords us untold opportunities to grow and mature. Life, by its very nature, is redemptive.

Your character is who you really are; your reputation is who people think you are. Your character is what God says about you; your reputation is what people say about you. Your character is the words that God will speak over you at judgment; your reputation is the words a professional minister will speak over you at your memorial service.

Don't live to build your reputation; live to build your character and integrity. Don't live to improve how people see you or what they think or say about you; live to become the man or woman God can uphold when the time comes for you to give an account of your life. Don't let your problems make you bitter; let your problems make you better. The most enduring organizations and the most revered and respected people are the ones who stressed integrity and who lived what they taught, even when life got hard.

You've heard it said that honesty is the best policy. Well, that's very true, not just in a spiritual or moral sense, but in a practical sense too. Even the non-religious people of this world know that once a person or a corporation abandons ethical principles of honesty and integrity, nothing of substance is really left and nothing that has been built will last. Over time, the pursuit of more—more money, more power, more this, more that—will become meaningless in itself and will eventually no longer satisfy even the greediest and most hedonistic among us. Things will come up empty. Power will become meaningless and shallow. Money won't fill the void inside the human heart. Pleasure will eventually cease to please. But knowing that one has done the right thing in the right way for the right purpose is worth more than gold. It will satisfy every desire of the heart, and will meet one's every legitimate need.

Without integrity, leadership at any level becomes mere management and ceases to be leadership at all. Whether we're talking about government, business, or religion, those who surrender integrity in order to pursue power or achieve a goal, regardless of its worth, no longer can claim to be leaders. True leaders and genuinely successful people (the "greats") are known as faithful and true. Their lives and careers are marked with trustworthiness and noble behaviors that stem from integrity. Their character is imbedded in moral truth that stays with them and manifests itself most clearly when they are faced with a temptation their better judgment won't allow to embrace.

As I just illustrated through the story of Joseph, character is who you are in secret when nobody is looking. It's doing the right thing when nobody is watching you. It's performing the thousands of little tasks that need to be done and that should be done, even when nobody notices that you do them and when nobody gives you credit. It's telling yourself the truth about yourself and being honest with everyone else as well. It's keeping your promises, even when it inconveniences you to do so. It's remaining true to your word and your guiding principles, and it's following through with the commitments you have made to other people.

Not long ago, my four-year-old son, Solomon, was invited to spend the night with one of his little friends who lived about an hour from our house. Even though this would be Solomon's first sleepover with friends, my wife and I made plans to take Solomon over for the night. We thought he would really enjoy the experience and have a great time. Besides, he really wanted to go. Before we left, I told my son I would come get him if he got scared or homesick.

Knowing Solomon, however, I fully expected that he would stay through the night, playing with his little friend until he finally collapsed of exhaustion late in the evening. After dropping my son off at his friend's house, I went to an important meeting I had scheduled for that same night. About 8:30, I got a call from my son. He had decided he did not want to stay. He wanted to come back home, and he wanted me to pick him up as soon as possible. As quickly as I could wrap up my meeting, I again made the drive to his little friend's house and drove Solomon back to our house. The whole thing consumed my night, as you can imagine.

Character is not as much preference as it is conviction.

Believe me, it wasn't convenient for me to drive for an hour to drop off my son for his sleepover. It wasn't convenient for me to drive another hour to get back to my meeting. And it certainly wasn't convenient for me to drive two more hours to pick up Solomon at his friend's house and take him all the way back home again. I had worked a long day, and I had another meeting scheduled for early the next morning. I really didn't want to spend four hours that night, running my son back and forth between his own home and his friend's house. But I made a promise to my son. I told him I would do something. I made a commitment to him. And, in the end, regardless of the inconvenience, it was more important for me to model integrity and demonstrate character to my son than it was to get a good night's sleep. What I did that night was simply the right thing to do.

Character is not as much preference as it is conviction. It is not as much coincidence as it is choice. In fact, you could say that character is the sum total of all the choices you make during your lifetime. Every minute of every day, you will stand at some type of fork in the road, facing a decision. Most of the time, those decisions will be inconsequential. Will you walk up the stairs or take the elevator? Will you have mayonnaise or mustard on your sandwich? But each day will also present you with decisions that are consequential, decisions that will mold your worldview and shape your destiny. They may seem small at the moment, and perhaps, one by one, they are small. But as they add up, they have a huge impact on your life. Will you walk away with the excess change the cashier returned to you after your transaction, or will you give it back to her? Will you boost your ego by responding to the flirtatious advances of your coworker, or will you protect the sanctity of your marriage and place professional boundaries on your relationships at work? Will you eat the candy bar while you shop and then "forget" to pay for it at the counter, or will you pay for it first?

As I stated earlier, every person makes a bad choice now and then. Thank God for His patience and mercy! But if you ever allow yourself to start compromising the principles you publicly advocate, you are on the fast track to becoming a hypocrite and a person of poor character. The man of integrity sets a high bar for himself and strives every day to live up to his own noble expectations, even if he falls short. He may fail to meet his own expectations from time to time, but he knows he will never rise any higher than the goals he sets for himself. Never forget, it's always better to set your standards high and come up a little short than it is to set your standards low and succeed every day.

Whether you like it or not, your character will be the foundation of your life, because bad character will yield a bad life and good character will yield a good life. The hard and deliberate process of building your character will have an outcome on the back end. What you need to realize on the front end of all that hard work is that you will form your character over time through the habits you develop in the midst of life's storms.

Albert Einstein, noted by everyone for his powers of observation, said, "Try not to become a man of success, but rather try to become a man of value."[34] Einstein knew what even a little child like my son knows: The highest goal you can have is to live faithful and true. Be true to yourself and true to God. Be true to those around you, even the strangers you encounter briefly along life's way. Try to do what is right in every situation, because integrity is really nothing more or nothing less than simply doing the right thing, no matter the situation and no matter the circumstance. As Alan Simpson, an eighteen-year veteran of the United States Senate, so aptly put it: "If you have integrity, nothing else matters. If you don't have integrity, nothing else matters."[35]

CHAPTER 10

ADAPTABILITY

CHANGE OR BE CHANGED

There is a profound difference between conformity and adaptability. The "greats" seem to instinctively understand this difference, and while they disdain conformity, they cherish the courageous ability to adjust to changing circumstances. Conformity is the negative quality of blending in, becoming average, refusing to stand out or capitalize on one's uniqueness. Adaptability is the positive quality of being able to sense the shift in wind direction and proactively adjust one's course to take advantage of that wind shift. While conformity is a weakness based upon fear of rejection, adaptability is a strength based upon confidence in oneself and in one's own judgment and abilities.

The key to adaptability is one's willingness to change. The "greats" understand that change is inevitable, and they realize that a person's capacity to accept change is a key element of growth and success. They also realize the world isn't standing still and they can't stand still either. They must change or be swept away in a tidal wave of change as it inevitably sweeps across the landscape.

The fact of the matter is that no human condition is permanent. There are seasons in life, just as there are seasons in nature. Back in 1965, The Byrds recorded a best-selling song that was written by Pete Seeger and based on the writings of King Solomon in the biblical book of Ecclesiastes. The song, "Turn, Turn, Turn," quotes a lot of the observations of Solomon, including his well known adage that *"to every thing there is a season, and a time to every purpose under the heaven"* (Ecclesiastes 3:1). So the smartest man who ever lived observed that the things of life change. They wax and wane. They move. Life seems to come in seasons. Solomon was saying, in effect, that happy and successful people need to understand this reality of living in the world, and they need to get with it. To resist change is to resist reality and invite utter disappointment, heartache, and failure.

Nothing in this life will last forever, and I guess this truth can be viewed as both an encouraging and a discouraging reality. While the storms of life are destined to move on, so are the beautiful things of life. But this is the way life is, and the "greats" recognize this fact rather than resist it. The wise people of this world embrace this reality rather than reject it. The primary truth I want to convey in this chapter is that change is inevitable, but it is possible to be happy in the midst of change and even to utilize change to one's advantage. The "greats" have learned to do this and have made their penchant for change one of their strongest assets in the pursuit of excellence.

Spencer Johnson wrote a phenomenal book on the subject of change. I highly recommend it. The book is entitled, *Who Moved My Cheese?* (New York: GP Putnams's Sons, 1998). Written as a parable, the book imparts some real insights into the subject of change and how to deal with it successfully. Until a person can deal with change in a useful way, he won't enjoy life to the fullest and won't be able to succeed in life either. But those who are prepared for change and those who can navigate it successfully are those who will travel through life with greater enjoyment and greater results. So learn to change quickly and learn to enjoy change, because things will change whether you want them to or not.

Until an accomplished person is willing to change,
his past achievements simply remain in the past.

The undeniable truth is that the faster you can turn loose of what used to work and embrace what's working now, the sooner you can enjoy where you are and where you are going with your life. The faster you can embrace the benefits of change and the positive aspects of growth, the sooner you can begin to enjoy your journey from today to tomorrow. Learn to celebrate change. If you can, you will be healthier, happier, and far more relevant. If you can, you will be able to appreciate the accomplishments you have made to date while anticipating greater achievements in the days ahead.

Past accomplishments can often serve as a reflection of one's abilities, but by themselves they are never a good predictor of one's future potential. Until an accomplished person is willing to change, his past achievements simply remain in the past. Sometimes I feel sorry for those people who gloat over their past achievements, because I know that when a storm finally hits and a cold front moves in, these people might not be able to change with their environment. They might not be able to recognize the shift in the winds or adapt to life's modifying seasons. These kinds of people often lose everything during seasons of change because they get swept away by the changes. Rather than riding the waves of change like an expert surfer, they allow the waves of change to break over their heads and sweep them away in a powerful undercurrent that eventually pulls them down and drowns them. They weren't prepared to move with that which is new, so they became victims instead of overcomers.

Know that conditions around you will change, and they will change constantly. Consequently, be patient with life and with yourself and refuse to give up. Keep doing what you are destined to do, but learn to do it in new ways. Adjust. Transition. Adapt. Hang in there, but learn to go with the flow. Learn to fit in with your culture and with the society in which you live. And learn from the advice of the apostle Paul who said, "*...Let us not be weary in well doing: for in due season we shall reap, if we faint not*" (Galatians 6:9).

One of the few elements of life that is unchanging is change. In fact, just about the only thing in life that doesn't change is the fact that things change. So if you want to be successful and relevant, you need to learn to embrace change, celebrate it, and make it part of your life. This very moment, everything within you and everything around you is changing. If you refuse to let your thinking and your methods change with everything else, you are going to become irrelevant very quickly and be left in the dust by those who are willing and able to adapt and evolve.

Right now, as you read this book, the very cells of your body are changing. At this precise moment, the earth is changing. Before you go to bed tonight, the laws of our land will change, the economy will change, communications will change, and somebody somewhere will invent a new computer chip or improve an existing one and technology will change. In fact, before you return to work tomorrow, some aspect of the way you do business will change, and before you rise in the morning, some aspect of the way you live life will change.

John F. Kennedy said, "Change is the law of life, and those who look only to the past or present are certain to miss the future."[36] When change occurs, therefore, you have two choices. You can co-operate with change or you can resist it. You can embrace it or you can fight it. You can learn to recognize the benefits of change and view change as an opportunity for growth and new experiences, or you can denounce change as the work of the devil and dig your heels in as you rapidly become the latest species of dinosaur to go extinct. The choice is yours. But the "greats" have learned to embrace change wholeheartedly. In fact, they see change as an ally, not a foe, as a friend, not an enemy. They view change through their paradigm of optimism and see it as a catalyst for growth and a launching pad for greater success. They don't see it as a threat or a challenge; they view it as a healthy opportunity to go where they've never been before.

Of course, there are different kinds of change. Some changes are natural and they occur in predictable cycles. The stock market goes up and down every day, the hot summer months are followed every winter with frost and snow, and while holiday shopping drains our wallets every December, our tax refund checks arrive every spring. We accept these natural cycles of life as ordinary, and we have little or no difficulty adjusting to the ebb and flow of the seasons of nature, the seasons of the economy, and the seasons of life. In fact, many of us actually look forward to these predictable forms of change, be-cause they keep us from becoming bored.

But other changes aren't so easy for some people to accept. The personal computer and all the gadgets created to work with it have forever changed the look and shape of everyday life. Debit and credit cards have basically made cash a thing of the past. Online shopping and electronic banking make it possible to live a somewhat normal life without ever leaving home or interfacing with a real human being. In my short lifetime, I have seen multiple changes in the way we live, the way we work, the way we get our news and information, the way we shop, the way we communicate, and the way we socialize, all because the world refuses to stand still and remain the same. It is sobering sometimes to contemplate the fact that these things will never go back to the way they were. The world is moving on. I have to decide whether I will move with it or wave goodbye to those old familiar things as the rest of humanity disappears over the horizon of progress.

Unfortunately, too many people do stand on their front porches, buggy whip in hand or Model T Ford in the driveway, and wave goodbye to progress. Too many resist change, and they resist change on various levels. Not only do they resist changes in music, fashion, and technology, but they also resist change in more fundamental things. They resist changes on their jobs, in their churches, in their neighborhoods, in their communities, and in society. But if you would honestly think about it, you would have to admit that changes in your own life have worked out for the good more often than the bad. Even though you resisted them at the time, they turned out to be positive modifications in the landscape of your life.

Just think about times in your own personal history when you experienced a major change. More than likely, you resisted that change at the time. In the very least, you probably deplored it. Maybe you were forced to move. Maybe you were transferred to a new job site. Perhaps your company changed suppliers. Perhaps new management took over the business where you were employed. Maybe your factory relocated or your office took on a new supplier. If you are like most people, you probably didn't like that change when it first occurred. Nevertheless, the change worked out okay, didn't it? In fact, most of the changes that have happened to you without your consent or pre-approval probably turned out to be beneficial for you. They turned out good.

I encourage you to keep that historical record in mind the next time you are confronted with change, because the same rule applies today. More often than not, change will be a good thing in your life. If you will keep that thought in the forefront of your mind, you can actually begin approaching each new change in your life with excitement and anticipation instead of fear and loathing. You can actually begin to look forward to the full effects of the change and you can embrace the change with a good attitude.

The key to greatness is to learn how to flow with and embrace change, because everything will eventually change.

The next time you find yourself confronted with a major change, ask yourself some honest and probing questions in order to learn whether you are approaching the change with a positive attitude or whether you are subverting the benefits of the change. Ask yourself: Am I doing things to resist this change? Am I secretly afraid of what might happen to me as a result of this change? What is it I'm afraid of losing because of this change? What price would I be forced to pay if I decided not to cooperate with the change? To get onboard with the change, what deliberate steps would I have to take that I am not taking right now?

The key to greatness is to learn how to flow with and embrace change, because everything will eventually change. You need to decide whether you want to move forward with life by seizing life's sometimes scary opportunities or whether you want to just sink your roots down and dare the forces of nature to try to move you. You can either change or you can be changed. The choice is yours.

Bill Gates didn't become one of the richest men in the world by resisting change. In fact, he has been one of the driving forces of change in recent times. History will attribute to him many of the great technological changes of the twentieth and twenty-first centuries. Bill Gates teaches that change is not an optional thing. We cannot take a vote to decide as a society whether we want change, and we cannot opt out of change as individuals. Change is coming to our world each and every day, typically in small, bite-sized pieces. Nevertheless, it is coming, and it is coming steadily and persistently through technology and every other imaginable way.

In fact, in the twenty-first century, we are changing at an unprecedented rate, and no place is changing faster than the United States. Part of the strength of the United States has been its ongoing love affair with change. Since before the founding of our republic, we have been a nation of innovators, entrepreneurs, explorers, and dreamers. As a people, we have embraced change while much of the rest of the world has been slowed down by its superstitions and its nearly immovable traditions. As a society, we have taken advantage of change and we have made it our national mantra. Though the global attitude toward change is finally changing itself, in the past, too many cultures have tried to hide from change and resist it. They have fought a losing battle in a vain attempt to resist change. They have tried to build walls to keep it out of their countries. But what many of these cultures are finally learning is that both individuals and nations have a decision to make: One can either embrace change and become better because of it, or one can resist change and be crushed by its inevitable advance.

Perhaps you've heard the story of the two frogs that were dropped into separate pots of water. One frog was dropped into boiling water; the other frog was dropped into room-temperature water that was gradually brought to a boil. The frog that was dropped into the pot filled with boiling water immediately jumped out of the pot. He was scalded a little, but he was alive. But the frog that was dropped into the room-temperature water remained in the pot while the temperature of the water was gradually increased, one degree at a time.

Eventually, the frog in the room-temperature water was boiled, because he stayed in the pot. The frog that was dropped into the boiling water was a little wounded, but he lived to croak another day. Other than the fact that one frog lived and the other one died, what was the difference between the two frogs and the way they handled the situation?

The first frog accepted change. When he was placed in the pot of boiling water, he immediately reacted to the difference in temperature and he did something about it. He jumped out of the water. The second frog resisted change. When he noticed the temperature of the water gradually increasing, he decided to do nothing. He decided to resist the change and try to "ride it out." So while the surviving frog changed, the dying frog was changed.

That's the way it is with change. We humans can either change or we can be changed. We can either adapt with the times and circumstances, or we can be crushed by the steamroller of change that is coming our way whether we like it or not. The second frog ignored the warning signs, but everything around him told him that things were changing and that he needed to change too. Whether it was fear or stubbornness, his resistance to change destroyed him. Resistance to change destroys many people, too.

Change is occurring everywhere, and it is occurring faster than ever before. Yes, even the rate of change is changing. Throughout most of the world's history, change has taken place very slowly. Cultures have been very hesitant to surrender their social institutions, cultural rituals, and familiar ways of life. Throughout ancient times and even the Middle Ages, the human mindset resisted change. And in some places of the world, like Afghanistan, one can still see how that mindset and historical resistance to change can grip an entire culture of people.

Beginning with the Industrial Revolution, change started coming more quickly to the world, particularly to those nations that participated in the industrialization of the planet. From the mid-nineteenth century to the mid-twentieth century, change came to the world at a rapid and unprecedented rate. In the field of technology, especially, there were phenomenal breakthroughs that fundamentally changed the way we live our lives, and these technological innovations came in rapid succession as the world's population began to understand the advantages of change.

In the first decade of the twentieth century, the automobile became a fixed part of human life. The mass production of automobiles began to make it possible for people everywhere to own and drive a car, thus dramatically improving their possibilities for travel. In the 1920s, the radio changed the way the world got its information. In the 1930s, the telephone became a mainstay in America and forever changed the way we communicate. In the 1940s, commercial aviation again altered the way we travel and made it possible for people to experience places and cultures that had been a mystery to them prior to this time. In the 1950s, the television became a fixture in virtually every American home, changing the way we view the world and the way we spend our leisure time and relate to our family members. In the 1960s, the first robot was invented and space travel and satellite technology began to impact every facet of our existence. And in the 1970s, the personal computer started emerging.

In each of these giant steps forward, there was significant change. While some people embraced these changes and built their lives upon them, other people resisted these advances and were left in the dust. Those who accepted change, however, realized its value to the human condition and the desire for more change became a driving motivation that accelerated the pace of change to the point we know it today. Demand for more and more inventions and innovations has driven the world's economies, causing factories to work overtime and research and development teams to burn the midnight oil.

Over time, the Industrial Revolution, which gave credence to change, has given way to the Information Revolution, and consequently the rate of change has become unprecedented. Whereas it used to take technology years or decades to change, today it changes at a rate that makes today's purchases nearly obsolete before you can get them home and get them unpacked. And what does the future hold? More change at an even faster rate! So my advice to you is to hang on and enjoy the ride. In fact, if possible, take advantage of it. That's what the "greats" do. But if you decide to fight change or to hide from it, you're going to be like a Model T at the Indianapolis 500. The speed of change and innovation is going to literally blow you off the track as it passes you by and leaves you in the dust of antiquity. Information is expanding. The world is changing. Make up your mind to change with it.

I cannot judge your heart because I do not know you, but if you are reading this book, it is probably because you want things to be better in your life. You want things to be different. The basic premise of this book is that, for things to get better in your life, you have to get better first. And the only way you are going to get better is by changing some things in your life. Nobody ever got better by remaining the way he was. To improve anything about yourself or your life, you must change some things about yourself or your life. If you refuse to change things in your life today, then tomorrow will simply be a repeat of today. In fact, you won't really have a tomorrow; you will only have a longer today. So if you are serious about getting ahead, if you are serious about modifying the direction of your life, if you are serious about making tomorrow better than today, you must change. You need to ask yourself, "What can I do today to make tomorrow different?"

Tom Peters, one of the authors of *In Search of Excellence* (New York, Harper, 2004), explains that change is disruptive, but that the disruptive nature of change doesn't make any difference. We all have to endure change whether we want to or not. Because Peters wrote about some of the world's most successful and innovative companies, he knows that we live in an era where the unbridled acceptance of change is the only course of survival and particularly the sole course for future growth. If you want your life, your relationships, your financial situation, your health, or your business endeavors to improve, you need to do something different. You are going to have to change. "Better" is always preceded by change.

When all is said and done, most of us want all the same things out of life. We want to be happy and healthy. We want to own nice homes. We want to drive nice automobiles. We want financial security for ourselves and our families. We want to provide our children with the best possible educations and a head start toward secure and fulfilling lives of their own. If these are your goals and you're not walking a course that is taking you toward them, you need to make some changes in the direction you are traveling or in the way you are moving forward. If you truly want the rest of your life to be the best of your life, you simply have to do something different.

There's a true story I ran across a few years ago that really drove home to me the importance of change and the absolute necessity for people to become adaptable in their thinking. This story has captivated me ever since I first heard it. It's about two brothers who were born during the 1960s and who grew up in Richmond, California, a beautiful community across the bay from San Francisco. Michael and Chris were well-behaved boys. They got good grades in school. They stayed out of trouble. They obeyed their parents.

Part of a large working-class family with eight children, Michael and Chris knew what it was like to go through occasional financial want, so the boys often had to go without the things that other boys their age enjoyed. At times, things got so financially difficult for their parents that Michael and Chris actually went without food. They were hungry. So they began to steal things to eat. From the age of five until their freshman year of high school, the two brothers would sneak crackers from the cupboard, shoplift cookies from the grocery store, take sandwiches from people, and even steal small amounts of money from their parents to buy food.

When Michael and Chris entered high school, however, they changed schools and were bussed across town for their classes. Then, at the conclusion of the boys' freshman year of high school, something happened that made one of the boys decide to change his life. Chris got his end-of-the-year report card and discovered he had made three A's and three F's. Realizing that his school only allowed three failing grades over the four-year program, Chris decided he wanted to turn his life around. He did not want to be forced to drop out of school. So he made up his mind to change some things.

It wasn't easy for Chris to change. Few people really supported him. Chris' brother, Michael, did not join him in his new endeavor. Chris' friends badgered him and abandoned him. The people who did not like Chris before the change continued to reject him. Chris took a lot of "flack" for his bold decision. Nevertheless, he decided to change his ways. He stopped stealing. He started studying and working hard. That moment became a pivotal point in Chris' life.

Michael also made a key decision at this time. As I have already noted, he decided to stay on the path he was walking. Nothing changed in Michael's life. Nothing changed in his thinking. While Chris finished high school and enrolled in college, Michael decided to join the Army. While Chris went on to law school, Michael returned from his tour of duty just to hang out in the streets with his old friends. While Chris worked hard, eventually becoming the deputy district attorney for Los Angeles County, Michael started

---

You have to choose to get better
or choose to get bitter.

---

hustling to earn money and started taking illegal drugs to numb the pain and fill the void in his life.

Eventually, Chris Darden became one of the lead prosecutors in the O.J. Simpson murder trial. Eventually, Michael Darden died of AIDS at the age of forty-two. A story of both triumph and tragedy, this true account of the divergent lives of two brothers enables us to see that who we are and what we become is not so much a matter of circumstance as it is a matter of choice. The choices we make will determine who we become, and the changes we either make or refuse to make will determine the course we walk in life and the epitaph that will be written on our tombstone.

You have to choose to get better or choose to get bitter. You have to choose to improve your life by improving yourself or you have to choose to stay the same by doing nothing or by actually moving backward. Whether you are fifteen or sixty-five, your decisions right now have the power to dramatically impact your future and to actually alter your destination in life. Your decision to be adaptable and to be able to sense the changing tides and take advantage of them is key to the quality of life you will know.

We learned from the frogs that a person can either decide to be different or decide to stay like they are. We learned from Chris and Michael that a person can either change or be changed. While Chris changed, Michael was changed. He was changed by the streets, he was changed by drugs, and he was changed by AIDS, which eventually killed him. While Michael lived the life of a criminal, Chris became a prosecutor who did something about the problem of crime. You can be part of the problem, or you can be part of the solution. You can be part of the new world, or you can foolishly cling to all that is outdated and irrelevant. It's up to you. But the decision to be a driving force for all that is worthwhile is basically a decision to change yourself so you can be in a position to change others and change the world.

Chris changed his attitude. He changed his priorities. He went from being an underachiever to being an honor student. He went from being a pessimist to being an optimist. And eventually, Chris changed his destiny. You can change your destiny, too, but not by keeping everything the same. You can only create a different outcome after you create a different approach.

When all is said and done, you have a choice, just like the two frogs or the two brothers from Richmond. You can live a life of frustration and mediocrity, or you can live a life that is worthy of who you are inside. Like Chris Darden, you can create a story through your life that can be an inspiration to others. But the most obvious fact is that you can't make things different in your life by keeping them the same. You can't turn your life around without changing directions. Don't be like most people who could have been happier, greater, wealthier, or more fulfilled. Start making the necessary changes today so you can become the person God wants you to be tomorrow. Be adaptable to new climates and new situations and don't be afraid to sow the seeds of change before the sun goes down. If you do, you will reap a harvest of blessing when it rises again.

CHAPTER 11

WISDOM

UNDER IT ALL

As I started my work on this book, I found myself living in a challenging time. Often, greatness is most notably manifested and is actually extracted from those who possess it by the context of the times in which they live and how they deal with the challenges that confront them. The great challenge of this present time is an economic one. Most countries of the world find themselves in the midst of a frightening financial meltdown. The United States is confronting what economists are calling a "double dip recession," one of the worst in our nation's history.

In the midst of this enduring recession, many sectors of the American economy are struggling, and perhaps no sector is struggling more than the housing industry. Last month, the sale of new homes hit an all-time low in this country, and the same low occurred for the sale of existing homes at about the same time. Right now, things look bleak, to say the least, for construction workers, appraisers, mortgage brokers, real estate agents, and all others who earn a living by buying, selling, building, and servicing the sale of new and existing homes.

With this harsh reality as the backdrop for the writing of this book, I am reminded of the opening phrase of the preamble to the Code of Ethics for the National Association of Realtors. The NAR, founded in 1908, is the professional, non-governmental organization that sets standards of conduct for the more than 900,000 dues paying real estate professionals who have voluntarily aligned themselves with the organization in order to safeguard the integrity of the real estate profession. As part of their responsibilities as members of the NAR, these 900,000 realtors must take a required course in real estate ethics, and they must pass a test in ethics in order to earn the designation "Realtor." Then, every four years, they must repeat the course and pass the test again. The focus of the course is the NAR Code of Ethics, which realtors are required to learn forward and backward and to which they are held accountable by their peers and the other realtors who live and work in this country. The opening sentence of the Code of Ethics is what interests me as I write this book. The opening sentence of that code simply states: "Under all is the land."

The founding members of the National Association of Realtors knew that, over time, the real estate industry would have its ups and downs. They knew that real estate laws would come and go. They knew that housing sales would wax and wane. They knew that realtors would rise and fall. But under it all was something that would never change: the land. They knew there was a foundational, reliable substance to their industry that would give it perpetuity throughout the generations and from one political climate to the next. As my father and yours so succinctly phrased it when they were teaching us the importance of home ownership, "They aren't making any more land."

The fact of the matter is that the housing market, like anything in the economy, will rise one year, only to fall the following year, only to rise again after that. New home sales will be up one month and down the next. Realtors and other real estate professionals will make more money than they can handle one year, only to lose that money the following year. Just as land is the solid, reliable, unchanging commodity that undergirds the real estate industry and gives that industry its reason-for-being, so wisdom is the solid, reliable, unchanging commodity that undergirds life and gives life its meaning. Other things may come and go, and one great achiever may possess one set of exemplary qualities while another great achiever possesses a different set of exemplary qualities. But wisdom endures. Without wisdom, nobody accomplishes anything of lasting value and nobody achieves greatness in any form. Wisdom, my friend, is the solid land under the feet of those who would reach for the sky.

When I think of wisdom, I am reminded of the little second-grade student who raised his hand in class to ask his teacher a question. "What did I learn today?" the boy inquired as the teacher was ending her session on basic addition and subtraction.

"That's an odd question, Johnny," the teacher replied. "Why would you ask me that?"

"Because that's what my parents will ask me when I get home," Johnny replied.

Little Johnny, at the tender age of 8, knew something that many adults have forgotten. He knew that life is a continual, never-ending learning process, and that learning must be ongoing if we are to truly "grow." I'm not talking about physical growth here, because physical growth is automatic. Johnny was already physically larger than he had been when he started the first grade, just a year earlier, and you and I are a lot bigger than we were when we were Johnny's age, even though we did nothing to spur that growth. But mental, spiritual, and social growth aren't so automatic. Growth in these important areas of life requires a deliberate and purposeful effort. While some people grow in these important aspects, most unfortunately don't.

The fact of the matter is that, unlike physical growth, mental growth depends upon the individual. Physically, you will only be a second-grader during one year of your life and then you will continue to march toward adulthood, like it or not. But unless you make a conscious effort to grow in the area of your mind and your heart, you can remain immature and ignorant forever. Unless you consciously take action to grow in knowledge and wisdom (the application of knowledge), you can remain mentally and emotionally dysfunctional for the rest of the your life.

If you "Google" the phrase "wisest man who ever lived," you will find that, in the minds of most people, this distinction belongs to Solomon, the legendary king who ruled the ancient nation of Israel about 3,000 years ago. A thinker as well as a leader, an author as well as a ruler, King Solomon was responsible for compiling the biblical book of Proverbs. In that book, he wrote, "A wise man will hear, and will increase learning; and a man of understanding shall attain unto wise counsels" (Proverbs 1:5). So Solomon, the wisest man who ever lived, knew that mental growth was a process, not automatic; it was increased incrementally, not gained all at once. He knew that today's efforts in gathering wisdom and knowledge would bring tomorrow's successes in life and enterprise, because wisdom is the land under our feet, the solid, immovable rock upon which dreamers can stand in order to reach for the great aspirations in their hearts.

I wish I could tell you that good things in life are automatic. I wish I could tell you that, if you would only believe and have faith in God and yourself, you could accomplish anything you set your heart to. I wish I could tell you that, if you would only pray passionately and work diligently, every problem in your life could be solved and every situation in your life could be changed. Unfortunately, I can't tell you that. I can tell you that faith is a vital prerequisite for success, and I can tell you that prayer is important. You can pray until your knees bleed and you can have faith until the day you die, but unless you follow your prayers by actually doing something to change yourself and your circumstances, life is going to continue to look the same tomorrow as it looks today. In fact, if you are unwilling to do something to improve your life, especially through the accumulation of wisdom, you might as well just take a snapshot of yourself and hang it on your refrigerator door, because you are going to look the same tomorrow as you look today. No matter how much you hope for better things and no matter how often you think positive

---

If you want your tomorrow to look different
than your today, you are going to have to
do something to make tomorrow different.

---

thoughts, you are going to remain unhappy, unfulfilled, overweight, poor, lonely, or whatever until you decide to get the information you need and take the action that is necessary to reverse the downward spiral of your life or break the log jam of "sameness" in your life.

Think about it this way: If you want your tomorrow to look different than your today, you are going to have to do something to make tomorrow different. Otherwise, you won't really have a tomorrow; you will only have a longer today. In order to make tomorrow different from today, in order to start the process of change and growth, you must learn something today that you didn't know yesterday. You must learn something today that will enable you to change your tomorrow, because, if your life isn't going where you want it to go as fast as you want it to get there, you don't have a money problem or a health problem or a relationship problem or a situation problem. You have a knowledge problem. You have stopped learning the things you need to know. Therefore, I encourage you to get the information you need, and then act upon it. That's wisdom.

John Wooden, the great basketball coach who won more national championships than any collegiate coach in history, said, "If I'm through learning, I'm through."[37] Wooden knew that just good enough wasn't good enough. He knew that learning is constant and that improvement must be constant too if we intend to do great things with their lives.

Someone once asked me a very audacious question: "Are you doing as well as you'd like to be doing?" I thought about that question for a moment before responding. The fact of the matter is that a "growing" person is never doing as well as he would like to be doing. There's always room for growth and improvement. But if you are like me and you would like to be doing better in one or more areas of your life, then you have just admitted to yourself that there's something you do not know. New knowledge and the application of that new knowledge is always the beginning of any new chapter in your life.

The wonderful thing about acquiring new knowledge is that it doesn't take a lot of time, but it does take a little effort. In order to learn something new that could change the course of your life, you only need to spend about an hour each day reading about the subject that interests you or you need to spend a little time here and there with people who know more about that subject than you do. Did you know that just 15 minutes a day devoted to the pursuit of knowledge can make you an expert on that particular subject in just a couple of years?

The acquisition of knowledge doesn't take a lot of time, but it does take a focused and purposeful effort. Successful people learn and grow because they have a thirst for knowledge, an innate desire to improve themselves, and a stubborn resolve that they are going to do something to change their temporary ignorance regarding the subject that interests them. In other words, they take responsibility for their own growth and improvement. They become teachable, and, like sponges, they become willing and able to soak up all the information they can glean from whatever reputable sources they can tap into. Unsuccessful people are different. They already know everything. At least, they think they do. They don't want to learn anything new, because they don't think they need to learn anything new. John Wooden also said, "It's what you learn after you know it all that counts."

When you were a child, like little Johnny in our earlier story, your teachers and parents were responsible for your personal growth. They taught you what you needed to know. But when you became an adult, you became responsible for your own personal growth and development. You became responsible for the acquisition of your own knowledge and wisdom. So be teachable. Until the day you die, which I hope is a long time from now, you should be like desert sand, soaking up every drop of new information you can find, learning to apply that information to the real-life situations and opportunities that confront you on an hourly basis, and then returning to the reservoir of wisdom to digest more of the information that can change your outlook, your perspective, your paradigm, and your destiny.

What you know is extremely important in life. I learned this principle years ago when the personal computer was just coming into its own. When my very first PC stopped working and I was forced to call a computer technician, he came to my home office to fix my broken computer and to teach me a life-changing principle all at the same time. Once I described the problem to him and showed him my desktop system, I know he took a grand total of five minutes to fix the thing. Almost as quickly as he arrived, he was packing his little toolbox and filling out an invoice to hand to me. While he was waiting for payment, I made sure my computer was working properly, and then I looked over the invoice he had handed me. $300.

I asked the guy why he was charging me $300 (a lot of money in those days) when it only took him five minutes to repair my broken computer. I asked him if he could itemize his expenses for me. After listening politely to my foolish request, the man took the invoice back from me and proceeded to write more detailed information on it. When he handed it back to me, I looked at what he had written, which was the breakdown of his charges. The bill was still $300, but the itemized charges he had noted on the amended invoice were $1 to tighten a loose connection and $299 to know which loose connection to tighten.

Knowledge is power, and this little illustration demonstrates that fact poignantly. The people in life who don't know things are always at the mercy of those who do know things, and those who know things hold all the power and make all the money. We go to doctors when we are sick, because doctors know, better than we do, just how the human body works and what medications and treatments can solve our physical problems. We take our legal problems to attorneys, because attorneys know, better than we do, just how the legal system works and what the various laws say about this and that. We take our cars to mechanics, because mechanics know the difference between an accelerator and an alternator. And we take our computers to tech geeks, because they know which loose connections to tighten.

Knowledge is power, but wisdom is the application of that power. So the one common denominator that unites all great people is their love of knowledge and their insatiable pursuit of wisdom. They want to know what they don't know. But perhaps more importantly, they want to understand how to apply the information they didn't have yesterday, yet which they acquired today. They realize that growth consists of more than just getting bigger, older, and heavier. They realize that growth consists of more than just gathering and accumulating more pieces of disconnected information. Real growth consists of increasing one's knowledge each day, each hour, and each minute, and then applying that information to real life in a way that changes one's behaviors and thus the outcome of one's life.

Wisdom, therefore, is really more than a *thing*; wisdom is an *action*. The pursuit of wisdom is the deliberate application of what we learn. If you and I aren't changed by the knowledge we gain and if our circumstances aren't eventually altered by the knowledge we accumulate, we really didn't apply knowledge. So, even though a person might have an abundance of facts in his head, he lacks wisdom if he hasn't successfully applied those facts to life.

The New Testament book of James encourages us to "*be ye doers of the word, and not hearers only, deceiving your own selves*" (James 1:22). James then goes on to reinforce his point by asking a rhetorical question: "What person looks into a mirror," he asks, "and then walks away and ignores what he has seen?" The implication here is that no sane person looks into a mirror and then ignores what he has seen. A person looks into a mirror to get an accurate reflection of who he is and what he looks like, then he follows that experience by adjusting whatever needs to be adjusted: his hair, his tie, his collar. Only a fool would see himself clearly and then walk away without actually doing something to correct the inadequacies he has discovered.

But James is not talking about external things like hair or superficial things like ties and collars; he's using this analogy to teach us something about life. Once we "see" something about ourselves, about God, about our circumstances, about our opportunities that we did not "see" yesterday, we ought to follow that revelation by actually doing something to apply the information we have just acquired. We must act on our discovery. That is wisdom.

This book is a book about the attributes of great achievers, but the one quality that lies beneath all the other qualities of greatness is the quality of wisdom. It is the foundation of greatness. The information I share regarding all the other attributes is good information and the illustrations and stories I use to convey those thoughts are memorable, I believe. But the thing you need to remember as you journey through the life-changing principles of greatness is that the information contained in this book has to be applied if it is to mean anything. Wisdom is nothing more and nothing less than the accumulation and the application of knowledge.

A truly wise person wants to change. He wants to grow. He wants to modify his perceptions, his abilities, and his insights. She wants to transform her circumstances, her opportunities, and her destiny. But nothing will ever change in a person's life until that person gains new knowledge and understanding about things that really matter and then aggressively acts upon that new information to alter his or her life. Therefore, realize that, no matter what your problem may be in life, you actually have an information and application problem. Just think about it, and you will see that I am right. You don't really have a marriage problem; you actually have a wisdom problem. You don't really have a health problem; you actually have a wisdom problem. You don't have a wealth problem either; you have a wisdom problem. There are few problems that cannot be solved with the right information and the proper application of that information.

The Bible teaches us that Jesus Christ, God's own Son, had to increase in knowledge and the ability to apply that knowledge. Reading about Him at a point in His life when He was just twelve years old, we learn that Jesus "*grew in wisdom and stature, and in favor with God and men*" (Luke 2:52, NIV). So if the Son of God himself had to learn on a daily basis and had to apply that acquired information as He gathered it, how much more do you and I need to seek wisdom in our lives?

The fact of the matter is that Jesus did not initiate His earthly work among men until He was approximately 30 years old. So from the time this observation was made about Him, Jesus spent an additional 18 years growing and learning before He finally stepped out into His destiny. Becoming wise is not a quick process, but it is a steady, methodical, daily process of learning what you do not know and using what you learn. Jesus' ministry, therefore, like all the achievements of the great people mentioned in this book, was a natural outflow of the increase of wisdom in His life.

As I mentioned in the opening paragraphs of this chapter, wisdom is the foundation beneath every other meaningful virtue. It is the solid ground under the feet of high-reaching individuals. As a mighty river owes its majesty to the hidden springs of the mountain brooks, so greatness owes its origins to the pursuit of wisdom. As we increase in wisdom, we will increase in favor with God and mankind.

But like any foundation, the foundation of wisdom must be built. It must be carefully laid, and it takes time.

So how does one go about pouring the slab? How does one go about laying the foundation of wisdom in his or her life? We all live in the same world, and we all know that wisdom is not highly regarded these days. People don't talk about wisdom. At a party, we don't huddle in a corner of the room to share nuggets of wisdom with each other, and we don't tend to think of people as being "wise," even though they might be. At work, during lunch or break time, nobody says, "Let's go get a cup of coffee and share some wisdom." And whenever we think of wise people, we tend not to think of ourselves or other "real" people we know; we think of the wise men who visited Jesus when He was a small child or we think of some bearded hermit who lives in a log cabin in the mountains. We just don't give a lot of credence to wisdom in this modern age. Unlike King Solomon, we refuse to set our affections upon wisdom and we fail to desire it or seek it.

In modern America, we seek other things. We seek new cars, bigger homes, riches, promotions, and fun-filled lives; we don't seek wisdom. But the irony here is that all these "things" can be ours if we will place them a little lower on our list of priorities and seek wisdom instead. Any man who devotes himself to the passionate pursuit of wisdom will, over his lifetime, enjoy more favor, promotions, and advancement than his peers. Any man who devotes himself to the passionate pursuit of wisdom will, over his lifetime, accumulate more things and enjoy more prosperity than those around him. The man of wisdom will realize his dreams. The woman of wisdom will experience more success. The person of wisdom will typically own a better home, drive a nicer automobile, and travel more extensively. More importantly, the man or woman of wisdom will have more friends who enrich and benefit their lives and they will bask in the acceptance of their peers, the respect of their enemies, and the admiration of all. People may not even realize what it is about the person of wisdom that makes that person so desirable, because wisdom is an intangible and often unidentifiable quality that usually goes un-

---

*Great people attract great things and do great deeds
because wisdom is the foundation from which they start.*

---

noticed and almost always goes unappreciated. Yet its quiet strength is the steel framing that supports the life of people of achievement. It is the land beneath their feet.

The ironic twist in life is that you can actually have most anything your heart desires if you can set the pursuit of that "thing" aside and seek wisdom instead. Then the good "things" and good experiences of life will flow toward you as you grow in knowledge and mature in wisdom. This is the lesson we learn from King Solomon, the wisest man who ever lived, and this is the lesson we learn from all the people of greatness who have changed our world and the course of human history. Great people attract great things and do great deeds because wisdom is the foundation from which they start.

Therefore, to begin your own journey from mediocrity to greatness, you must begin by adding to your understanding in that arena of life that commands your attention. You must gradually and incrementally learn what you need to know, and then discipline yourself to apply what you have managed to learn. In other words, you must grow in wisdom and knowledge and in favor with God and man.

You must have a foundation to stand upon before you can reach for nobler things.

If you want your children to grow up to be successful, you must accumulate the wisdom you need in order to be a good parent and mentor. If you want your marriage to "sizzle," you must accumulate and apply the knowledge you need in order to understand your mate and to meet his or her needs so that your mate, in turn, will happily meet all of yours. If you want your life to be meaningful and excellent, rather than bland and predictable, you must learn what few people know about life and then go out and live your own life according to what you have learned. If you want your business to rise above the fray, you must "see" something that nobody else sees and then act upon that discovery in a way that nobody else is acting. If you want to be healthy until you are well beyond life expectancy, you must eat in ways other people aren't eating and sleep in ways that other people aren't sleeping. If you want your church to grow and to truly impact the world, you must step out of the corral of predictability and do something that will command the attention of both God and man. In other words, predictable and ordinary behavior flowing from predictable and ordinary thinking will only produce predictable and ordinary results. To rise above the predictable and the mundane, you must do something that is unpredictable and wonderful. But you must first know what to do before you can do it, and that's where information becomes your greatest commodity and wisdom becomes your greatest friend.

We are taking the time here to explore the virtues of wisdom, because wisdom is the foundation upon which all other qualities of greatness rest. It is the key to happiness, prosperity, and success. Everything you desire in life will be attained through the acquisition of wisdom or lost through its neglect. Let me illustrate through a true story just how central wisdom truly is to greatness and achievement.

Some time ago, I was running late for an extremely important business meeting, a meeting that had enormous implications for my future and my personal dreams. In spite of the fact that I had planned ahead and that I had prepared diligently for this important meeting, I was still running late because I could not find my car keys. I looked everywhere. Realizing that I was not going to find the keys without help, I called my wife to see if she could give me any direction, but she didn't answer her cell phone. So I found myself in a real dilemma. On the one hand, I had an automobile in the parking lot, but no key to make it work. On the other hand, so much time had passed while I was searching for my keys, I no longer had the time to call a cab or to call somebody at my office to come get me. I was really in a pickle.

About that time, my wife pulled her car into the driveway, and I found my keys in the glove compartment of her car. I quickly grabbed my keys, jumped into my own car, and took off for the meeting. Along the way, as I was driving, I started thinking about what had just happened to me. I realized that, in spite of all my planning and preparation, I almost missed one of the most important meetings of my life. And the only thing that had been keeping me from getting where I wanted to go was a tiny, little key. A single key was the difference between where I was and where I wanted to be.

Wisdom is the "little key" that unlocks everything for us in our lives. It is the stepping-stone that takes us from one level of increase to another. The lack of it is often the only thing keeping us from excellence and achievement. The presence of it is always the difference between the forgotten man and the memorialized icon. But just as dew can be found in one flower, yet not in another, because one opens its cup to take in the precious moisture while the other closes itself and the drop runs off, so it is with wisdom. God rains down His wisdom as bountiful as the dew. If we lack wisdom, it is not because it is unavailable to us. Rather, it is because we do not know how to open our hearts and minds to receive it. Never forget that it is the law of life that nothing will ever change in your life or mine until we actually do something to change our lives, until we deliberately accumulate the life-giving wisdom that is all around us and take action on the knowledge we have gained.

I needed just one key to start my car the day of my meeting, but there are lots of keys in this book. You may need all of them to get where you want to go, or you may need just one or two to be able to leave where you are, crank your engine, and begin your journey toward greatness. Yet regardless of how many of these keys may be present in your life and how many need to be added to your personal resume, it is vital that you seek and gain wisdom first, because wisdom is the eternal and everlasting foundation to life.

Make a decision today that a deliberate and passionate pursuit of wisdom will mark your life. Make a decision that you will devote some time every day to learning and growth. Make a decision that you will expand your knowledge base by reading, studying, and spending time with people who inspire you. Make a decision that you will multiply your understanding by actually applying what you learn.

Derek Bok, the former president of Harvard University, said, "If you think education is expensive, try ignorance."[38] Starting today, let the search for knowledge become the passionate pursuit of your life and let the acquisition of wisdom become the focus of all your available time. If you do, today is the day that can alter your very destiny. Today is the day you can begin to make the rest of your life the best of your life.

CHAPTER 12

GENEROSITY

BLESSED TO BE A BLESSING

Those who are familiar with my work know I travel frequently and spend almost every Sunday in a church pulpit somewhere, teaching the things I have shared in this book. The churches where I speak are great churches, and they are filled with great people. But these churches, like all charitable concerns, are dependent upon and sustained by the freewill offerings of the people who attend there.

Over the years, I have seen some amazing churches that do some wonderful things in their communities and the world. I also have seen churches with tremendous potential that are stymied in their effectiveness by the limited giving of their constituents. Although some people give until it hurts, other people give very little or nothing at all, and this obviously limits the churches that depend upon this giving to finance their operations.

In my conversations with some of those people who limit their giving or fail to give at all, I have heard all kinds of reasons why they find it difficult to support the causes they believe in. Some are facing genuine hardships in their lives; others offer shallow excuses. But almost all of the limited givers who talk to me conclude with the same explanation for their motivations: "If I only had more money, I could give more." Oftentimes, I hear the same explanation from those who have put their personal goals and pursuits on hold: "If only I had more money, I could do what God has put in my heart to do."

Prosperity is more about one's mindset than it is about one's financial bottom line.

Money is definitely the fuel that drives the engines of ministry. It also is the fuel that drives the engines of dreams. Unfortunately, people everywhere seem to lack it. Most people I know seem to be under such a heavy load of debt and seem to carry so many financial obligations and responsibilities that there's no money left over to invest in their dreams. And there's certainly no money to give away. So unless something changes—unless they win the lottery or inherit a large sum of unexpected cash—these people cannot see anything changing significantly in their lives.

Prosperity is more about one's mindset than it is about one's financial bottom line. People who have a lot of money seem to look at money differently and think about money differently than the average person, and most of these prosperous people held those attitudes long before they built their large portfolios. In fact, I personally believe most self-made millionaires became wealthy primarily because of their generous attitude toward money. I am also convinced very few people will ever find themselves in a comfortable financial situation until they change the way they think about money.

God wants to bless us, and He wants to make us a blessing in the earth. Although most people are not wealthy, and although the Bible tells us that most people who fill our churches are simple, common people (see 1 Corinthians 1:26), there is nothing in the Bible that tells us we need to remain in our "commonness." In fact, the Bible teaches from Genesis to Revelation that God desires to uplift His people in every way, including financially.

So what is prosperity? What does it mean to be prosperous? Prosperity is simply having enough to do what God calls you to do. It means having enough to survive and to take care of yourself and those who are dependent upon you. But it goes beyond this basic definition to include the ability to thrive—to pursue the dreams that are in your heart and to reach out assisting others with their needs and pursuits. It means having the resources to make a difference and leave an impression on the world. It means having the resources to fulfill the call of God upon your life, with plenty left over for your descendants and for the people and causes God places in your life.

Prosperity is simply having enough
to do what God calls you to do.

One of the primary motivations in the life of any person is the desire for financial independence. People just want to have enough money to be able to stop worrying about money. They just want to have enough money to stop thinking about it night and day. But ironically, the thing that seems to be the biggest problem for the most number of people is really one of the simplest problems to solve in life, because there are few areas of life where the rules are more evident and where the laws are more fixed. Acquiring and keeping money is not complicated, even though it may be difficult. Acquiring and keeping money requires a proper attitude toward the commodity of money and a few basic behaviors that have proven to be successful over the years.

In modern America, there are a lot of people who started with little or nothing, yet they are financially independent today because they possess this necessary attitude—they have learned not to worry about money. They know how to use money for their advantage and make a real difference in the lives of others. But there are a lot more people who do worry about money. These people rarely seem to worry about having too much. Instead, they worry about having too little, and their lives are suffering as a result of this constant concern.

In psychology, a worry about money is often referred to as a "deficiency need." In other words, thoughts about money primarily tend to motivate people when those people experience a lack of money or when they otherwise feel a deficiency in the area of financial security. A person who has sufficient amounts of money tends not to think about money at all or to be motivated by it as much. To put it another way, a person who has enough money tends not to dwell on it while the person who doesn't have enough money tends to think about it all the time. In fact, nobody thinks about money more than poor people. A person who believes he doesn't have enough money to secure his life, to provide adequately for his family, or to pursue his reasonable dreams is the person who will be obsessed with money. Money can dominate his thoughts, his feelings, and his actions, and those dominant thoughts can dictate the thrust and direction of his life every day.

This is why people with money problems often experience problems in other areas of their lives as well. Arguments over money—the lack of it and what to do with the limited resources at hand—are one of the primary issues behind marital strife and divorce. Problems over money also cause business failures and ruin friendships. And more than a few people have committed suicide because of the overwhelming stress created by their obsession with a lack of money.

I want to reiterate that the lack of money is one of the simplest problems to solve. I'm not saying it's one of the easiest problems to solve, because a financial turnaround always involves a lot of time, self-discipline, sacrifice, and change. But the process is not complicated to understand or implement; the process of becoming prosperous is simple, and the first step in this simple process is to change one's thinking about money.

One of the primary mental obstacles to achieving financial independence is the deep-seated superstition that money is somehow evil. Deep down inside, we loathe it. In our heart of hearts, we wish we could be like the birds that fly in the sky or the little animals that play in the trees. We wish we could live without money. The only reason we pursue it is because it is essential to human life in this world. We need it to eat. We need it to get around. We need it in order to provide ourselves with shelter, clothing, medical care, and all the other necessities of life. Unlike the birds and the squirrels, we don't eat worms or build nests in trees. We have to have money. But deep within our souls, we wish we didn't need it, because we regard it as "evil." We also look at people who have money as being "evil." There's no way in our minds that those people could have acquired their "evil" wealth without being a little sneaky, dishonest, or cruel.

Some of this mindset comes from our childhood conditioning. From the time when we were young, we can remember our parents fighting over money. We can remember our fathers becoming angry when money was wasted, because it was so precious and sacred. We can remember our dads telling us that "money doesn't grow on trees," and we can remember the secret guilt we felt because our parents had to spend their precious, limited money to feed us, clothe us, educate us, and keep us warm. We also remember learning at an early age that "money is the root of all evil." The pursuit of it causes crime. The desire for it causes greed. The accumulation of it leads to lascivious living and a callused lack of concern for the plight of others.

But I'm here to tell you that money is not evil. In fact, money can be a good thing. Money can buy lots of wonderful things like homes, food, automobiles, and clothes. Money can be exchanged for medical care, a quality education, a memorable family cruise, or a trip to our nation's capitol. Money is not good or evil; it is a commodity, a "thing." Money has no life of its own and no moral character of its own. It is nothing more and nothing less than a tool in the hands of the one who holds it.

This "tool," however, does have great power. Like nuclear energy, it can be harnessed to do tremendous things. This tool can bring dreams to life. This tool can give substance to the desires of the heart. Therefore, the man with money can stop dreaming about the things his heart desires; he can actually have the things his heart desires. With money, one man can build a house of prostitution. With the same amount of money, another man can build a homeless shelter or a church. Money is like a brick. Bricks can be used to build torture chambers or schools. The brick has no morality in itself. It is a dead and lifeless object. But in the hands of someone with a plan, a brick can be used to give substance to a noble idea or a wicked one, to a grand imagination or an evil one.

Money is not good or evil in itself. While one man will use money to do evil in the world, another man will use money to do good. Perhaps the greatest power that money possesses is the power to reveal the hidden desires of people's hearts. For instance, if two brothers should suddenly inherit a million dollars each, the first brother might give half his inheritance to charity and use the other half to improve the quality of life for his family. On the other hand, the second brother might quit his job, divorce his wife, and start living the "high life" with his drinking buddies. Money doesn't change people; it simply gives people the power to finally become what they have always been deep down inside.

In reality, money has a life of its own. It is attracted to people who treat it well, but it flees from people who abuse it. Those who understand money, who appreciate money, and who have a positive and balanced attitude toward money are the people who seem to find it and create more of it. They also are the people who discover the most productive ways to hold onto their money and even leave it for subsequent generations. On the other hand, those who acquire money rapidly, without first developing the proper mindset toward it, are those who tend to waste it, squander it, or use it for inappropriate purposes. This is why the rich often get richer and the poor often get poorer. Wealth was created by God (see Genesis 2:11), so it has a certain spiritual nature to it. It flows toward those who use it well, but it flows away from those who use it poorly. It flows toward those who respect it, value it, and learn how to use it properly. But it flows away from those who think it is nothing more than a portal to instant gratification.

Money gives you choices in life. As I have said, it gives you the ability to live what your heart has always imagined, to live your life the way you have always pictured your life to be. Money opens doors to your dreams that might forever remained closed without it. But money also has a negative aspect to it. Like any powerful thing, money can be destructive when those who desire it become obsessed with it.

The reason God created money and the reason He wants to bless us with financial resources in this world is so we can become His hands in the world to do His bidding and to fulfill His purposes. Wealth, therefore, must always be accompanied by generosity if money is going to be a positive force in our lives. When you understand this eternal concept and when you grasp both the necessity and the power of generosity, you will begin to understand what God had in mind when He first created wealth. The "greats" understand the power of generosity. I want you to understand the power of generosity too.

According to the Bible, money is a good thing. Money is never referred to as "evil" in God's Word. It is the love of money that is the root of all evil (see I Timothy 6:10), because love involves obsession. God likes it when money becomes a tool in our hands for doing good things for ourselves and others, but He doesn't want anybody to obsess over a temporal, earthly thing. This is why the first

---

Like any powerful thing, money can be destructive when those who desire it become obsessed with it.

---

commandment says, "*Thou shalt have no other gods before me*" (Exodus 20:3). The true God wants to be first in our lives, and He wants to sit on the throne of our hearts. All the external things He has given us in this world are intended to remain external to our lives. They are intended to serve a purpose and then pass away. God created man's heart to be His throne room, and He won't share that throne with anyone or anything.

We should never lose sight of the fact that money is just a tool designed by God to help us fulfill our purpose in the earth. When we forget this fact and allow the truly important things in our lives to be relegated to a subordinate role while money is elevated to a role of ultimate superiority, we invite disaster. Money itself is not evil. In fact, money is necessary. God designed money to be the fuel that drives all aspects of economic life. But money will never be more than a mere thing, and we must never forget that fact. Consequently, it is not the abundance of money or the lack of money that interests God, but one's attitude toward money. The person who understands, respects, and handles wealth can often be entrusted by God to handle more of it. On the other hand, the man who frets over it and bends his ethical standards to acquire a little bit more is the man who is not worthy of handling more. The way we acquire money and the way we use money determine its effect on our lives.

Whether you like money or fear it, the fact remains that money is necessary. If you are reading this book, then you need money to live. You need it to eat, pay your rent, feed your family, provide yourself with medical care, and support your ailing parents. You need it to pay for fuel for your car, electricity for your home, stamps for your mail, and shoes for your feet.

Even the work of God is dependent upon money, because God set things up that way. Sure, God is the ultimate force behind ministry, and what He blesses will succeed. But God never bypasses the monetary system. If He wants a husband and wife to build a new church, He provides them with the money they need to do so. He doesn't make a church building grow out of the ground. If He wants a young couple to go overseas to work as missionaries, He provides the financial resources to make that possible. He doesn't just zap them over to the Philippines. Faith doesn't bypass the monetary system either. When your cable bill comes due, the cable company won't accept a prayer and a New Testament as payment. They want money. So if God wants you to have cable service, He will have to provide the money you need to pay for it.

God lives in the real world because God created the real world. Yes, He created the spiritual world too. But the spiritual and natural worlds aren't in competition; they exist side by side and operate under the same laws. The same Architect designed both of them, so the eternal laws that work in the spiritual world also work in the physical world. The law of sowing and reaping and the law of generosity lie at the heart of God's financial promises to His people in the earth. Our Creator has a lot of wealth at His disposal, and He wants to shower that wealth upon His children so they can live abundant lives and fulfill their individual purposes in the world. God helps His people do these things by providing them with money, and God supplies money through the generosity of those people He uses.

Because God is the creator of wealth and the designer of generosity, you can be generous in lots of ways. You don't have to be rich to possess a generous spirit. You can be generous with your time or your talents. You can be generous with your knowledge. But if you want to be generous in the most practical way possible, it helps to have money, because most human needs can best be satisfied with money. Even King Solomon agrees with this assessment when he says, "… *Money answereth all things*" (Ecclesiastes 10:19).

Generosity and financial prosperity go hand in hand. Do you have a desire to buy Bibles for believers in China? Then you need money. Do you have a burden to help send a young missionary couple to Peru? Then you need money. Do you want to reach more people in your community with the Gospel? Then your church will need money to pay for advertising, special events, outreach ministries, and so forth. Do you want to touch the world with the Gospel? Then the many excellent missionary organizations around the world will need your money. Nothing else will pay the bills.

God may own the cattle on a thousand hills (see Psalm 50:10), but He keeps those cows in your barn (your wallet). Consequently, you need to open up your wallet and let some of those cows loose. It's obvious that the more cows you have (financial prosperity), the more cows you can release for God's purposes. It's also obvious that the fewer cows you have (financial lack), the less you can make available to the Lord. As long as you are barely getting by, few of the needs that God lays upon your heart will ever be met through your hands.

We have a misconception that poverty is godly and that wealth is evil. This fallacy is not rooted in the Bible. Rather it is rooted in poor theology dating back to before the time of Christ, when somebody got the idea that the physical, material world is evil and that only the spiritual world is pleasing to God, so spiritually hungry people began to renounce anything physical. They began to give away all their earthly possessions. They began to leave their families, homes, and jobs, and by the fourth century, they began to live in monasteries. Some of them even went so far as to renounce food and water. All of this was intended to "earn" them salvation and to get closer to God. But if you know anything at all about basic theology, you know that salvation cannot be earned. God is not impressed with our meager efforts at self-righteousness. And He is not displeased with the physical world. In fact, He created the physical world and said that it was "good."

God doesn't want us to become weird or to drop out of society. He just wants us to live our lives in the physical world in such a way as to please Him. He wants us to put our trust in Him as we go about our daily lives and to be faithful in the basic responsibilities He has assigned to us. God did the necessary work to procure our salvation; we can't add anything to His efforts by our own foolish renunciations of those things He created for our benefit and pleasure.

The ironic thing is that somebody had to pay for those monasteries. Somebody had to work, earn money, and give that money to provide the place where the "spiritual" people could go to renounce material wealth. Likewise, a lot of modern people who think that wealth is evil have a way of migrating straight toward churches when they need food or money to pay their light bills. A little hypocritical, don't you think?

The apostle Paul declared, "…*God is able to make all grace abound toward you; that ye, always having all sufficiency in all things, may abound to every good work*" (2 Corinthians 9:8). The following verses in that chapter speak about God's faithfulness to provide "seed" (a biblical symbol for money) to those who will take that seed and sow it back into His work. In other words, He will provide financial resources for those who will be generous toward His work and His purposes in the earth. If you are faithful with the resources He entrusts to you, He will cause you to "abound" and have "sufficiency in all things." Why? So you can "abound to every good work."

No person can give to "every good work" out of an empty pocket. We need abundance in order to be able to give. God is willing to give to us abundantly (prosperity) if we will become willing to share that wealth with those who need it most in a way that is responsible, effective, and pleasing to God (generosity). So if you have "just enough," you will never be able to be generous at the level God wants you to be generous. You need to prosper in order to be a fully generous person. That's why God wants people to prosper instead of struggling every day just to get by.

Right now, if you heard about a need that deeply touched your heart, could you do anything about it? Could you meet that need? Could you write a check for $250,000 to feed hungry children in Peru? If somebody suddenly appeared in your life who had a legitimate need for food or clothing, could you make a real difference in that person's life? If your church had an opportunity to buy a prime piece of real estate at a key intersection in your community, could you call the pastor and ask him, "Will a check for $1 million do?"

You are blessed to be a blessing, and if God's people could get this, they would begin to ask God to help them do whatever it takes to become prosperous. They also would begin to be generous right now with the resources they currently have in their possession. The things the Church or charitable organizations could do with a significant amount of money staggers the mind. Most of these institutions have learned to get by with very little, because few people have learned to be truly generous. They have learned to squeeze a nickel until the buffalo screams. But if these churches and charities suddenly had all the money they needed because of the generosity of many prosperous people, they could really make that money go a long way.

I don't understand how anybody could oppose the biblical doctrine of prosperity when they fully understand it. If good people had the money to funnel into the hands of other good people who needed it to fulfill their visions for serving others, these generous souls could literally change the face of the world. They could truly apply the teachings of Christ instead of praying that others might do it. They could feed the hungry, clothe the impoverished, house the homeless, educate the ignorant, help find cures for despicable diseases, prolong lives, and make things easier for the suffering. But without the necessary resources, these noble intentions go unmet, and the people who want to do something about these human conditions are frustrated. The fact of the matter is that we cannot fully live the way God wants us to live and or do the things He wants us to do without being generous. And we can only be generous when we have something of value in our hands to give away.

Let me invite you to visit an interesting and inspiring website, www.givingpledge.org. This site was established by Bill Gates and Warren Buffet, and the concept behind the website is to challenge America's wealthiest individuals and families to commit to giving the majority of their wealth to philanthropic causes and charitable organizations of their choice either during their lifetimes or after their deaths. According to Warren Buffet, the site is just gaining traction, yet there already has been a tremendous response. In a press release dated August 4, 2010, Buffet explained, "At its core, the Giving Pledge is about asking wealthy families to have important conversations about their wealth and how it will be used. We're delighted that so many people are doing just that—and that so many have decided not only to take this pledge but also to commit to sums far greater than the 50 percent minimum level."[39]

As you can see from Buffet's explanation, those families who accept the challenge must pledge a minimum of half their wealth to charity, but many have exceeded this minimum requirement. The full list of those accepting the challenge can be found on the website. But here's my point: Generosity is a prerequisite for true greatness. Great people are great partly because they are generous, and they understand the power and the efficacy of giving. They see a personal responsibility and possess a strong personal desire to get personally involved in finding solutions for some of society's most pressing problems. They know their money can be a tool that gifted people can utilize to fulfill this objective.

Those people who think like Buffet and Gates are people who understand money, its value, its power, and its purpose. They are people who appreciate money and who understand the concepts of wealth and generosity and how these are interrelated. They know they have been blessed with good fortune, and they are profoundly grateful. Just as the gifts are great, they feel a greater responsibility to use those gifts well.

The average American, on the other hand, has become a slave to money. Rather than being a conduit that God can prosper for the purpose of blessing others, the typical man on the street has become obsessed with finding money and hoarding it. Such people don't see money as a tool for doing great things and changing lives, but as a mechanism for securing their own futures and fulfilling their own selfish desires. So they work hard in order to increase the quality of their lives, then they find themselves in a position where they are forced to work even harder to sustain the lifestyles they have grown accustomed to. Money—the accumulation of it and the preservation of it—controls their lives. And there's never enough.

If the average American suddenly felt a call from God to go to Africa, that person couldn't respond to the call because of a lack of resources. If the person wanted to stop working for a while in order to spend time with his grandchildren, he couldn't. If he wanted to volunteer at his church, write a book, or get in an RV and trace his roots across America, he couldn't do those things either. Why? Because he doesn't have the money! Either he hasn't become prosperous or he has consumed all his prosperity on riotous living. But could you imagine what we could do for ourselves, for our families, and for God if we could turn that situation around? What would happen if we could make money and make it work for us instead of us working for it? With money, we could resurrect our dreams, give life to our talents, and pursue our individual purposes in life. Also, we could be a real blessing to others and change a multitude of lives and situations along the way.

---

*We have to recognize and embrace the fact
that God wants to bless us.*

So how do we develop wealth so we can be generous in the way God wants us to be? First, we have to recognize and embrace the fact that God wants to bless us. Before we can have a proper attitude toward money, we must realize that prosperity is a divine blessing from above and a trust from God. Of course, it's up to us how we respond to that blessing and how we use the wealth God puts at our disposal, but the wealth itself comes from the Lord. He has given us the talents that we can turn into money. He has given us the relationships that have been instrumental in building our wealth. He has given us the opportunities and the open doors that we utilize every day to get ahead. God has blessed us and wants to bless us even more so we can increase our giving. He uses the material resources of this world to establish His spiritual kingdom in the lives of men. He always has, and He always will.

Let me digress for just a moment to comment further about God's use of money. I believe that most people, even believers, disassociate God from money and money from God. In their minds, the two lie at opposite ends of the moral spectrum. But that's just not true, and the Bible emphatically teaches us that this is a false conclusion. In fact, money (how it is earned and how it is used) is one of the biggest subjects in the Bible and was the focus of 15 percent of the teachings of Jesus. God doesn't despise money. In fact, money is the fuel He uses to drive the engines of ministry and accomplish His work in the world.

If God wanted something done, I suppose He could send an angel to do His bidding, or He could simply speak the Word and it would happen miraculously. But instead, God asks His people to get involved in His work so they can be His partners in building His kingdom in the earth. Since no man has all the time, talents, or resources necessary to do all the great works that God wants done, He appoints some people to lead, some to plan, some to do the physical labor, some to organize, some to pray for the work, and some to finance the enterprise. If people don't give, the work won't progress.

The fact that ministry ventures require financial fuel helps separate the truly inspired works of God from the well-intentioned works of man. If a visionary cannot inspire people to give, he cannot raise the necessary financial support to fund that enterprise, and the enterprise will die a natural death from lack of resources. This helps eliminate a lot of things God doesn't really want. Also, money is representative of a man's time and is one of the most precious commodities that people possess. No man will be willing to part with his hard-earned cash unless he loves God and fully believes in the concept of the mission, the people leading the mission, and the goal of the mission. The fact that God has financed His work through the tithes and offerings of His people since the Israelites left slavery in Egypt shows us that He wants His work to progress. And He wants to separate his own worthy efforts from the not-so-worthy efforts of men by making finances a necessary part of the equation.

The Bible is full of God's perspective on prosperity. In the Old Testament, Moses declared, "*But remember the LORD your God, for it is he who gives you the ability to produce wealth...*" (Deuteronomy 8:18 NIV). Joshua wrote, "*Do not let this Book of the Law depart from your mouth; meditate on it day and night, so that you may be careful to do everything written in it. Then you will be prosperous and successful*" (Joshua 1:8 NIV). King Solomon wrote, "*The blessing of the Lord brings wealth, and he adds no trouble to it*" (Proverbs 10:22 NIV) and again, "*A good man leaves an inheritance for his children's children, but a sinner's wealth is stored up for the righteous*" (Proverbs 13:22 NIV). Jabez, the little known figure of 1 Chronicles 4:10, prayed, "*...Oh, that you would bless me and enlarge my territory! Let your hand be with me, and keep me from harm so that I will be free from pain...*" (NIV). And God granted his request.

The New Testament also has a lot to say about wealth and God's desire to bless His people financially. In Luke 6:38, Jesus declared, "*Give, and it shall be given unto you; good measure, pressed down, and shaken together, and running over, shall men give into your bosom....*" The apostle Paul wrote, "*And God is able to make all grace abound to you, so that in all things at all times, having all that you need , you will abound in every good work*" (2 Corinthians 9:8 NIV). When the aging Paul was writing to his young protégé, Timothy, he told him, "*Command those who are rich in this present world not to be arrogant nor to put their hope in wealth, which is so uncertain, but to put their hope in God, who richly provides us with everything for our enjoyment. Command them to do good, to be rich in good deeds, and to be generous and willing to share . In this way they will lay up treasure for themselves as a firm foundation for the coming age, so that they may take hold of the life that is truly life*" (1 Timothy 6:17-19 NIV).

These are just a few samplings of biblical references to prosperity and generosity. The basic conclusion of the Bible is that God's people should be careful not to put their trust in material things. At the same time, they should expect to be showered with material blessings so they can enrich the lives of others and thus fulfill God's purposes in the world. As Paul further explains in 2 Corinthians 9:10, God provides seed for the sower. In other words, God will give seed to the man who is willing to scatter that seed so it can produce a harvest. In the context of Paul's teaching regarding financial generosity, this analogy is intended to convey the truth that God will give money to the man who is willing to put that money to work so it can produce a spiritual harvest in the earth.

When God knows you will sow money, it is His good pleasure to provide it. He will typically bless us financially through the unique destiny he has put within our hearts. As we recognize that destiny and develop it, that distinct ability in our lives will usually become the vehicle through which the Lord showers His blessings upon us so that we, in turn, can shower blessings upon others in His behalf.

When you look at the miracles God performed in the Bible, those miracles were quite extravagant. God likes to do things in a big way. Since generosity is a form of worship, God wants us to worship Him in a big way, as well. He wants our worship through generosity to be extravagant. Of course, God wants us to be wise in handling our money, and this brings us to our second principle for developing wealth. We can develop wealth by handling wisely the resources God puts in our hands.

I don't believe God wants us pinching pennies, but I do believe He wants us to use wisdom in the utilization of our resources. God is infinite, but wealth is not infinite. Wealth is a created "thing." Consequently, there are only so many dollars in the world, and there are only so many dollars that will pass through our hands. If we don't handle our money with prudence, we will squander a great deal of the precious "seed" God has placed at our disposal to build our dreams and to bless His kingdom. This is why the Bible has so much to say about stewardship, as well as prosperity. God wants to prosper us, but not until we can handle what He gives us. He will give us all we can handle, but not more than we can bear.

Spending money wisely for the glory of God is a legitimate form of worship. It is respecting God and the resources He has placed in our hands. It is appreciating God's gifts and making the most of them. This is why the good steward and the generous giver must not think in terms of giving some of their money to God; they must think in terms of giving all their money to God. One's resources come entirely from God, and all one's resources belong entirely to God; therefore, all one's resources should be used for God's glory.

In the Bible, giving is encouraged. In fact, it is commanded. The basic requirement for giving was 10 percent (the tithe), but that's not enough. In reality, the other 90 percent belongs to God, too. The way you use that 90 percent, the way you invest it, and the way you utilize it in your life says everything about you and your relationship with God. In fact, if I could peek into your checking account ledger or study your credit card statement, I could learn everything about you and your spiritual life. Those few minutes would reveal to me your priorities, your level of commitment to the Lord, your dreams and ambitions, your problems, and your theology. In fact, a few minutes of analyzing your financial records could tell me more about you and your deepest thoughts than a psychiatrist could learn in a thousand hours of therapy. The way you make your money and the way you spend your money tells me everything I would ever need to know about you. So just think about what those facts reveal to God. It's not just the 10 percent that you drop in the offering plate or send to the American Red Cross that reveals the real you; it's the other 90 percent that you spend here and there that reveals your character and the future outcome of your life.

God is pleased to enrich your life. In fact, no matter how much you have, God desires to give you more. But He doesn't want to give you money to waste. He wants you to do something meaningful and significant with that money. He wants you to change your life and the lives of others. As He sees that He can trust you to do the right things with money, He will release more of heaven's bounty to you. He wants you to use His wealth to provide richly for your family, to achieve the destiny he has planted within your heart, and to change your corner of the world by changing the lives of people around you, one life at the time.

My wife, Christine, and I have learned the value of giving. Throughout our adult lives, we have deliberately sought out men and women of faith and potential whom we could bless with our resources. We have given away money, vehicles, motorcycles, furniture,

A lifestyle of giving is one of the highest levels of living that is possible.

and even food. We have paid for mortgages, tuition, and vacations for other people. We are givers because we believe in the principle of giving. We truly desire to be conduits of God's blessing. Of course, we are goers, as well. We are out there doing the work of the ministry, where we must learn to receive as well as give. We are blessed to be able to see the benefits of generosity from both ends of the spectrum. We have learned that wealth and income, regardless of where it originates, always must be used for kingdom purposes.

The more you give, the more God gives back to you. A lifestyle of giving is one of the highest levels of living that is possible. It also is one of the most exciting lifestyles available. Someone once said, "Your candle loses nothing when it lights another." So if you want to make an impact or be loved, respected, admired, and emulated, then learn to give. If you become a giver, you will truly glorify God with your life and be used by Him in this world.

When you think of generous people, who comes to mind? I think of people like Bill Gates, Warren Buffet, and Oprah Winfrey. These people are leaders. They are successful. They are "great." Can you see that there is a direct correlation between generosity and greatness, between giving and achieving one's own dreams? These people didn't learn to be givers after they became successful. They had generous spirits before they became successful, and that's precisely why they became successful. Whether they did so consciously or not, and whether they have personal relationships with God or not, these people and others like them have fulfilled the purposes of God in the world through their generosity. God has been delighted to place more and more resources in their hands.

Effective leaders—the kind of people that others feel honored to follow—don't gather things just for themselves. They cultivate a lifestyle of generosity and spend their lives enhancing the lives of others. They understand that money is a resource to be used and distributed, not a reward to be pursued for its own sake and then stashed away. To the "greats," to be generous with wealth is to accomplish something of value in life. The only way they know to develop and maintain an attitude of generosity is to get into the habit of giving.

They "let go" of their money. They support their churches with tithes and offerings, they assist individual people by helping them navigate the difficulties of life, they make dreams come true for promising protégés, they help charities fulfill their missions, and they develop the potential they find in others.

God placed giving into the system to eradicate the spirit of greed and teach us the true value of wealth. Are you generous? Have you given to someone else, particularly to someone you view as being "above" you, not "beneath" you? If not, would you like to nurture the quality of generosity in your life? Then give something away, and start right now. But give something away that is valuable to you. If it doesn't hurt, it's not real giving. So give until it hurts. Give away some of your wealth or something that is precious to you. Give it to someone who can benefit from it. Invest in another person, so your money can outlive you and someone with potential can be propelled forward. One of the most significant things a person can do in this world is to help another person navigate the difficulties of life or ascend to greatness.

I once heard John Maxwell say, "No one stands taller in the climb to success than the person who is willing to bend over to help someone else." When you add value to another person by showing generosity toward them, you will actually benefit more than the recipient of your kindness. In the end, you will incur the favor of God upon your life.

A woman stopped at a traffic light at a busy intersection in her hometown. When she noticed a homeless man with a cardboard box, standing at the corner to solicit funds from the motorists approaching the intersection, she rolled down her window and handed him a $1 bill. "I'm giving this to you, not because you deserve it," the woman said, "but because it pleases me to give."

So the man asked her, "Then why not make it $10 and really enjoy yourself?"

It makes you feel good to do something nice for someone else, because God made you to do good things for other people. King Solomon, said, "*The world of the generous gets larger and larger; the world of the stingy gets smaller and smaller. The one who blesses others is abundantly blessed; those who help others are helped*" (Proverbs 11:24-25 THE MESSAGE).

Giving is a source of tremendous joy, so there is incredible value in giving, not only for the one who receives, but more so for the one who gives. This lifestyle of giving cannot be mustered from sheer self-control; it must be mustered from the heart. If you are serious about developing a spirit of generosity and a lifestyle of sharing with others, you should begin right now to do something every day to bless others. What you give doesn't have to be money, but it does have to be something of worth to you, so that it costs you something. And, yes, when it is appropriate and you have it, you also should give money. You should give money to your church and those productive ministry organizations that gain respect, you should give money to worthwhile charities, and you should give money to individuals who need a helping hand or who need assistance in achieving their dreams.

Andrew Carnegie, steel magnate and humanitarian, also said, "No man becomes rich unless he enriches others."[40] So don't wait until you have $1 million. Don't tell yourself, "When I get rich, then I'll be generous." Stop fooling yourself. If you can't be generous with $100, you won't be generous with $1 million.

A person's income level has very little to do with generosity and nothing to do with giving. Some of the most generous people I know are those who don't have a lot of money. Even though they seem to barely make ends meet, they give faithfully to their churches and to charities they believe in. Something within them just won't allow them to stand idly by and watch a friend suffer. When they don't have extra money, they're cooking meals for people, helping a neighbor fix his car, or stopping by to encourage somebody who lives alone. On the flip side of the coin, some of the stingiest people I know are those who have lots of money. They give little or nothing to charity, and they don't have eyes to see either the needs or the potential in other people.

This dichotomy in attitude can be seen simply by studying a map of our country. For example, the state of Mississippi, where I was born, ranks 49th among the states in personal income, yet Mississippi ranks sixth in charitable giving. This tells us something. This tells us emphatically that there is no direct link between generosity and income levels. In fact, it confirms for us that some of the poorest people are also some of the most generous. On the other hand, the state of New Hampshire ranks sixth in personal income, yet 45th in charitable giving. I don't mean to pick on the good people of New Hampshire, but there are a lot more people up there with the capacity to give who refuse to give.

More money won't make you generous. The United States as a whole easily leads the world in personal income, yet the people of this blessed land give only 3 percent of their income to charity, and 80 percent of those Americans who have earned at least $1million dollars per year make no accommodations in their wills for worthwhile charitable causes. On the other hand, if you already possess a generous heart, more money can enable you to do more of the good things you desire to do, and I believe that God would be pleased to place those added resources in your hands. Perhaps that's why He has so materially blessed men like Bill Gates and Warren Buffet, who believe it is despicable for a wealthy man to give less than half his earthly riches to those he doesn't even know.

Somebody once said, "People give, not from the top of their purses, but from the bottom of their hearts." Generosity is a heart thing, not a bank balance thing. It is a habitual thing, not a forced or coerced thing. It is automatic, not contrived. It is followed by joy, not remorse. The three greatest joys you will ever derive from whatever financial success God allows you to achieve are the joy of achieving your purpose in life, the joy of enriching the quality of life for those you love, and the joy of seeing others benefit directly from the blessings imparted by your hands. When you can see these three things flourishing in your life, you will indeed be, like George Bailey in *It's a Wonderful Life*, the richest man in town. You also will be rich in heaven. There will be great treasure stored up for you there.

So do what King Solomon did. Build your own house (he built the royal palace in Jerusalem), but build a house for God at the same time (Solomon also built the great temple in Jerusalem). Don't seek to raise your standard of living. Instead, seek to raise your standard of giving. Solomon himself explained, "*One man gives freely, yet gains even more; another withholds unduly, but comes to poverty*" (Proverbs 11:24 NIV). The generous man will be made rich outwardly with increased wealth of his own. He will be made rich internally by the personal satisfaction he derives from generosity, the respect he commands in his community, and the reverence he commands from his children. The tightfisted man will have none of these truly valuable things.

A spirit of generosity transforms the way you see things. A man's paradigm of life is everything, because it shapes what he believes, thus shaping what he does. What a man does, over time, becomes his destiny and legacy. While stingy people see the world only through eyes of selfishness and greed, viewing people as an impediment to more riches or as the next batch of "suckers" in their scheme to get more and more, generous people see the world as a place where they can make a difference and leave a lasting footprint. Solomon again noted, "*A generous man will himself be blessed, for he shares his food with the poor*" (Proverbs 22:9 NIV).

Of course, the best example of pure generosity is found in the most famous and oft quoted verse in the entire Bible, John 3:16. This verse reminds us, "*For God so loved the world, that he gave his only begotten Son….*" From this famous verse of Scripture, we see the foundations of generosity. God himself was a "giver." In fact, God was the very first giver. He gave "before the foundation of the world" (see Ephesians 1:4), because that is when He determined to sacrifice his only Son as payment for the sins of mankind. So when we become givers, we take on the nature of God himself. Note from this familiar verse of Scripture the three things that God wants us to always remember about giving. Note that God gave until it hurt. Note that God gave His very best, not a token of His heavenly resources. And note that God isn't asking us to do something He wasn't willing to do first.

God is a giver, and He gave His very best until it hurt.

God is a giver, and He gave His very best until it hurt. He also gave before anybody gave back to Him, with no assurance that He would ever receive anything in return. In the same manner that God sacrificed His Son, He wants us to sacrifice things that are precious and meaningful to us. He wants us to sacrifice our time, convenience, comforts, and resources until it hurts so we can enrich the lives of many in the same way that His sacrifice has enriched the lives of billions.

Obviously, you and I can't give people eternal life, but we can give what we have. Peter expressed it perfectly when he and John healed the lame man at the temple gate: "*Silver and gold I do not have, but what I do have I give you: In the name of Jesus Christ of Nazareth, rise up and walk*" (Acts 3:6 NKJV). You can only give what you have. In Peter's case, he had no money, but he had God's anointing to heal. In your case and mine, we have no ability to heal, but we typically have money. We should give what we have. If we have no money at the moment, we can give other things, especially our time and a helping hand. Like Peter and John, we also can give without expecting anything in return. That's true generosity.

Always remember that, in God's economy, you reap what you sow, not where you sow. If you sow love, you will receive a harvest of love in your lifetime. If you sow forgiveness, you will reap a harvest of forgiveness. If you sow kindness, you will reap kindness. If you sow mercy and patience, you will receive mercy and patience. If you sow finances, you will reap monetary blessings. God will make sure that you reap what you sow. But He usually won't repay you through the hands of the one who received your kindness, your patience, your forgiveness, or your financial generosity. God will repay you through the hands of another. So I can expect to get back what I sowed. In fact, I can expect to get back more than I sowed. I just can't expect to get it back from the person who received it from me. That's God's law.

Oprah Winfrey is one of my favorite examples of a giver. Oprah lives a lifestyle of giving and of generosity. Although I don't necessarily share her beliefs in every area of life (I don't share all the beliefs of anyone I've mentioned in this chapter), I do think she is a model citizen when it comes to this particular aspect of life. In fact, in the area of giving, I think she is a wonderful role model. In an effort to inspire others, Ms. Winfrey openly talks about her generosity and how her money has enabled her to do great things for a lot of people. Of course, she is a very prosperous woman. In fact, Oprah Winfrey is one of the wealthiest women in the world. This is a perfect example of what I have been talking about since the opening paragraph of this chapter: Generosity works best when we have the financial prosperity to give it punch. We can start being generous today, even before we have wealth. But with financial wealth, we can do so much more for people and thus far more for God in this world.

Never underestimate the influence and impact your generosity can have on others. Something you have in your possession today can become so much bigger in the life of another person, but most people never grasp this concept. Not only can the act of giving change the life of the person blessed by your giving, but the object given can multiply in the hands of another. That which you currently hold in your hand may look very small to you, but it can look incredibly large in the hands of someone who truly needs it, and it can become the catalyst that turns that person's life around. Thus, it can come back to you later in the form of utter amazement or an overpowering sense of purpose when you actually see what your generosity has contributed to the life of another.

So understand the power of generosity and how it works. The little boy in the sixth chapter of John's gospel understood the power of generosity when he gave his five loaves of barley bread and his two fish to the disciples of Jesus. Once the disciples had given that fish and bread to Jesus, it was tremendously multiplied and was sufficient to feed more than 5,000 people. The gift of this food, though seemingly small in the eyes of the apostles, was really quite significant to the little boy. This was his food. It was all he had to eat that day. Without it, he would probably spend the entire day in the heat without any nourishment. He would truly be famished when he got home that evening. So he gave until it hurt, and though his gift was small by our standards, it was a true sacrifice for him. God took that act of generosity and made it something huge. Not only did He feed thousands of people with it, but He used the example to impact the lives of billions of people over the centuries through the four accounts of this story in the gospels.

This is the power of generosity. Something small released from the hands of a giver can become something truly significant in the hands of the receiver. Eventually, it can become a tool God uses to change countless lives and destinies of those who are touched by it indirectly.

Some of you might say, "Well, I don't believe in all this prosperity stuff." My reply would be, "That's too bad. I'm sorry to hear that." Then I would ask you, "Are you shrinking your beliefs to accommodate your current lack of wealth, because those who have wealth feel differently about the matter? Are you forfeiting your dreams to accommodate your present realities, or are you just afraid to believe in grander things so you won't have to risk failure?"

The truth is every dollar in your hand can become a door of hope and opportunity for someone else. You never know what the gift of your five loaves and two fish can trigger in the life of someone else. Because you gave, a marriage might be restored. Because you gave, a soul might be saved. Because you gave, an addict might be helped in overcoming his addiction. Because you gave, a malnourished child might eat tonight. When you realize the incredible impact you can have through your generosity, your faith will leap into action and your generosity will come alive. But until you "see" the power of generosity, you will make every excuse for your selfishness and offer every justification for your unwillingness to part with your precious cash.

As I wrap up this analysis of the twelve traits that I think contribute most forcefully to greatness, please know that I have purposely chosen to mention personal responsibility first and generosity last in this series of exceptional qualities. While personal responsibility is the place you must start the journey, generosity is the end goal, the purpose for achieving success. If your pursuit of significance is about you and you alone, then you are wasting your time and you will never really achieve a genuine level of success or renown. At best, you can only hope to become a rich old miser who has a long list of enemies and a gnawing sense of emptiness. To be great you must do what you do for a higher purpose.

Your success, although it will certainly benefit you and your loved ones, must do something more than merely expand the square footage of your house or increase the size of your investment portfolio, which your greedy relatives will fight over and squander after your death. To be truly meaningful, your pursuit of greatness must make a difference to you, must reshape the thinking of your family members (especially your children), and must leave a mark on the lives of others long after you are gone.

My final word to you is to get busy with giving. Don't wait for things to be perfect, because the roof will always need repairs and the tires will always need replacing. If you wait until you have abundance, you will never start to give. Learn the joy and the discipline of generosity. Don't lean on your feelings, because you will never "feel" like giving. And don't succumb to your fear of lack, because fears will always haunt you. Instead, confront your fears and refuse to heed them. Give generously. Give regularly. Give now. God wants to bless you, so you can bless others on His behalf.

Please allow me to conclude these thoughts with a prayer I hope you will pray along with me as your own personal appeal to God.

Father, in Jesus' name, I thank You I am anointed to prosper. My eyes are open to see creative ways to increase financially. My ears are open to hear the best deals. My heart is pure so You can channel finances through me. I am on the path of perpetual increase.

I covet earnestly the gift of faith. I boldly declare this gift operates in me now, and I walk in higher levels of faith and kingdom integrity. I live in daily expectation of increase and favor on my life. Money comes to me. My nature attracts money. The fear of lack has been broken in my life and has no more power over me. I am a steward of kingdom wealth, and my life is a clearinghouse for Your work in the earth.

Thank You, Father, for loading me up daily with benefits. It pleases You when I prosper. Therefore, persecution does not discourage me. I summon increase, health, peace, wisdom, abundance, integrity, the gift of faith, and prosperity to come to me now, in Jesus' name. I use my wealth to advance the kingdom according to Deuteronomy 8:18 (NKJV): "*And you shall remember the LORD your God, for it is He who gives you power to get wealth, that He may establish His covenant which He sore to your fathers, as it is this day.*" Therefore, I give generously and extravagantly to help others. Amen!

CONCLUSION

STUPIDITY

IGNORING THE OBVIOUS

Earlier in the book we talked about wisdom. Let's conclude this book by talking about stupidity. Since we looked at the subject of wisdom from a biblical perspective, particularly from the perspective of King Solomon, let's wrap things up by looking at stupidity from a biblical perspective, calling again upon the observations of Solomon.

The Bible never actually uses the words "stupid" or "stupidity," but the various writers of Scripture did talk about foolishness. King Solomon, in particular, had a great deal to say about fools. In his mind and in the minds of the other biblical writers, a fool was someone who knew the truth, yet lived his life contrary to it in the unfounded hope that somehow he could defy the odds and become the first human being to prosper by ignoring the obvious. Solomon spoke about the fool often in the pages of Proverbs, but James, the brother of Jesus, probably summarized the fool best when he said he is "*like a man who looks at his face in a mirror and, after looking at himself, goes away and immediately forgets what he looks like*" (James 1:23-24 NIV).

Stupidity (or foolishness), of course, is the opposite of wisdom. Everything that wisdom is, stupidity isn't. And everything that wisdom isn't, stupidity is. I like the way Forrest Gump put it when he said, "Stupid is as stupid does." Actually, I guess it was Forest's mother who said that. Nevertheless, the point is well made: A "stupid" person is a person who lacks intelligence or common sense. His actions violate his intended goals, and his repeated behaviors take him farther away from his goals, not closer to them. A fool is someone who looks truth in the face and yet rejects it. A very observant person once said that stupidity is doing the same thing over and over, then deciding to do it one more time in the hope that there might be a different result. Unfortunately, there won't be a different result. In life, there are fixed laws, and one of those fixed laws is that you have to do something different to get a different result. Too many people want things to be different, but they don't want to change. And that's stupid.

God can work miracles. I've seen too many miracles in my life to believe otherwise. But I also know that all the promises of God are conditional. We have to do something to meet God's conditions before His promises will work in our lives. We have to do something to demonstrate we believe God's words. Then He will take action on our behalf to prove that His words are true. God has good things in store for me, but I have to do something to activate God's blessings in my life. You do too.

If you want to be thinner, for example, you have to eat healthier. God will help you, but you have to help yourself first. If you want to be wealthier, God will help you, but you have to help yourself by learning to think differently about money. If you want more friends, you have to be friendlier. If you want a stronger heart, you have to exercise. If you want to learn a new language, you have to study. If you want a different outcome, you have to take a different course. In short, you have to do things in a different way if you want things to be different in your life. Stupidity is continuously doing the same thing while praying for a different outcome and dreaming of a better life.

The premise of this book is that successful people, great people, march to the beat of a different drum. They think differently. They behave differently. Their priorities are different. Their standards are different. This is why they rise above the fray. This is why they transcend mediocrity. They feel differently about things. They look at things from a different perspective. They live their lives backward instead of forward. They seek to give instead of get. They are out front instead of lagging behind.

God created you to be great. He created you to be unique and different. In some areas of life, He intends for you to be just like all the other people around you. He intends for you to keep your home, raise your children, go to work, mow the lawn, and check the mail. He wants you to fit in and to be part of society. But in at least one area, He wants you to be unique. He made you to be different in that area because there is something different you are supposed to do with your life. You know what that difference is, even though you may be resisting it, denying it, or running from it.

The simple truth is that you cannot develop that unique aspect of your life and nurture the greatness that God has placed within you by hiding among the masses, doing what they do and thinking like they think. You need to take a step upward and assume your rightful place in God's order. You need to accept the responsibility for your unique calling in life and for the passion that beats within your heart. Then you need to make the necessary changes inwardly that can enable you to live that passion. You also need to make the necessary changes outwardly that can set you apart from all the people who refuse to recognize and develop their own potential for greatness.

There is great reward at the end
of this journey to greatness.

Life is filled with choices. Now that you know what it takes to climb from mediocrity to excellence, you have a choice to make. You can either stay where you are and leave things the way they are right now, or you can start changing things in your life immediately. You can start being generous. You can start acting on your passion. You can begin moving the ball forward. You can start reversing the downward trek or stagnant condition of your life.

It's up to you now. To leave things like they are while dreaming about the way things could be in your life is absolute foolishness, because it will lead you nowhere and only leave you feeling guilty and frustrated. On the other hand, to start living the things you have read about in this book will take time and a great deal of effort. You probably won't have a lot of support, especially in the beginning, and your journey will be lonely at times.

That's the way it is with greatness. That's the way it is with wisdom. That's the way it is on the highway to success. Few people make the journey, because the journey is lonely and difficult. In fact, few people even start the journey, because the road is uphill and not well traveled. Most people are traveling in the opposite direction, and it's tough to swim against the tide.

But there is great reward at the end of this journey to greatness. There is great satisfaction, significance, fulfillment, and legacy. Most importantly, for the person who determines to make the necessary changes, there is a great deal of joy, because the journey is downright fun. I hope you will make it. I hope you will look in the mirror and realize you are a person with great potential. You just need to change a few things, and although those changes might not be easy at first, you will know you are on the right road, and that road leads somewhere worth traveling to. I hope to see you at the finish line. I hope you finish your course and win your race. You're great!

ENDNOTES

1   For more background on Tim Allen, check out his website at www. timallen.com.

2   Wayne Dyer quote from Thinkexist.com, accessed May 16, 2011, http://thinkexist.com/quotation/all_blame_is_a_waste_of_time-no_matter_how_much/323289.html.

3 Lou Holtz quote from quotationsbook.com, accessed May 16, 2011, http://quotationsbook.com/quote/7608/#axzz1MXWNoAPE.

4   Henry Ford quote from BrainyQuote.com, accessed May 16, 2011, http://www.brainyquote.com/quotes/quotes/h/henryford122817.html.

5   "Top 10 Most Expensive Paintings Ever," chiff.com, accessed May 16, 2011, http://www.chiff.com/a/painting-top-ten.htm.

6   Eleanor Roosevelt quote from Thinkexist.com, accessed May 16, 2011, http://thinkexist.com/quotation/no_one_can_make_you_feel_inferior_without_your/204263.html.

7   Story of Ty Cobb taken from book by Al Stump, *Cobb: A Biography* (Chapel Hill, NC: Algonquin Books, 1994).

8   Ken Hemphill quote from moneyandthebrain.com, accessed May 16, 2011, http://moneyandthebrain.com/index.php/motivation/quote-center?start=60.

9   Nelson Mandela quote from Thinkexist.com, accessed May 16, 2011, http://thinkexist.com/quotation/as_we_are_liberated_from_our_own_fear-our/144636.html.

10   Arthur Schopenhauer information taken from TheQuotationsPage. com, accessed May 16, 2011, http://www.quotationspage.com/ quote/25832.html.

11   Geena Davis quote from BrainyQuote.com, accessed May 16, 2011, http://www.brainyquote.com/quotes/quotes/g/geenadavis371447. html.

12   Calvin Coolidge quote from Thinkexist.com, accessed May 16, 2011, http://thinkexist.com/quotation/no_person_was_ever_honored_for_ what_he_received/10456.html.

13   Agnes George DeMille quote from FinestQuotes.com, accessed May 16, 2011, http://www.finestquotes.com/quote-id-22478.htm.

14   Eleanor Roosevelt quote from Thinkexist.com, accessed May 16, 2011, http://thinkexist.com/quotation/the_future_belongs_to_those_ who_believe_in_the/13262.html.

15   Burke Hedges, "Dare to Dream," *Upline Magazine* May 1998, accessed May 16, 2011, http://www.opnetint.com/dare_to_dream. htm.

16   Mike Murdock quote from The Wisdom Room, accessed May 16, 2011, http://www.thewisdomcenter.tv/applications/shop/scripts/ prodView.asp?idproduct=136.

17   Background on Jim Carrey taken from Thespiannet.com, accessed May 16, 2011, http://www.thespiannet.com/actors/C/carrey_jim/ jim_carrey.shtml.

18   Albert Einstein quote from Thinkexist.com, accessed May 16, 2011, http://thinkexist.com/quotation/imagination_is_everything-it_is_ the_preview_of/260229.html.

19   John D. Rockefeller quote from Great-Quotes.com, accessed May 16, 2011, http://www.great-quotes.com/quote/86441.

20   C. M. Depew, "The Most Foresighted and Adventurous of the Captains of Industry," *New York Times* August, 13, 1919, accessed May 16, 2011, http://query.nytimes.com/gst/abstract.html?res=F609 17F8385C1B728DDDAA0994D0405B898DF1D3.

21　Charles C. Noble quote from Thinkexist.com, accessed May 16, 2011, http://thinkexist.com/quotation/first_we_make_our_habits-then_ our_habits_make_us/201923.html.

22　Anna Mulrine, "Medal of Honor Recipient Salvatore Giunta Tells His Story," *The Christian Science Monitor* September 16, 2010, accessed May 16, 2011, http://www.csmonitor.com/USA/ Military/2010/0916/Medal-of-Honor-recipient-Salvatore-Giunta- tells-his-story.

23　Sophocles quote from QuotationsBook.com, accessed May 16, 2011, http://quotationsbook.com/quote/770/#axzz1MXWNoAPE.

24　Abraham Lincoln quote from Thinkexist.com, accessed May 16, 2011, http://thinkexist.com/quotation/things_may_come_to_those_ who_wait-but_only_the/145511.html.

25　Lao-tzu quote from The Quotations Page, accessed May 16, 2011, http://www.quotationspage.com/quotes/Lao-tzu/.

26　Michael Moncour quote from The Quotations Page, accessed May 16, 2011, http://www.quotationspage.com/quote/989.html.

27　Thomas J. Watson quote from BrainyQuote.com, accessed May 16, 2011, http://www.brainyquote.com/quotes/authors/t/thomas_j_ watson.html.

28　Peter Drucker quote from Thinkexist.com, accessed May 16, 2011, http://thinkexist.com/quotation/whenever_you_see_a_successful_ business-someone/167688.html.

29　Henry Ford quote from QuotationsBook.com, accessed May 16, 2011, http://quotationsbook.com/ quote/13723/#axzz1MXWNoAPE.

30　Richard Buckminster Fuller quote from Thinkexist.com, accessed May 16, 2011, http://thinkexist.com/quotation/you_can_never_ learn_less-you_can_only_learn_more/223480.html.

31　The story of Terry Fox can be found at http://terryfox.org, accessed May 16, 2011.

32 Dr. Norman Vincent Peale quote from BrainyQuote.com, accessed May 16, 2011, http://www.brainyquote.com/quotes/quotes/n/normanvinc100962.html.

33 Thomas Carlyle quote from AllInspiration.com, accessed May 16, 2011, http://www.allinspiration.com/Life/Quotes/Life%20Quotes%20%28Subject%29/life_quotes_greatness_%26_great_things.html.

34 Albert Einstein quote from Thinkexist.com, accessed May 16, 2011, http://thinkexist.com/quotation/try_not_to_become_a_man_of_success-but_rather_try/6989.html.

35 Alan Simpson quote from Thinkexist.com, accessed May 16, 2011, http://thinkexist.com/quotation/if_you_have_integrity-nothing_else_matters-if_you/343397.html.

36 John F. Kennedy quote from the John F. Kennedy Presidential Library and Museum, accessed May 16, 2011, http://www.jfklibrary.org/Research/Ready-Reference/JFK-Quotations.aspx.

37 John Wooden quote from HoopsU.com, accessed May 16, 2011, http://www.hoopsu.com/99-wisdoms-from-wooden.

38 Derek Bok quote from Thinkexist.com, accessed May 16, 2011, http://thinkexist.com/quotation/if_you_think_education_is_expensive-try/188916.html.

39 Quote from Warren Buffet can be found at www.givingpledge.org in the press release dated August 4, 2010. Accessed May 16, 2011.

40 Quote from Andrew Carnegie from GoodReads.com, accessed May 16, 2011, http://www.goodreads.com/author/quotes/23387.Andrew_Carnegie.

PRAYER OF SALVATION

God loves you—no matter who you are, no matter what your past. God loves you so much that He gave His one and only begotten Son for you. The Bible tells us that "...whoever believes in him shall not perish but have eternal life" (John 3:16 NIV). Jesus laid down His life and rose again so that we could spend eternity with Him in heaven and experience His absolute best on earth. If you would like to receive Jesus into your life, say the following prayer out loud and mean it from your heart.

Heavenly Father, I come to You admitting that I am a sinner. Right now, I choose to turn away from sin, and I ask You to cleanse me of all unrighteousness. I believe that Your Son, Jesus, died on the cross to take away my sins. I also believe that He rose again from the dead so that I might be forgiven of my sins and be made righteous through faith in Him. I call upon the name of Jesus Christ to be the Savior and Lord of my life. Jesus, I choose to follow You and ask that You fill me with the power of the Holy Spirit. I declare that right now I am a child of God. I am free from sin and full of the righteousness of God. I am saved in Jesus' name. Amen.

If you prayed this prayer to receive Jesus Christ as your Savior for the first time, please contact us on the Web at www.harrisonhouse. com to receive a free book.

Or you may write us at:

Harrison House • P.O. Box 35035 • Tulsa, Oklahoma 74153

ABOUT THE AUTHOR

Dr. Dave Martin is known by many around the world as America's #1 Christian Success Coach. He has embraced his assignment to teach others how to walk in the fullness of God's plan by pursuing, possessing and teaching the scriptural keys to biblical success.

His Ultimate Life Seminars attract thousands of people each year from across the country and around the world. He regularly appears on INSP, TBN, Daystar, and many other television programs.

Dr. Dave is the author of several bestselling books including *The Force of Favor* which teaches people to recognize, accept, and walk in the favor of God, and *Name Your It*, a teaching on the power of a seed. Most recently he released *Creating the Ultimate Life*, a 20 CD series and workbook, which teaches you to "Stop making a LIVING and start making a LIFE!"

Dr. Dave is a husband, father, author, inspirational speaker, successful businessman, and national television host.

He speaks regularly in churches, colleges and business organizations. Dr. Martin's powerful life improvement messages have been embraced by God's people, political figures, kings and presidents, professional athletes, actors, and Fortune 500 Companies.

His wife, Christine, is a powerful teacher speaking regularly in conferences and women's meetings.

Their international headquarters is located in beautiful Orlando, Florida.

EXPERIENCE THE LIFE-CHANGING TEACHING OF

DR. DAVE MARTIN

"Dave Martin has been a real blessing to our church and ministry with his message of hope, life, and victory. I just want to encourage you when you are looking for someone to speak for you, call Dave Martin. He will bless your people and support your church. I promise he will do you good!"

PASTOR JOEL OSTEEN
LAKEWOOD CHURCH • HOUSTON, TX

"Dave Martin's teaching has transformed not only myself but my family and business life as well. I appreciate his wisdom and incredible sense of humor. He captures your attention and allows you to create a new crease in your brain in regards to leadership"

GILLIAN ORTEGA
MARY KAY INC.

"I encourage every pastor to get in touch with Dr. Dave because he will rock your church and take it to a whole nutha level in wisdom, success, and finances."

PASTOR ED YOUNG
FELLOWSHIP CHURCH • DALLAS, TX

To schedule Dr. Martin at your church, conference or special event call today!

407.770.2020
OR VISIT US ONLINE AT
WWW.DAVEMARTIN.ORG

p.o. box 608150 • orlando, fl 32860 • 407.770.2020 • www.davemartin.org

ADDITIONAL MATERIAL
ONLINE FROM DR. DAVE MARTIN
www.DaveMartin.org
OR CALL US TO ORDER AT
407.770.2020

Follow me.

Keep in touch with live events, timely coaching and ministry in your area!

Twitter   Facebook   Vimeo

@drdavemartin   /davemartininternational   /drdavemartin

The Promises in the Bible are as Powerful and Relevant Today as they were 2000 Years Ago...

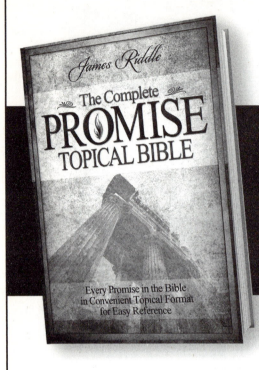

Harrison House

A new topical Bible from
Best-Selling Author

James Riddle

that contains EVERY
Promise in the Bible
in Topical Format
for Easy Reference.

6" X 9" Paperback–928 Pages
$21.99
ISBN: 978-1-60683-311-7

The Complete Promise Topical Bible lists every single promise in the Bible, in topical format for easy reference. Each promise is recorded from various Bible translations and includes a personalized, Scripture-based declaration of faith. By studying these promises and speaking them back to the Father God, you will establish your faith for those promises to be a part of your life.

Let God's Word become so rooted in your spirit that you will not be able to turn from the truth or give up, no matter how difficult your situation. God has made a way for you to overcome! Over 1,800 Scriptures are listed in this topical reference Bible.

**To Order Call (800) 888-4126
or Visit www.HarrisonHouse.com**